Developing Flex 4
Components

Using ActionScript 3.0 and MXML to
Extend Flex and AIR Applications

Developer's Library

Praise for
Developing Flex 4 Components

"So many Flex books gloss over the details of component development, or focus just on MXML. Mike Jones has bucked tradition and written a book that can actually help beginning as well as experienced Flex developers. Mike covers topics that are not found in other books. This book is not on my shelf, it's on my desk next to my keyboard."

—Adrian Pomilio
UX Developer, Railinc Corp., Cary NC
www.uiandtherest.com

"Finally, a book that covers Flex components from the ground up. I've been working with Flex for several years, but I have to admit that I've never quite grasped component development fully, let alone their styling, packaging, and distribution. Thanks for this book, Mike; it was long overdue!"

—Stefan Richter Editor
FlashComGuru.com
Founder, muchosmedia ltd

Developing Flex 4 Components

Developer's Library Series

Visit **developers-library.com** for a complete list of available products

The **Developer's Library Series** from Addison-Wesley provides practicing programmers with unique, high-quality references and tutorials on the latest programming languages and technologies they use in their daily work. All books in the Developer's Library are written by expert technology practitioners who are exceptionally skilled at organizing and presenting information in a way that's useful for other programmers.

Developer's Library books cover a wide range of topics, from open-source programming languages and databases, Linux programming, Microsoft, and Java, to Web development, social networking platforms, Mac/iPhone programming, and Android programming.

Developing Flex 4 Components

Using ActionScript 3.0 and MXML to Extend Flex and AIR Applications

Mike Jones

✦Addison-Wesley

Upper Saddle River, NJ • Boston • Indianapolis • San Francisco
New York • Toronto • Montreal • London • Munich • Paris • Madrid
Cape Town • Sydney • Tokyo • Singapore • Mexico City

Developing Flex 4 Components

Many of the designations used by manufacturers and sellers to distinguish their products are claimed as trademarks. Where those designations appear in this book, and the publisher was aware of a trademark claim, the designations have been printed with initial capital letters or in all capitals.

The author and publisher have taken care in the preparation of this book, but make no expressed or implied warranty of any kind and assume no responsibility for errors or omissions. No liability is assumed for incidental or consequential damages in connection with or arising out of the use of the information or programs contained herein.

The publisher offers excellent discounts on this book when ordered in quantity for bulk purchases or special sales, which may include electronic versions and/or custom covers and content particular to your business, training goals, marketing focus, and branding interests. For more information, please contact:

U.S. Corporate and Government Sales
(800) 382-3419
corpsales@pearsontechgroup.com

For sales outside the United States please contact:

International Sales
international@pearson.com

Visit us on the Web: informit.com/aw

Library of Congress Cataloging-in-Publication Data
Jones, Mike, 1969 July 14-
  Developing Flex 4 components : using ActionScript 3.0 and MXML to extend Flex and AIR applications / Mike Jones.
      p. cm.
  Includes bibliographical references and index.
  ISBN 978-0-321-60413-2 (pbk. : alk. paper) 1. Internet programming.
2. Application software—Development. 3. Web site development—
Computer programs. 4. Flex (Computer file) 5. ActionScript (Computer program language) I. Title.
  QA76.625.J664 2011
  006.7'6—dc22
                                              2010044919

ISBN-13: 978-0-321-60413-2
ISBN-10: 0-321-60413-X

Text printed in the United States on recycled paper at RR Donnelley & Sons in Crawfordsville, Indiana.

First printing January 2011

Editor-in-Chief
Mark Taub

Senior Acquisitions Editor
Chuck Toporek

Senior Development Editor
Chris Zahn

Managing Editor
Kristy Hart

Project Editor
Lori Lyons

Copy Editor
Sheri Cain

Indexer
Erika Millen

Proofreader
Apostrophe Editing Services

Technical Editors
Adrian Pomilio
Neil Webb
David Williamson
Stefan Richter

Editorial Assistant
Romny French

Page Layout
Nonie Ratcliff

❖

To my wife Emma, who put up with my erratic work schedule and sleepless nights as I wrote this book.

To my lovely baby daughter Freya, for lifting my spirits with her perfect smile.

❖

Contents at a Glance

Table of Contents

We Want to Hear from You!

You can visit our website and register this book at

www.informit.com/title/9780321604132

Be sure to visit this book's website for convenient access to any updates, download the book's sample code, or errata that might be available for this book.

As the reader of this book, you are our most important critic and commentator. We value your opinion and want to know what we're doing right, what we could do better, what areas you'd like to see us publish in, and any other words of wisdom you're willing to pass our way.

When you write, please be sure to include this book's title and the name of the author, as well as your name, phone, and/or email address. I will carefully review your comments and share them with the author and others who have worked on this book.

Email: chuck.toporek@pearson.com

Mail: Chuck Toporek
        Senior Acquisitions Editor, Addison-Wesley
        Pearson Education, Inc.
        75 Arlington St., Ste. 300
        Boston, MA 02116 USA

For more information about our books or conferences, see our website at
www.informit.com

Preface

With the advent of the Flex framework, Adobe provided an application-orientated framework to make the production of rich, immersive solutions aimed at providing end-user benefits beyond just "looking cool."

To achieve this, Adobe focused on a component-based approach to the Flex framework, making the development of this new breed of Rich Internet Applications (RIAs) easier and faster to develop. However, although there is a veritable chocolate box of components to choose from within the Flex framework, it appeared to be like dabbling in the black arts if you wanted to create your own components.

That's where this book comes in. It provides you with the knowledge and experience to help you develop new components for Flex 4. So much has changed since Flex 3, and this book makes it so you can speed up your own team's development processes and understand how you can create, package, and distribute your components to a wider, more public audience.

Audience for This Book

As with all technologies, as they grow in functionality, the desire to develop bigger, brighter, and better solutions with them reaches a tipping point. At that point, two things happen. First, there is a sudden increase in popularity, and second, the roles and responsibilities that existed for the teams who use these technologies start to specialize.

The Flex framework is no different. When Flex first appeared, you were generally just classed as a Flex (or RIA) developer; however, as projects grew in scope and teams expanded, the necessity to specialize in some aspect of RIA development became apparent. To this end, you can now find that most Flex developers will tell you that they are a "Flex developer, but I specialize in Enterprise," or "I specialize in data visualization." Personally, I specialize in component development. Not too long ago, I was called in on a Flex project by various clients for just this purpose. They had the core Flex development team in place, but they needed a component specialist to build specific, discrete functionality within a "black box" set of components.

Now, it's unlikely you are currently specializing in component development. But you are obviously interested in finding out more, if nothing else. And for that, I warmly welcome you to an exciting segment of Flex development.

What type of person do you need to be? Well, beyond the requirements detailed next in the section, "Who Should Read This Book," you need to think both in the macrocosm and the microcosm. By this, I mean you can understand the entire Flex framework from an operational sense by understanding it from a component level. That way, you can make efficient and generic components that operate in the majority of use cases and situations. By generic, I mean little or no external constraints to function; something that is discussed in Chapter 9, "Manipulating Data."

Who Should Read This Book

There isn't one archetypal person who should read this book; you may be a pure ActionScript developer, a Flex application developer, or someone who sits within both camps. See if these questions apply to you:

Are you comfortable with ActionScript 3.0?

Do you understand object-orientated programming?

Do you have experience with the Flex framework and Flash Builder?

Do you have a burning desire to create your own components?

If you answered yes to the majority of these questions, you are the kind of person for whom I wrote this book. Even if you answered yes to only a couple of questions, you might want to look through a few chapters to see if you're comfortable with the content from both a conceptual and code perspective, just in case.

Who Shouldn't Read This Book

If you're not comfortable working with ActionScript 3.0 or rely on the timeline and graphical drawing capabilities of Flash Professional CS5 to create applications, you will probably find this book a bit of a struggle. It's also not aimed at developers who want to create components to use within Flash Professional CS5 or components that don't leverage the Flex framework.

Finally, this book isn't aimed at designers. Although there are visual elements to component development, this is a code-centric book that covers only the visual aspects of component development in Chapter 10, "Skinning and Styling," and Chapter 11, "Creating Flex Components with Flash Professional CS5," and even then, it is still code heavy.

What You Need to Know

To get the most out of the concepts and ideas discussed in this book, you must have a good understanding of ActionScript 3.0, object-orientated programming, and be comfortable with the Flex framework. You don't need to be an advanced ActionScript/Flex developer, but if you don't understand things like the propagation and bubbling within the event model, or working with collections and arrays, this may be a tough read for you.

You also need Flash Builder 4 and Flash Professional installed. The trial versions of each is fine, and you can find the relevant links to download these products in Appendix A, "Flex Resources." Although you can create components using nothing more than the Flex SDK and a text editor, I made the decision to use Adobe tools, because they are easier to install and get going with.

If you're comfortable with ActionScript 3.0 but are still getting up to speed with the Flex framework, I suggest checking out the "Flex in a Week" video tutorials, which are available on Adobe.com (www.adobe.com/devnet/flex/videotraining/). This gives you a good foundation, especially when it comes to learning the ins and outs of MXML.

How This Book Is Organized

This book is broken into three parts. Part I, "Overview and Installation," introduces the Flex 4 component architecture and looks at all the components available to use as the basis of, or as an element of, your own components. It also covers installing Flash Builder 4, if you haven't had the opportunity to already do so.

Part II, "Developing Components," deals with actually developing your own components. Here, you learn how to create your own events and dispatch them and handle data passed into your components from an external source. You work with view states, transitions, and effects and provide support for styles and skins. You also discover how to harness the timeline and drawing tools of Flash Professional CS5 to easily create even more visually rich components.

Part III, "Distribution," looks at distribution. It focuses on how to integrate your components with Flash Builder to provide visual feedback, customized property panels, and code hinting, and how to package and deploy your components for public use. Finally, this book closes by looking at how to document your components for both reference and external documentation generation, giving your component the capability to survive in the wild without relying on you to explain how it operates.

The following is a general summary of each chapter:

- **Part I, "Overview and Installation"**: This part runs through installing and setting up Flash Builder and gives you the theory and history of the components within Flex. You also learn about the differences between the Halo (Flex 3) and Spark (Flex 4) component frameworks and what actually happens when you declare a component within your application.

  - **Chapter 1, "Getting Started"**: This chapter, like all first chapters, deals with setting up your development environment. There is a quick overview of Flex and Flash Builder aimed at ActionScript 3.0 developers who use Flash and want to try Flex. This chapter also includes how to install Flash Builder 4 on Mac OS X and Windows.

  - **Chapter 2, "The Flex 4 Components"**: This chapter introduces both the Halo and Spark components and provides you with a history of how and when components came about in relation to the Flash Platform and, more specifically, to Flex.

  - **Chapter 3, "Anatomy of a Component"**: This is the last "theory" chapter. Here, you see how a component is structured, the phases it goes through before it is finally rendered to the screen, and the three common development routes for creating components.

- **Part II, "Developing Components":** This part contains the core chapters that deal with developing components. Here, you create your first component and see how you can leverage both ActionScript and MXML in doing so. You also learn how view states, transitions, effects, events, and metadata are implemented within a component. You also learn how you can manipulate and store data within your components when assigned both internally and externally.

    - **Chapter 4, "Creating Your First Component":** This chapter enables you to create a component and test it. It also covers creating the component in both ActionScript 3.0 and MXML and explains the benefits of both options.

    - **Chapter 5, "Managing States":** You've probably used view states many times within your Flex applications, but how do you actually declare a new view state and, more important, how do you implement that within your components?

    - **Chapter 6, "Effects and Transitions":** Working with view states is one thing, but to provide a more fluid user experience, you need to know how to harness the power of effects, both in isolation or as a transition between view states.

    - **Chapter 7, "Working with Metadata":** Metadata is often overlooked within the Flex framework after you go beyond the core metadata tags. This chapter shows you how to add element- and class-based metadata and how to actually create your own metadata tags.

    - **Chapter 8, "Events and Event Handling":** ActionScript 3.0 operates off of an event-based model, as does Flex. This chapter shows you how to implement, dispatch, and handle events within your components, and how to create your own custom events and why these are important.

    - **Chapter 9, "Manipulating Data":** Components are generally only as good as the data they are given. In Flex, you can leverage numerous complex data collections within your component. This chapter looks at collections, cursors, data manipulation, and renderers so that you can make your components as flexible as they need to be when it comes to data requirements.

    - **Chapter 10, "Skinning and Styling":** The vast majority of components have a visual aspect. In Flex 4, you now have access to FXG, which enables you to declare your skins using MXML style syntax. This chapter shows you how to add skin support to your components, implement skin states, and add styling support. It also shows you how to access various attributes from your component within the skin.

    - **Chapter 11, "Creating Flex Components with Flash Professional CS5":** Not every component created for use within the Flex framework needs to be created purely in code. This chapter looks at how you can leverage the drawing tools within Flash Professional CS5 to create components that can communicate and contain normal Flex components.

- **Part III, "Distribution"**: This final part deals with how you integrate, package, and distribute your components to other members of your team or to the public at large. We first look at how to integrate your components with Flash Builder; next, you learn how to package your components so that they can be easily distributed without the need to include source code if you choose not to. Finally, we look at documentation and how you can make other developers' lives more pleasurable by documenting your components.

  - **Chapter 12, "The Flex Library Project"**: This chapter looks at exposing and setting parameters that tie in to the Flash Builder framework, through manifests, design view extensions and specific metadata you can easily add support for your components to make implementation quicker and more streamlined.

  - **Chapter 13, "Component Integration in Flash Builder 4"**: The Flex Library project enables you to convert your components in to an easily distributable format, enabling you to package and distribute your components without having to include the source code, among other things.

  - **Chapter 14, "Documentation"**: The final piece in the distribution jigsaw is documentation. Although it is the last chapter, , you discover why documentation should be the first item on your mind as you code.

  - **Appendix A, "Flex Resources"**: This appendix includes listings for the resources used in this book, and blogs, articles, and videos that provide additional information.

By the end of this book, you will have the necessary skills and knowledge to create any component that you want. The only limitation will likely be your imagination. Couple these newfound skills with the ability to package your components to provide other developers with a truly professional experience through Flash Builder integration and complete documentation, and you will have truly earned the title of Flex Component Developer!

About the Sample Code

The source code for the projects in this book are available as a downloadable Zip archive (.zip), which you can access by clicking the Resources tab on the book's catalog page at www.informit.com/title/9780321604132.

The Zip file also contains a README file, along with folders containing the projects for each chapter. To work with the samples, you need Flash Builder 4.0 and Flash Professional CS5 installed. (See Appendix A for the URLs.)

Acknowledgments

I want to take this opportunity to thank my wife, Emma, for enduring the late nights and long weekends when all she got out of me was the occasional grunt as I typed away on this book in my office. Thanks to my cats, Jpeg and the late great Figo, for their continued affection while working on this manuscript.

Thanks to Chuck Toporek, Romny French, Chris Zahn, and the rest of the team at Pearson for their support, guidance, patience, and the belief I could actually write a book.

A big thanks to my technical reviewers—you know who you are—for providing invaluable feedback and suggestions and the numerous revisions the book went through to get to the format that you, the reader, are now holding.

Finally, I thank my beautiful daughter, Freya, for nothing more than being perfect. This is for you, Freya-bear.

About the Author

Mike Jones has 14 years of experience developing for the Flash Platform. He was first introduced to Flash (then called Futurewave Splash) in November 1996, by his then Visual Arts studio manager while at a university. Suffice it to say, Flash made sense to Mike, and he literally ran with it and never looked back.

These days, Mike is a Platform Evangelist at Adobe and spends most of his time speaking with customers, presenting, and blogging and tweeting about the Flash Platform. Although developing is Mike's first love, he never refuses the chance to speak at user groups and conferences about components, the Flex framework, AIR, and the Flash Platform in general.

A regular speaker at Flash on the Beach on topics such as "Flex Development in 60 Minutes" and Flex component development, anyone who has met Mike knows he speaks passionately about these technologies, which is the same passion that has kept him engaged as Flash and Flex have grown over the years. When he isn't speaking or developing, Mike posts his thoughts and musings on Flash technologies on his blog (http://blog.flashgen.com). He lives in Haslemere, England, with his wife Emma, new baby daughter Freya, and his cat JPeg.

Overview and Installation

1

Getting Started

This chapter gives you a better understanding of what Flex is, both as a technology and as a development environment (Flash Builder). This chapter also includes how to install and configure Flash Builder for developing components.

Flex

In the beginning, Flex was a J2EE application server that "lived" on the server and took flat, plain text files and produced compiled content (an SWF) from them when a visitor requested the relevant file. This was fine, but it had its limitations. It was expensive—really expensive. Plus, as a developer, it was a fairly niche skill to have. Unless you worked for an organization that was large enough to buy a copy of Flex, or had a client willing to do likewise, it was fairly unlikely that you would get the opportunity to learn how to develop for the Flex server product. That said, Flex was becoming the technology of choice for rich reporting and data visualization web applications; however, it was a big-ticket item, so in the grand scheme of things, the market for Flex wasn't huge.

Eventually, Adobe (as Macromedia) made a landmark decision. It realized that, as a server-side only product, Flex was unlikely to set any sales records, or more important, provide a ubiquitous way to develop and deploy Rich Internet Applications (RIAs). Adobe, instead of End of Life-ing Flex,[1] refocused Flex from a server-side solution to a developer toolset. This enabled developers to create, test, and deploy applications created entirely in Flex without needing the original costly server-side product. That decision may have just changed the way we forever develop and deploy web applications.

---

[1] End of Life is the polite term used when a product is no longer going to be developed.

What Is Flex?

In a nutshell, Flex is an application framework built with, and harnessing, ActionScript 3.0 that leverages the Flash Player as its deployment platform on the web. More recently, it can now harness the capabilities of the Adobe Integrated Runtime (AIR) for the development of desktop-based applications.

To make the development process as streamlined and time efficient as possible, Flex enables you to create applications with ActionScript 3.0 or combine it with MXML. MXML is a subset of the XML language and, as such, conforms to the basic structure and rules that apply to XML. The advantage MXML has over pure ActionScript is two-fold. First, you don't need to be an ActionScript guru to create Flex applications because MXML takes most of the complexity out of the equation, leaving you to simply develop your application. Second, because of its hierarchical nature, MXML is easy to understand from a structural and relationship point of view, which makes the design and development of user interfaces efficient and conceptually easy to visualize compared to ActionScript.

From a pure development perspective, Flex has additional benefits, especially to those who work in teams or collaboratively. By harnessing the power of MXML, a section of your team can rapidly develop the graphical user interface (GUI) elements of your application separately from the actual logic. This has several advantages, such as enabling you to use the actual GUI as the basis for any prototyping and interactive client concepts without generally having to wire in the full functionality of your application. MXML is easy to restructure compared to ActionScript, and much of the low-level functionality that you would normally create with ActionScript is already present, be that layout management, styling, effects, and events or my personal favorite, Tooltips.

A common misconception is that MXML and ActionScript are two mutually exclusive languages used by Flex. This isn't the case. MXML exists only within the "eye of the compiler." When you compile a Flex application, any MXML is initially compiled/converted to ActionScript before finally being compiled into an SWF. You don't, by default, see this in between the ActionScript stage because the compiler does this in the background and then discards it after it creates the final SWF. You can set a compiler flag that keeps the generated ActionScript if you want to see what your MXML becomes when it's converted into this intermediary ActionScript phase. (See Appendix A, "Flex Resources," for some compiler commands and flags.)

Flex SDK

The Flex Software Development Kit (SDK) is the core of Flex development. It contains the Flex framework, which is provided as both source code (in the form of ActionScript classes) and compiled libraries (in the form of SWCs). (For more information about the SWC format, see Chapter 12, "The Flex Library Project.") The SDK also contains sample files and the relevant standalone and browser plug-in debug Flash players. Additionally and more important, it contains the **mxmlc** compiler, which compiles Flex applications, and the **compc** compiler, which creates SWCs. (Again, see Chapter 12 for details about the compc and the SWC format.)

The Flex SDK is free to download and use as a development tool. However, it is a "warts and all" solution that requires you to know and be comfortable with executing applications with the command line or via an automation tool, such as ANT. That said, this is the bare minimum that you need to start developing Flex components and applications.

In addition to being free to download, the Flex SDK is now part of the open source movement and, as such, you can submit updates and bug fixes to improve it. To do so, head over to http://opensource.adobe.com and download the latest build of the Flex SDK.

The command line isn't for everyone, so if all that sounded like a chore, don't worry. Adobe realized that most developers want the capability to develop Flex applications in a purpose-built editor, so it created Flash Builder (formerly Flex Builder). Before we move on to Flash Builder, let's look at probably the longest and most contentious debate regarding the Flex frameword: the Flex versus Flash debacle.

Flex Development Versus Flash Authoring

If you are reading this because your expertise is in Flash and ActionScript, you need to know a few things before we proceed. As mentioned earlier, Flex is, at its core, just a set of ActionScript 3.0 classes. Therefore, if you were to lock yourself in a room with nothing more than the Flash Authoring tool (or a text editor, for that matter), you too could probably produce something that works in a similar vein as Flex. And if you were truly committed, you could probably write something in Python or Java that would let you use an XML-derived language to quickly and easily define layout controls for your applications. The thing is, you don't actually need to do that; Macromedia/Adobe already did that hard work and produced Flex.

Also, there is nothing stopping you from creating content in Flash and including it within your Flex applications. Chapter 11, "Creating Flex Components with Flash Professional CS5," looks at how to leverage Flash for that very purpose.

Most of the Flash versus Flex debate centers on the development tools, primarily Flash Builder and Flash (or Flash Authoring, as it is officially referred to). For ease of distinction, my use of Flex refers to the Flex framework; Flash Builder refers to the Flex Authoring tool; and Flash refers to the Flash Authoring tool unless indicated otherwise.

Flash Builder Has No Drawing Tools or Timeline

The visual tools in Flash Builder are not reflective of the Flash Authoring tool because they are targeted at different solutions. The Flash Authoring tool is, at this point, aimed at more visually creative solutions. On the other hand, Flash Builder is more application-oriented, but it's not any less creative. Flash has a host of visual tools for the creation of assets. Flash Builder has a visual layout system, but it cannot create content visually because it has no toolset that's comparable to Flash. Flash Authoring has a timeline; the Flex framework technically doesn't. That is not to say that Flex cannot manipulate content over time; it is just that Flex uses programmatic means to achieve this. Flash uses ActionScript and can export backward-compatible content for earlier versions of the

Flash Player. The Flex 4.x framework uses MXML and ActionScript 3.0 and, therefore, only targets the Flash Player 10 and beyond.

Flex SWFs Are Massive

In general, Flex applications have a large footprint. This is because Flex is framework-based and, therefore, needs this framework to operate. Recently, however, Adobe has updated the Flash Player to enable application caching on users' machines, so if they have already been to a site that uses this, it will download the Flex framework and cache it within the Flash Player. Then, when they visit your web application, it will only need to download the actual content, not the framework. This change in Flex applications brings Flex SWF file sizes in line with pure Flash Authoring SWF sizes.

Flash Builder Has No Symbol Library

Although it is true that Flash Builder doesn't have a symbol library, it does enable you to create simple MXML objects (sometimes referred to as application components) that are fairly close in concept to Flash's symbol library. The advantage Flash Builder has over Flash symbols is that there is no risk of hiding source code within a Flex application because of its plain-text nature. This makes for ease in searching compared to the risk of losing where code is instantiated when it is attached to symbols or timelines.

At the end of the day, they both have their benefits and deficits. It isn't about which is better or how much you can achieve with A or B because of your 1337 s|<!11z. It's more about picking the right technology and toolset for your requirements, although that would clearly be Flash Builder and the Flex framework. ☺

Let's look at Flash Builder in detail and install it so that we can start making some cool things.

Flash Builder

When Flex first emerged, its development environment was based off of Dreamweaver and code named Brady (after the Brady Bunch).[2] Versions 2 and 3 of Flash Builder were called Flex Builder to draw symmetry between this new development tool and the Flex framework. However, because Flex Builder could be used to create pure ActionScript applications that didn't use the Flex framework, Flex Builder was renamed Flash Builder

---

[2] Initially, there was going to be an alternative development tool code, named Partridge, that was more approachable for Java developers because it was built on the Eclipse platform. However, for one reason or another, Partridge never saw the light of day until Flex Builder 2 was announced and Adobe made its dramatic turn from server-side to client-side development of Flex applications. With the arrival of Flex 2, it heralded the demise of the original Dreamweaver-inspired Flex development environment, which, although serviceable, was clunky and more Dreamweaver than Flash Builder.

to coincide with the launch of the Flex 4 framework, positioning it under the Flash Platform banner alongside Flash CS5 and Flash Catalyst.

What Does This Actually Mean to You?

Flash Builder is an Integrated Development Environment (IDE), which means that it provides all the tools necessary to develop and deploy Flex applications. However, if we stopped there, there isn't that much to separate this from the Flex SDK. Interestingly, Flash Builder actually contains the Flex SDK and provides a more user-friendly workflow that makes the development of Flex applications easier because it provides productivity tools and features to assist you when developing.

Built on the Eclipse platform, Flash Builder comes in two versions: Standard and Premium. The Premium version has a memory profiler, unit testing, and network monitoring. If that weren't enough, these versions come in two variants. You can either install the standalone version of Flash Builder, or if you already use the Eclipse platform for other development needs, you can install Flash Builder as a plug-in on top of your copy of Eclipse. Honestly, the way you choose to install Flash Builder is entirely up to you because there is no other difference between the two options. The more important decision you need to make is whether you need the added functionality offered by the Premium version. At this point, it is probably prudent to mention that, unlike the SDK, Flash Builder isn't free, but it won't break the bank, either. The Standard version of Flash Builder is probably the cheapest piece of development software that Adobe sells.

Wrapping the Flex SDK

Flash Builder can use more than one version of the Flex SDK, so as updated versions are released, you can include them within your Flash Builder IDE and select the one you want to use on a global and project basis. Flash Builder 4 comes with the Flex 3.5 and 4.0 SDKs already installed. Although you can just plug in new versions of the SDK (from Adobe's open source site, for example), it does not add additional functionality, wizards, or tools to Flash Builder beyond those already present; so, don't view this as an easy path to upgrading Flash Builder. Now that you have an understanding of the basic makeup and mechanics of Flash Builder, let's actually download and install it.

Installing Flash Builder

Installing Flash Builder is virtually identical on Windows and Mac OS X. This is partly because Eclipse already works on these operating systems. For brevity, I explain how to install Flash Builder on OS X and, where applicable, I indicate the key differences if they exist on Windows. As mentioned in the previous section, Flash Builder comes in two variations: a standalone and plug-in version. I won't go over the installation of both, because there isn't a huge difference. But, if you are already using Eclipse for the development of other forms of web or desktop software, you can obviously choose whether you want to include Flash Builder as part of that workflow or use it in isolation as the stand-alone version.

Downloading Flash Builder

Flash Builder is available as a 60-day free trial that can be downloaded directly from the Adobe website. The download isn't huge, but it is fairly substantial (about 500MB). So, you might want to get it going while you read through this chapter, and after it's downloaded, go back through the section, "Starting the Installation of Flash Builder."

To install Flash Builder, the first thing you need to do is download the Flash Builder installer for your respective operating system. Windows and OS X users can download it from Adobe's download page (www.adobe.com/go/flex_trial).

Select your operating system from the drop-down box, scroll to the Download button, and click it to start downloading the free trial. If you want to receive an email or two to get you started with the Flex framework, check the appropriate boxes as you move down the page. If you want to download the plug-in version of Flash Builder instead of the standalone, scroll to the bottom of the download page; you'll see a text link that takes you to the plug-in page. There, you can download it in the same manner.

Starting the Installation of Flash Builder

After your download completes, locate the installer and start it. For most of you, this is as simple as double-clicking.

When the installer fires up, you are presented with the initial installer screen, which includes the End User License Agreement (EULA) that everyone—myself included—ignores and clicks right on through via the Accept button (see Figure 1.1). In a bid not to break with convention, accept the agreement...only if you agree with it, that is. Proceed to the next screen.

On the next screen, enter a serial number or run Flash Builder in trial mode (see Figure 1.2). Whichever option you select presents you with a drop-down list of language options. Pick one and click Next.

The Adobe login screen appears (see Figure 1.3). This is an optional screen, so if you don't want to log in to Adobe, just click the Skip button. (Logging in can help you access help and other features, but you can log in later, if needed.) If, on the other hand, you want to login or register an Adobe ID, select the relevant option and, once authenticated, click Next to proceed.

You're halfway through the installer set up. On the screen shown in Figure 1.4, you choose where to install your copy of Flash Builder. Personally, unless there is some administrative reason or quirk that requires you to install it in another folder, just click Next, and leave the installer to put Flash Builder in the default installation directory on your machine.

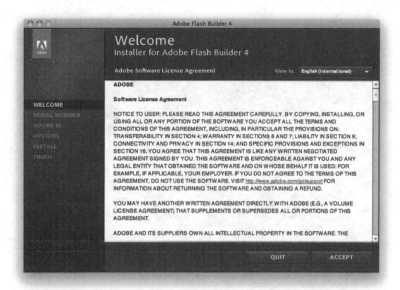

Figure 1.1   Flash Builder start screen and license agreement (OS X)

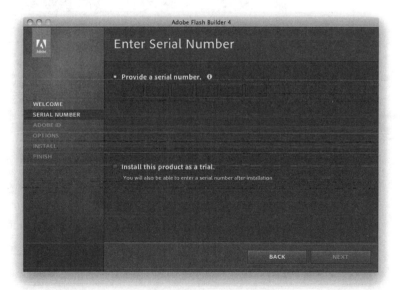

Figure 1.2   Choose whether to enter a serial number or install as a trial.

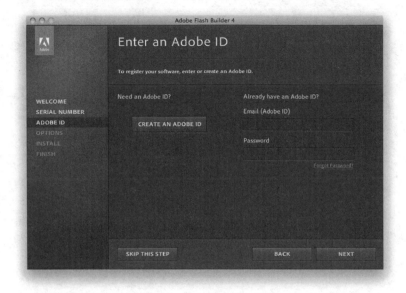

Figure 1.3   Adobe ID login screen

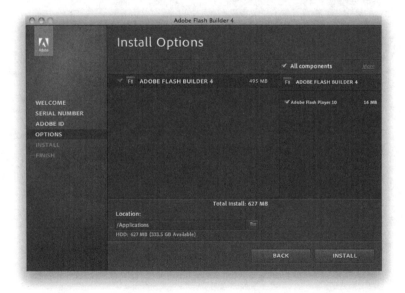

Figure 1.4   Flash Builder installation options (OS X)

The default installation paths are as follows:

- **Windows 32bit:**C:\Program Files\Adobe\Flash Builder 4
- **Windows 64bit:**C:\Program Files (x86)\Adobe\Adobe Flash Builder 4
- **Mac OS X:**/Applications/Adobe Flash Builder 4

If you're happy, it's time to start the actual installation. If anything is incorrect or you change your mind about a particular option, you can use the Back button to return to the relevant screen and make changes. Just click Next to get back to the Install Options dialog after you make your corrections. Click the Install button to start the actual installation, and grab a cup of tea or coffee while it installs.

After you finish your refreshing beverage, the installation will likely be complete. (It doesn't take that long, but if you grab the drink now, you can settle in for the remainder of this chapter without being disturbed.) If all went according to plan, you should be looking at the Congratulations screen (see Figure 1.5). Close the installer by clicking the Done button. You just successfully installed Flash Builder, and we can now fire it up for the first time.

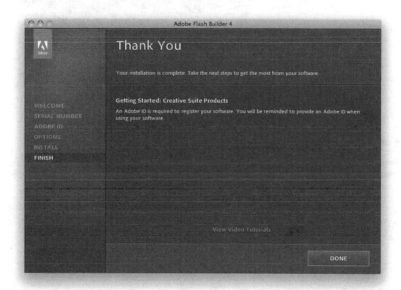

Figure 1.5   Congratulations! Flash Builder has installed A-OK.

Failed Installations

If you have problems or if the installer fails during installation, note the error you receive, and head over to Adobe's Support Center for Flex (www.adobe.com/support/flex/). The Installation Help tab can likely offer you a solution. However, problems seem to be few and far between these days, so you shouldn't have anything to worry about.

Launching Flash Builder

As part of the post-installation process, the installer placed shortcuts to Flash Builder on Windows (Start > Program Files > Adobe). On OS X, the installer opened a Finder window of the Flash Builder folder, so you can make an alias for it, if you want. To open Flash Builder on OS X in the future, you'll find it located in the Applications Directory. (If you opted to install it in another location, it will be located where you placed it.)

When you are ready to proceed, click or double-click (depending on your personal setup) the Flash Builder application to start it. This might take a few seconds because Flash Builder needs to create the default files on its first run through. After the splash screen disappears, you see the Flex Start Page within Flash Builder (see Figure 1.6). Feel free to explore the Flex Start Page tutorials. After you look around, we'll create your first project so that you are ready to develop.

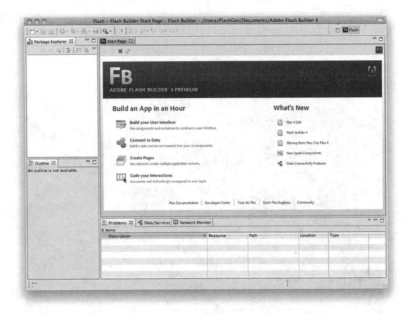

Figure 1.6   Flash Builder initial Start Page (OS X)

Creating Your First Project

Now that you've familiarized yourself to the IDE, you can set up the IDE and get ready to create components. There aren't any specific guidelines on how to configure Flash Builder for component development. But I've made my fair share, so I've had the opportunity to test various setups, and I think the way you will learn to develop components with Flash Builder is simple, practical, and—above all—productive. With that in mind, let's start creating our first project.

As the IDE is functionally identical on both Windows and OS X, I use OS X for all the screen shots from here on out; where applicable, I provide file locations and shortcut keys in both Mac and PC format.

From the File menu, select New > Flex Project (see Figure 1.7). Don't worry about the other options in that menu. We'll cover the various entries as we go.

Figure 1.7   New Flex Project entry (OS X)

After you click the Flex Project entry, the project wizard launches. The first dialog is fairly straightforward. The only thing you need to do is give your project a name (see Figure 1.8).

A few pointers here: Your project name cannot have spaces; it should be descriptive of the project but not verbose; it cannot contain special characters beyond underscores or hyphens; and I recommend not using any numbers. Also, it is common to format the name in CamelCase; that is, capitalize each individual word that is concatenated together, just like the word CamelCase is in this sentence. If you want to prefix or suffix your project name, that casing is up to you. If you want more information on naming standards within ActionScript and Flex, Adobe provides a coding standards document that you can read at your leisure; see Appendix A for the URL.

With this information in mind, give your project the name **DFC_DevelopingComponents**. For now, leave the rest of the settings set to their defaults. Throughout this book, we create a few projects, so the screen shown in Figure 1.8 and the following ones will become second nature to you.

Figure 1.8   Initial Create a Flex Project screen

Click Next to proceed to the next step in the process.

On the next screen, we have the default output folder into which our Flex-compiled files are placed. Notice that it is called bin-debug. This is because, by default, Flex compiles the SWF binaries with the debug information included; therefore, the name of the folder because they are binary files with debug information: bin-debug. You can leave these settings as is (we cover this later). Click Next to proceed to the next step in the project-creation process.

Figure 1.9 holds a lot of information about your project. Here, you can add external source directories to the project through the Source Path tab. Think of this as providing access to assets and classes without actually importing them. You can also link library items via the Library Path tab. At this point, I'm not going to explain the library elements because we use them and external sources in Part II, "Developing Components," and Part III, "Distribution," of this book.

At the bottom of the screen shown in Figure 1.9 are three text fields that hold the defaults for the project structure. First, you have the main source folder. By default, this is src. Flash Builder previously enabled you to just dump your content in the root of the project, but that can get messy and cause issues when deploying your applications. So, in Flash Builder, the default root for all your assets and content was set to src.

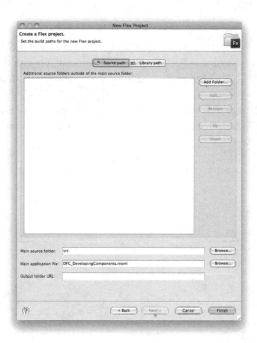

Figure 1.9   Final step in creating a new
Flex project

The next field is the main application file. Notice that it has the same name as the project. Again, you can change this, keeping in mind the restrictions and advice given earlier for project names. Many developers rename the main application file to Main.mxml, including myself. For clarity here, we keep the name the same as the project.

Finally, the output folder URL is generally populated only if your Flex project is used with a server-side solution and, therefore, needs to be pathed and deployed slightly differently than a nonserver-side project and can safely be left blank. As with the previous screen, I wanted you to view this screen so that you were aware of its existence and that we will revisit it in the future. Click the Finish button to complete the wizard.

As soon as the wizard completes, you see two things happen: The Package Navigator now contains your new project, which has been expanded, and the DFC_DevelopingComponents.mxml has been opened in a tab next to the Flex Start Page (if you still have the Start Page open).

Summary

This chapter introduced Flex the framework and Flex the SDK, and briefly overviewed the differences between Flash and Flex from a development perspective. You also downloaded and installed Flash Builder and created your first project. You are ready to move on!

That's it for this chapter. We are now ready to get deep into the Flex components, so put the kettle on and make another hot drink. Make one for me while you're at it. ☺

The Flex 4 Components

This chapter explores the core Flex components and the way in which they are grouped together. This will give you a better understanding of what you have access to, straight out-of-the-box and will provide the knowledge necessary for selecting the right component for your requirements as you start to develop your own.

This will also be your first step in developing components as you start to explore the Flex framework. Don't worry if some details are slightly confusing at this point; I go into greater detail as you progress through the subsequent chapters.

Components: A Potted History

Some of you may already have an idea of why components are so valuable in a development process. Others may have never used them or have had a bad experience. Whatever your take on them, you're reading this book, so you're obviously interested in learning more about the development of components and what you can actually achieve with them.

Following is a brief history of Flash-based components so that you can see how far they have come in a relatively short time. Macromedia (now Adobe) first introduced components in version 5 of the Flash Authoring tool. Back then, they were called Smart-Clips, and although they enabled developers to encapsulate functionality in both a visual or nonvisual manner, they weren't particularly flexible and usually required an above-average understanding of ActionScript to tweak them to suit your project needs. Fortunately, Macromedia realized they weren't as useful as had anticipated and, with the advent of ActionScript 2, it overhauled (read started from scratch) the SmartClip architecture to provide a set of controls that were easy to employ, simple to configure, and provided a greater degree of flexibility compared to the original SmartClips. To emphasize the change, and use an accepted term of reference, Macromedia also rechristened them as components.

The only downsides to these new ActionScript 2 components were that they were quite large from a file size point of view; there was a tipping point in a project in which the file-size cost was outweighed by the ease of inclusion and use of the components.

This was because all the components were descended from one base class and built upon this base functionality. Thus, putting one component into a project required the entire component framework that it inherited from or was composed from. On small projects, like banner ads, this was not always an option because of the tight size constraints that some banners demanded. Also, the styling and skinning aspect of the visual components left a lot to be desired. Although simple size and style changing were relatively easy to achieve in most cases, anything more complex required a greater understanding of the component framework and an even greater level of patience. Therefore, they were easy to use and build upon, but Flash solutions started to look uniform because of the lack of ease when it came to customizing the look and feel.

There was also a split in technologies that could produce Flash Player content. The Flex framework joined the Flash Authoring tool, which, although it shared the same compiled SWF format and Flash Player requirements, had additional requirements over those already included in the ActionScript 2 components for Flash. This posed a problem because Flash components wouldn't play nicely with Flex applications that used their enhanced equivalents, and the same applied to Flex components when applied to Flash content. Fortunately, at this time, Flex was a server-side product and fairly new. As such, it had a relatively small developer base compared to the user base of the Flash Authoring tool.

With the advent of ActionScript 3.0, things changed again. Components in the Flash Authoring tool (in this case, Flash Authoring) were overhauled again, and the decision was taken to address the styling and file-size issues. The components were redesigned to be lightweight and easy to style and skin through Flash Authoring's visual tools. Flex, on the other hand, kept the established component framework and streamlined it. I suspect you're thinking that, if this is the case, you'll never be able to use components from Flash within Flex. That, thankfully, isn't the case. Chapter 11, "Creating Flex Components with Flash Professional CS5," covers just that.

With the release of version 4 of the Flex framework (referred to as Flex 4), a new component architecture was developed that addressed some of the more cumbersome processes that Flex 3 components suffered from—primarily from a layout and styling perspective—but it also provided a clear hierarchy for component developers: the Spark component architecture. This new component framework is an extension of the original Flex 3 component architecture, or Halo, as it is commonly known. The Spark components are specifically targeted at Flash Player version 10 and, for the vast majority, they mirror all the Halo components.

This is not to say that you can use only Spark components in your Flex 4 projects. Actually, you can happily mix and match both Halo and Spark components. However, the overall file size is impacted and goes up because you are including classes specific to both component frameworks in your application.

With the development of version 4 of the Flex framework, Adobe has created a more visually driven development tool called Flash Catalyst. This is aimed at designers who want the same level of design fidelity when moving from their screen/application designs to an interactive Flex-based application. Think of this as converting a design from a flat image file in to a Flex MXML file with all the relevant components wired up without needing to write any code.

Using Flex Components

With the advent of Flex 4, the component framework has been given a massive overhaul, and the result is that you now have two component variants with which to work: the original Flex 2/3 components (often referred to as Halo) and, new to Flex 4, the Spark component set. Don't worry too much about the overall differences at this point; Chapter 3, "Anatomy of a Component" discusses this.

With that in mind, it is worth understanding how this impacts application development. First, additional namespaces help determine the package separation within the overall Flex 4 framework but, in the case of Halo and Spark, you have to be explicit in your namespace declaration to define which version of a particular component you want to use, as shown in the following code example:

```
<?xml version="1.0" encoding="utf-8"?>
<s:Application xmlns:fx="http://ns.adobe.com/mxml/2009"
               xmlns:s="library://ns.adobe.com/flex/spark"
               xmlns:mx="library://ns.adobe.com/flex/mx">

  <mx:Button id="haloBtn" label="I'm a Halo Button" />
  <s:Button id="sparkBtn" label="I'm a Spark Button" />


</s:Application>
```

As you can see, the older Halo components are still declared using the mx namespace, whereas the newer Spark components use a single s namespace. Also, note that the default namespace for noncomponent-specific elements, like script blocks and style tags, within the Flex framework now use a namespace prefix of fx.

One thing that catches a lot of people out when working with components is that instantiating a component in MXML and defining its initial property values is a fairly straightforward process. However, when replicating this in ActionScript, the process isn't as clear cut, as the following two code snippets show.

This example has a Label component with a selection of attributes defined inline in MXML, and it's clear and succinct:

```
<s:Label id="myLbl" width="50" text="OK" click="confirm(event)"
backgroundColor="0x0000ff" />
```

If you now look at the same Label component defined as ActionScript, you start to see how the ease of assigning values to MXML attributes is not always as straightforward when done in ActionScript:

```
import spark.controls.Label;
public var myLbl          :Label = new Label();

myLbl.width = 50;
myLbl.text = "OK";
myLbl.addEventListener(MouseEvent.CLICK, confirm);
myLbl.setStyle("backgroundColor", 0x0000ff);

addElement(myLbl);
```

Although ActionScript is initially more comfortable for most new Flex developers (especially if they are coming from an ActionScript or JavaScript background), it is more verbose to achieve the vast majority of simple tasks. That's not saying you should do everything in MXML—far from it—but you should evaluate the merits of both before making a final decision on which to use.

The main items to take away from this example are that in MXML you use id whereas in ActionScript you tend to use the variables name, in this case, myLbl. id is accessible but not until the item has been added to the target display list. Another thing you probably noticed is that you access event types directly in MXML and they are implicitly added to the EventDispatcher, whereas you have to explicitly do this with addEventListener(type, handler) in ActionScript. The event parameter in MXML is optional, but I recommend you always include it (that is, confirm(event)). Otherwise, you may come unstuck if you dispatch the same type of event to the same handler from an ActionScript implementation because the event object isn't optional in this case.

While in component development, you are more likely to produce your components as ActionScript classes, there is a lot to be said for using MXML for simple components or as facets of a large component structure. Remember that, even though your component may be defined in MXML, you can still import and instantiate it in ActionScript if required.

Don't worry if you are more comfortable in MXML than ActionScript or vice versa, because the code snippets throughout this book provide you with enough information to understand what is happening "on both sides of the fence," so to speak. Before we get ahead of ourselves, let's look at the entire component set that you have access to in Flex 4.

Component Family Tree

All the Flex 4 components are broken down in to five distinct groups. (Technically, there is a sixth, but I'll come to that in a bit.) These five groups are **Controls**, **Navigators**, **Layout**, **Charts**, and **AIR**. They are composed of both Halo and Spark components, with the exception of Charts and the AIR components, which, at this point, are still primarily based on Halo.

In total, there are 105 components; however, the vast majority is overlapping, whereby there are both Halo and Spark equivalents of the same component. Now, you may wonder why there are duplicates within the framework. Obviously, one reason is that not all Flex projects can take advantage of the full Flex 4 framework, and Spark is only available in applications that target Flash Player 10, so people maintaining older applications can continue to use the Halo components and target Flash Player 9 and the Flex 3 framework. However, as you update your applications, you can slowly replace most Halo components with Spark versions.

That said, there is not an equal divide between Halo and Spark components, nor are they all identical. One reason for this is that the Spark architecture is more design orientated and enables for greater separation and flexibility between the visual and functional aspects of the component. Another reason is that creating the original Halo components required a long development cycle and converting and creating comparable Spark components isn't something that was quick to do. Therefore, development of the Spark component set is an ongoing process, and it's likely to take a few updates to fully replicate all the Halo elements.

After reading this book, if you want to have a crack at those components still absent from the Spark side of the component framework, you are more than welcome to pitch in. Because the Flex framework is open source, nothing can stop you from creating and submitting code for the component framework to the Flex project. Be aware, however, that this isn't something you should take lightly because these need to be industry-grade commercial components. If you're still keen to get involved, make sure you read all the documentation on Adobe's open source site so that you are abreast with the developments within the Flex framework as it moves forward. Oh, and *always* read the source code. You'd be surprised how much more information you can glean from the private comments and class format/flow than you can from the standard documentation.

Before I digress and preempt the next chapter, let's get back to the five component groups. As mentioned, you have Controls, Navigators, Layout, Charts, and AIR, and the coverage by each component framework is shown in Table 2.1

Table 2.1   **Coverage by Component Framework**

Type	**Halo**	**Spark**
Controls	30	21
Navigators	8	2
Layout	17	11
Charts	10	0
Total	**65**	**34**

I separated the AIR components, which appear in Table 2.2. The reason I kept them separate from the main components is because they are project specific, meaning that they are only available when working with a Flex project that is targeting the desktop. Note that, although I marked them as Halo-based components, they, like all the Halo components in Flex 4, provide hooks to certain aspects of the Flex 4/Spark architecture, which enables them to capitalize on enhancements within the framework over all.

Table 2.2   **AIR Coverage**

Type	Halo	Spark
AIR	6	0

Don't be fooled into thinking that only 50 percent of the Halo components have Spark equivalents—this isn't true. Although the Halo components do not support the same design separation and flexibility as the Spark components, they do support the use of FXG in Flex 4, which is something we look at in Chapter 10, "Skinning and Styling."

You may still be thinking that there is an obvious disparity between the Halo and Spark components. The reason for this is that the vast majority of the complex data lists—DataGrid (and its variants), the Tree component, and a few of the position-orientated controls—are missing from Spark, such as HorizontalList.

There are two reasons for this: Some have yet to be added to the Spark framework (the complex data lists are a case in point here), and how Spark deals with layout. In Halo, layout is baked into the respective base class of certain controls, whereas layouts in Spark have been removed and placed within a standardized and self-contained set of layout classes that you can apply to any Spark component.

You may be forgiven in thinking that because the Spark components aren't feature complete yet, you should happily continue using just the Halo components until both Halo and Spark have achieved parity. But, you'd be missing out on all the advancements within Flex 4 and, in some respects, you'd just be providing a rod for your own back if you used only the Halo components.

Flex 4 has been designed so that Spark and Halo can exist and operate within the same application framework, and although Spark is missing some of the common component types, it does bring a slew of new ones for you to capitalize on. An obvious one within the Controls group is the VideoPlayer component. Not only do we now have a video player component, but also because of the underlying Spark architecture, it is easy to skin, style, and lay out the interface without having to dig into the overall code. It also incorporates the new Open Screen Media Framework (OSMF), which enables you to "easily provide pluggable components used for high-quality playback experiences," to paraphrase Adobe.[1] Another addition to the Spark components is the RichText and RichEditableText components. These incorporate the new Text Layout Framework (TLF), which harnesses the improved text rendering within Flash Player 10 and, in turn,

---

[1] Open Source Media Framework. www.opensourcemediaframework.com/.

enables these components to provide support for multilingual, bidirectional text that retains print fidelity and offers standard input and gesture controls for copy, paste, cut, and so on. This is not present within Halo.

Some components don't necessarily need to be converted over to the Spark framework; these components will continue to happily function as Halo versions. I suspect as future iterations of Flex are released, the likelihood is that Halo will be deprecated, and everything will be available within the Spark. However, until that day, feel free to mix and match between Spark and Halo as you see fit.

Before we look at what each of these five groups is comprised of, you may recall I mentioned a sixth group of components. These are the custom components, such as the components that you and I create for use within our applications. When using Flash Builder in Design View, you'll see the Custom Component folder at the top of the Components panel and, within it, any components you have created or imported into your Flex project. It also contains a few component placeholders for use with Flash CS5, but we get to that in Chapter 11.

With that in mind, let's look at these component groups in more detail to see what they contain. One thing to be aware of is that I won't point out which components are from Halo and which reside within the new Spark component set unless there is a fundamental change in functionality or operation. If you want to know which component belongs to which component version, look at the initial image in each section because they contain a list of both the Halo and Spark components separated by version.

Control Components

This group contains the vast majority of what most people assume components are when they talk about the Flex framework. Here, we have the building blocks for pretty much anything you need for the capture and provision of user-driven interfaces. As you can see in Figure 2.1, there are a lot of them, but what they all have in common is that they are visual components. I won't go through every one in detail because that would just replicate the Flex framework documentation. I will, however, highlight where items within the Spark component set differ from the Halo version be that in name, underlying functionality, or omission.

Within the Controls group, there are subgroups of components; these are arbitrary groups that either share common functionality (for example, loaders) and/or are extensions of a common base component (various buttons, for example). So, let's look at these in detail, starting with the Loaders.

Loaders and Displays

The vast majority of the components in the Controls group are visual by default except those that load content into them, often referred to as loaders. These components rely on the content they load into themselves to provide their visual aspect. A few control components have to load their content before you can actually view them within your application. For example, the SWFLoader and Image components are both transparent unless they have content to load and display. The `VideoDisplay` component (not to be confused with the `VideoPlayer` component) is identical and won't display a background if it doesn't have a video file loaded into itself. Figure 2.2 shows the `Image`, `SWFLoader`, and `VideoDisplay` components side by side with content loaded into them. It would be pointless to show you what they look like without data, because you'd be looking at a blank image, so I'll leave that up to your imagination.

Figure 2.1   Control components

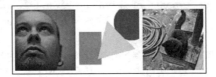

Figure 2.2   From left to right: An Image
displaying an image of me (don't I look cute?),
a SWFLoader, and a VideoDisplay component
displaying the data they have loaded

There is a debate over whether the `ProgressBar` component should be included in this group of loaders and displays. Technically, it doesn't load anything. It generally only exists and is viewable during the process of loading something. After the process finishes, most developers either hide or remove it from the display. However, unlike the SWFLoader, Image, and VideoDisplay components, it does have a default visual look and feel.

Data Consumers

Strictly speaking, all components are data consumers, because they all need to get their data from somewhere other than themselves to be useful. However, lists, grids, and tree components are the true data consumers within the Control components. The complete set of true data consumers is composed of the List, HorizontalList, DataGrid, AdvancedDataGrid, OLAPDataGrid, TileList, Tree, ComboBox, and DropDownList; all these can consume and display complex data through differing visual layouts (see Figure 2.3). You can also use DataGroup and SkinnableDataContainer, but these are more commonly used as facets of a component or as the base class for more interactive items.

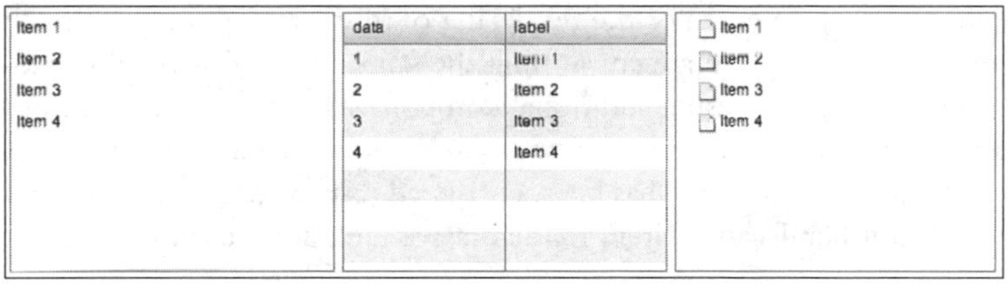

Figure 2.3   From left to right: The same flat data displayed
by List, DataGrid, and Tree components

Out of all the components mentioned in this section, the two that stick out are ComboBox and DropDownList because visually they are more similar to the various button components. I include them here because they support complex data and are technically list-based controls. Although they don't directly inherit from any of the ListBase classes, facets of their composition do. You may also wonder what the difference is between the ComboBox and the DropDownList. Well, it has to do with the actual prompt area of the component. In a ComboBox, this is a TextInput component, so a user could edit the text displayed within it, whereas the DropDownList uses a Label component as its prompt area, thereby offering a noneditable display.

These components can accept a vast selection of data formats to use as a data provider. However, the most commonly used are arrays and collections. If you use an Array, you can simply use individual values, anonymous objects, or instances of typed objects. The same can be applied to collections. Where they differ is how you access and interact with the data; arrays, as you are probably aware, use a zero-based index, whereas collections deal with items. So, accessing the same data from an array and a collection looks something like this:

```
// access data from an Array stored in index 2
private var myObj :Object = myArray[2];

// access the same data when it is stored in a collection
private var myOtherObj :Object = myCollection.getItemAt(2);
```

Collections come is various guises, but the common ones are `ArrayCollections` and `XMLCollections`, and you get a better look at data consumers in Chapter 9, "Manipulating Data."

By default, lists, grids, and trees accept values that can be used as "name, value pairs." These pairs are constructed of a `label` and a `data` property. If one of these is omitted, they will use the other property for both. This doesn't limit you to passing simple data objects to these components. They can accept complex data and display it for you. If you have multiple fields within a data object that you want to display, you can employ `ItemRenderer`.

What makes item renderers truly special is their capability to enable the inclusion of additional components to enhance the rendering of this data. Figure 2.4 shows two `Tree` components side by side. Both are consuming the same data. However, the one on the right has been enhanced by using additional components (in this case, an `Image` component) to display the content as image thumbnails. As you can see, the left one just shows a simple icon whereas the one that has been enhanced displays the actual image. Don't worry if you're not familiar with item renderers; we look at them in Chapter 9.

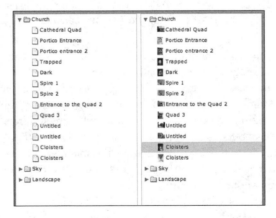

Figure 2.4   Standard Tree component and one
using an ItemRenderer to display thumbnails
of the images it represents

Having looked at the enhanced functionality that the lists offer you, let's look at some of the simplest components within the Controls group, the buttons.

Button-Based Controls

In may come as no surprise to discover that the vast majority of the Control components are button based; starting with the `Button` component, we then have the `ToggleButton`, `CheckBox`, `LinkButton`, `PopUpButton`, `PopUpMenuButton`, and `RadioButton` (see Figure 2.5). We don't end there, though; a lot of additional components incorporate buttons to provide functionality that requires some form of visual feedback; this includes the entire set of list-based components you just saw and `ComboBox` and `DropDownList`. That said, most people associate the functionality of a button with something that actually looks and responds like a button, that *button-ness* we all recognize and appreciate for the ease with which you can simply drop them into your applications and wire them up.

Figure 2.5   The various button components clockwise from the top left, Button, ToggleButton, Radio, CheckBox, LinkButton, PopUpMenuButton and PopUpButton.

Now, whereas `Button`, `ToggleButton`, `Checkbox`, and `LinkButton` can be dropped into an application and used as is, `PopupButton`, `PopUpMenuButton`, and `RadioButton` all require additional data (or in the case of the `RadioButton`, a `RadioGroup` component) to operate as expected. This is because they provide a higher level of functionality compared to the simple "click" and "toggle" of the first three button components.

The pop-up components are similar to `ComboBox` and `DropDownList` in functionality, but both `PopUpButton` and `PopUpMenuButton` can have their main content display area clicked to dispatch an event. `PopUpButton` enables you to define what will be displayed when it is clicked, whereas `PopUpMenuButton` includes a menu as part of its functionality, but it is also clickable.

Steppers, Sliders, Pickers, Choosers

Having looked at lists and buttons, you are nearing the end of the Controls. All that is left are the specialist components that, although unique, are still extremely useful: `NumberStepper`, `Spinner`, `Sliders`, `ColorPicker`, date, and separate scrollbar components (see Figure 2.6). Some of these are specific items that provide an extra level of functionality when a unique but valuable task or process is required.

The Date components, `DateField` and `DateChooser`, provide easy solutions when you need to set time-based criteria, like holidays or a birthdate. The sliders, both the `VSlider` and `HSlider`, provide a means by which the user can filter or adjust data that has a maximum and minimum value, such as the volume of a video player. `NumericStepper` offers the same type of filtering but through pure numeric values, which enables a user to fine-tune a value but still remain within the bounds as defined by your application.

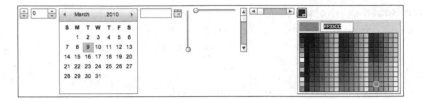

Figure 2.6   Spinner, NumericStepper, DateChooser, DateField, VSlider,
HSlider, VScrollBar, HScrollBar, and ColorPicker (open)

Spinner, although a separate component in its own right, is the up/down buttons in NumericStepper. It enables you to incorporate either within your components that require the ability to step up and down within the data provided.

ColorPicker provides a quick and easy mechanism for selecting a color value. The real value of all these components is that they transparently restrict the user's choice to a limited set from a vast set of options without strong-arming them. This is what makes them so unique and useful, especially if you consider how time-consuming the creation of these components could be.

Last but not least, you have the scrollbar components, both vertical and horizontal. Although these are not new to Spark, scrollbars play a bigger role in component control and layout through the Scroller component, which is something that will become clearer when we look at the Spark layout components.

Text Controls

The capability for you to display and enable the insertion of text (whether it is plain or HTML text) into your applications is a fairly important one, so I saved these components until the end of this section. These are the text components, starting with the Label component and working our way to the rich functionality that is the RichTextEditor. In between, we have the Text, TextInput, TextArea, RichText, and RichEditableText components.

Label is a single line noneditable text component that's useful for displaying simple headings and entries. The Text component is almost identical, but it has the added advantage of displaying multiline content. However, as with the Label component, this text is not editable. The TextInput and TextArea components are basically the Label and Text components' editable equivalents; there is one key difference between the Text and TextArea components, however.

Like the list components, the TextArea component has built-in scrollbars, so if the content exceeds their bounds, they are displayed automatically. When the scrollbars are used, they have an impact on layout. By this, I mean if your component requires a vertical scrollbar, its inclusion may force your component to also display the horizontal scrollbar. It is a quirk that you learn to anticipate, and it tends to occur only when you are using components with strict size requirements. You can easily avoid this if you don't need scrollbars by setting `horizontalScrollPolicy` or the `verticalScrollPolicy` to `off`, as Figure 2.7 and the following code to create it shows.

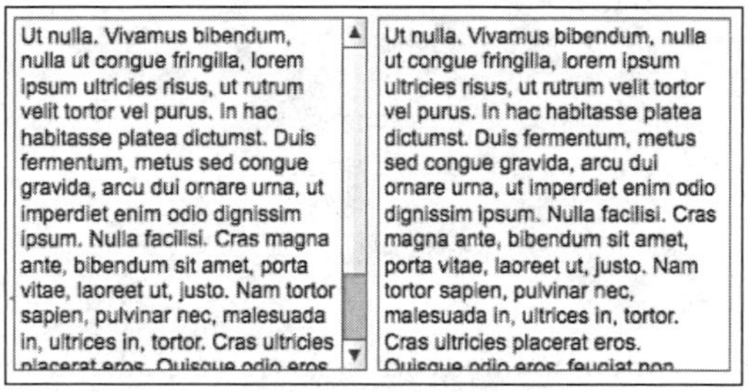

Figure 2.7   Text components displaying
the same content, the right image having
both scrollbars disabled

```
<?xml version="1.0" encoding-"utf-8"?>
<s:Application xmlns:fx="http://ns.adobe.com/mxml/2009"
            xmlns:s="library://ns.adobe.com/flex/spark"
            xmlns:mx="library://ns.adobe.com/flex/mx"
            minWidth="955"
            minHeight="600">

    <s:layout>
        <s:HorizontalLayout horizontalAlign="center" verticalAlign="middle" />
    </s:layout>

    <fx:Script>
        <![CDATA[
        [Bindable]
        private var _dummyCopy :String = "Ut nulla. Vivamus bibendum, nulla ut
                                    congue fringilla, " +
        "lorem ipsum ultricies risus, ut rutrum velit tortor vel " +
        "purus. In hac habitasse platea dictumst. Duis fermentum, " +
        "metus sed congue gravida, arcu dui ornare urna, ut " +
        "imperdiet enim odio dignissim ipsum. Nulla facilisi. Cras " +
        "magna ante, bibendum sit amet, porta vitae, laoreet ut, " +
        "justo. Nam tortor sapien, pulvinar nec, malesuada in, " +
        "ultrices in, tortor. Cras ultricies placerat eros. Quisque " +
        "odio eros, feugiat non, iaculis nec, lobortis sed, arcu. " +
        "Pellentesque sit amet sem et purus pretium consectetuer.";
        ]]>
    </fx:Script>
```

```
        <s:TextArea id="scrollBarsEnabledText"
                    x="10" y="10"
                    height="200" width="200"
                    text="{_dummyCopy}"/>
        <s:TextArea id="scrollbarsDisabledText"
                    x="218" y="10"
                    height="200" width="200"
                    horizontalScrollPolicy="off"
                    verticalScrollPolicy="off"
                    text="{_dummyCopy}"/>
</s:Application>
```

Up to this point, the text components we have seen are all available within Halo and Spark, but two new components are only available within the Spark framework: RichText and RichEditableText. Designed as a multipurpose text field, they enable for the display of both plain and rich (HTML) text, as the name implies. However, unlike the Halo text components whereby you just assign your data to either the text property, for plain text, or the htmlText property for richer formatted text, these rich text components use the new Text Layout Framework (TLF), giving you the ability to have multiple text styles and orientations (you can display all forms of bidirectional text in the same component via TLF), control the tab stops, formatting, and flow. The payoff for this is that it requires a slightly more verbose approach to assigning data to one of these components; but, as Stan Lee so wisely said, "With great power, comes great configurability," or something like that.

The following code shows a simple RichText component with formatted text. The rich text components and TLF give you pretty much pixel-perfect control over layout and formatting, but it takes a while to get used to all the properties that you can tap:

```
<?xml version="1.0" encoding="utf-8"?>
<s:Application xmlns:fx="http://ns.adobe.com/mxml/2009"
               xmlns:s="library://ns.adobe.com/flex/spark"
               xmlns:mx="library://ns.adobe.com/flex/mx"
               minWidth="955" minHeight="600">
    <s:layout>
        <s:HorizontalLayout horizontalAlign="center" verticalAlign="middle" />
    </s:layout>

    <s:BorderContainer>
        <s:layout>
            <s:HorizontalLayout paddingBottom="5" paddingLeft="5"
paddingRight="5" paddingTop="5" />
        </s:layout>
        <s:RichText width="300">
            <s:content><s:p>As you can see you declare formatting by
prefixing common tags with an <s:span fontFamily="Courier">s</s:span>
                in the same manner as you would form normal Spark
                elements.</s:p>
```

```
                <s:br />Strangely enough forgetting the <s:span
                fontStyle="italic" fontWeight="bold">'s' prefix</s:span>
                is the commonest point of frustration when applying
                formatting inline.<s:br />
                <s:p><s:span fontWeight="bold">Remember</s:span> if in
                doubt always prefix your elements!</s:p>
            </s:content>
        </s:RichText>
    </s:BorderContainer>
</s:Application>
```

For clarity, I wrapped this code in a `BorderContainer` so that it shows the bounds of the `RichText` component and applied a `HorizontalLayout` to it just to add a bit of padding. One more thing before we move on from these rich text components, in case it wasn't blatantly obvious from the name, `RichEditableText` components are the same as `RichText` components except that you can edit the text.

Beyond the various display and input text types, you have one special component that provides extra functionality over and above simple display and input of text: `RichTextEditor`. This composite component is more akin to a mini-application in its own right. It is ideal when you want to enable users to input large amounts of textual information and provide formatting and style control (see Figure 2.8). It's perfect for things like nontechnical administration systems, such as content-management systems.

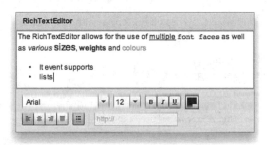

Figure 2.8   RichTextEditor component

Navigator Components

The navigators are, as the name implies, a collection of components that enable a user to move through your content. This can be in a linear or nonlinear fashion. Primarily menu-esque in design and operation, they provide a wealth of options when you need to create a system of display or movement between content areas. Most navigator components have a property called `direction` that enable you to specify the orientation of the actual component, so it's as easy to have a vertical `TabBar` as it is to have a horizontal one. Figure 2.9 shows the navigators.

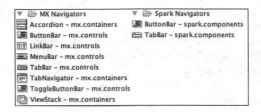

Figure 2.9   Navigator components

As you can see from Figure 2.9, you have access to a selection of button-driven navigation bars. Most of these are just an extension of the various button components. However, these components do not create the buttons themselves; as a developer, you need to provide a data source for them, and they in turn will create the number of buttons based on each unique data source.

The following code provides enough information for the `ButtonBar` in Figure 2.10 to create and lay out the relevant buttons. If you want to create a stateful navigation system to indicate to the user which item is currently active, you could use a `ToggleButtonBar` or a `MenuBar`.

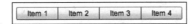

Figure 2.10   Basic ButtonBar with four buttons

```
<?xml version="1.0" encoding="utf-8"?>
<!-- Providing a ButtonBar component with a Array of simple data types (Strings)
 --/>
<s:Application xmlns:fx="http://ns.adobe.com/mxml/2009"
    xmlns:s="library://ns.adobe.com/flex/spark"
    xmlns:mx="library://ns.adobe.com/flex/mx"
    minWidth="1024" minHeight="768"
    creationComplete="application1_creationCompleteHandler (event)">

    <fx:Script>
        <![CDATA[
            import mx.events.FlexEvent;
            private var _dp      :Array = ["Item 1",
                                          "Item 2",
                                          "Item 3",
                                          "Item 4"];

            protected function
application1_creationCompleteHandler(event:FlexEvent):void
```

```
            {
                    myBtnBar.dataProvider = _dp;
            }


        ]]>
    </fx:Script>


    <mx:ButtonBar id="myBtnBar" />
</s:Application>
```

The `ToggleButtonBar` operates identically to the `ButtonBar`, but the elements it displays are set to toggle—kind of obvious, really. The `MenuBar` is similar in nature to the `ToggleButtonBar`, but it has a rollover state that can be toggled. When the user passes his mouse over an entry, that entry is highlighted. The `MenuBar` component also supports the display of hierarchical menus; these are created and displayed based on the data structure provided (see Figure 2.11). Like many data renderers, you can render other components within the menu component to supply enhanced functionality.

Figure 2.11   ToggleButtonBar and MenuBar
navigator components

Moving on from the button style navigators, you have the `TabBar` and `TabNavigator`. These differ from each in that the `TabNavigator` and its contents are tied together, whereas the `TabBar` and its content can be physically separated by other layout concerns, and if you were inclined, other items and components. Beyond this visual difference, they both function in a near identical manner.

Next is a tab navigator of sorts: the `Accordion`. This component provides you with a control that can contain numerous view containers within a fixed area. This is useful when you need a multiview system and space is cramped. It has a minor defect, however; each content item requires space within the `Accordion` for its header and, therefore, adding multiple containers reduce the overall space that each can use within the `Accordion`. You can add scrollbars to your content views, but this isn't a good user experience, so avoid it. If you do want to take advantage of an `Accordion` within your application, don't pack it with content views; otherwise, you may discover it becomes difficult, if not impossible, for a user to interact with it.

The last navigator component is the `ViewStack`. This navigator has no visual aspect. It operates in a similar manner to view states (see Chapter 5, "Managing States," for more information about view states) but provides a more flexible implementation by componentizing it.

Layout Components

Now that you have looked at the more visual Flex components, let's explore those responsible for handling positioning and layout (shown in Figure 2.12). As mentioned at the beginning of this chapter, one of the core differences between Spark and Halo components has to do with how layout is managed. In Halo components, the layout of a component is baked into the component itself, whether within a concrete class that the subsequent child components inherit and assign orientation to, like the HBox and VBox, or through a specific implementation within a particular component, like the Canvas. The core issue is that layout components don't implement the process as a common set of rules; they each implement it as they see fit. The knock-on effect is that it is difficult to lay content out in a more controlled and flexible manner—heaven forbid you want the Halo TileList to lay your content out in anything other than a grid of equally sized elements.

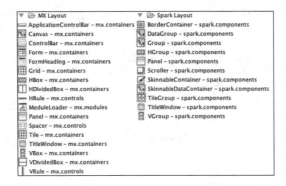

Figure 2.12   Layout components

A decision was made to rectify this shortfall and bring the component model of Spark in line with the overall layout strategy of Flex 4. All layout control was decoupled from the components and moved to a higher level set of classes that implemented layout in a consistent manner across the entire application, be it for a view or a single component control. The advantages are that you can easily define your own layouts and assign a layout dynamically at runtime, and the Layout manager will apply it in exactly the same manner as the standard layouts that come with Flex 4. This is pretty much impossible to do with the Halo components; beyond setting the orientation from horizontal to vertical or absolute, you'd have to get into some heavy subclassing.

To achieve this, Adobe went back to the drawing board and looked at the Halo's layout components. That's not to say that the Halo components were left unaltered. To allow the Halo components to operate within these new layout rules, they had to have some additional interfaces added to add support for this new approach. Because of this separation of layout from the component itself, it also meant that some components no longer existed within Spark for the same reason that they do in Halo. Take the HorizontalList mentioned earlier. In Spark, you just declare a `List` component and provide it with a horizontal layout as its layout property. Although this may appear to be more work, the dynamic nature of layouts means it is cleaner and more flexible to implement it in this manner, because you could just as easily switch out the horizontal layout for a tile layout at runtime if you wanted, which is something you cannot do with the Halo `List` or `HorizontalList`.

The Halo layout components, like `Grid`, `Tile`, and `Panel`, are probably a bit more self-explanatory compared to the Spark equivalents. Some of you could probably hazard a guess at `Canvas`, `HBox`, and `VBox`. The `Canvas` is a blank area with absolute positioning, whereas the `HBox` and `VBox` both lay out content based on either horizontal or vertical alignment. The `HDivided` and `VDivided` boxes, like the `HBox` and `VBox`, have two or more dividers that align their content in either horizontal or vertical panes. A few components may not initially resonate at all. The `ModuleLoader` is probably one of these. This component deals with loading modules—surprise, surprise! Modules are a special type of SWF file; to do them proper justice is beyond the scope of this book. However, if you want to know more about any of these components, or any classes within the Flex framework, you should certainly check out the internal help system in Flash Builder or head over to Adobe's Livedocs for Flex. (The URL is in Appendix A, "Flex Resources.")

The `Form` component is unique in so far that it formats any other component that is placed within it and provides a label for it. This is handy if you are building registration forms or the like, because it makes the actual creation quick and efficient. The actual labels it uses are a component called a `FormItem`. Now, you don't have to use a `FormItem` in a `Form`, but it makes sense to. By default, `Form`s are vertically aligned, so everything will be placed from top to bottom. However, by incorporating additional layout components, you can influence the layout of the form.

The rest of the layout components have to do mainly with formatting the elements and how they appear within a container. To this end, you have `HRules`, `VRules`, a `Spacer` component, a couple of control bars (`ApplicationControlBar` and `ControlBar`), and a `FormHeader` component. Again, most of these are self-explanatory. The `HRule` and `VRule` provide a one-pixel line either horizontally or vertically. The `Spacer` component acts just like the old shim pixel gifs that were used to fine-tune a layout in HTML back in the day, and the `ControlBar` is just an area to lay out other components, such as buttons and labels. Figure 2.13 presents two `Panel` components: one with a `ControlBar` (shown on the right) containing two buttons and the other (left) *au naturale*.

The `ApplicationControlBar` is pretty much identical to the `ControlBar` component, but it provides chrome and the ability to display a drop shadow and, as the name implies, `ApplicationControlBar` components generally are used as part of the main application layout as opposed to placing controls within another layout container. Unfortunately, at this point, the Spark components do not have an equivalent to the `ApplicationControlBar` or `ControlBar`. However, you can replicate it by using an `<s:HGroup>` and laying your content out as required. So, that's the Halo side of the layout components; let's compare those to the Spark ones.

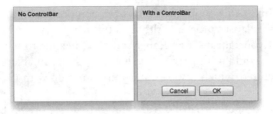

Figure 2.13   Ordinary panel component and one
containing a ControlBar composed of two buttons

One thing you will have likely noticed is that only two components are comparable to the Halo layout components: Panel and TitleWindow. Looking at the components in Figure 2.12, you can see that, from a Spark perspective, the vast majority of these components seem to revolve around the <s:Group> component. They all do. Group is basically a nonskinnable, nonstyleable container to place components within.

You may be thinking, "Why was the name changed when the Halo container component does the same thing?" It all has to do with MXMLG, Flex 4's new MXML-based graphics library and the center of the entire Spark "design in mind" approach, as you'll see in Chapter 10. Suffice it to say that a lot of stuff is going on under the hood of the new layout components and, once you are familiar with them, it's unlikely that you'll go back to the older Halo versions. Note that none of the Spark layout components contain scrollbars—you have to literally wrap a Spark layout component within a Scroller component to provide scrolling support. Again, this may sound a trifle counter-intuitive, but it makes sense; check out the following code example. After all, why pay the file-size hit for scrollbars if your application doesn't use them? Within Halo, you don't have a choice; you can only turn them off, but they're still there in the code base.

```
<s:BorderContainer width="100" height="200">
    <s:Scroller width="100%" height="100%">
        <s:VGroup width="100%" height="100%">
            <s:Button label="Button 1"/>
            <s:Button label="Button 2"/>
            <s:Button label="Button 3"/>
            <s:Button label="Button 4"/>
            <s:Button label="Button 5"/>
            <s:Button label="Button 6"/>
            <s:Button label="Button 7"/>
            <s:Button label="Button 8"/>
            <s:Button label="Button 9"/>
            <s:Button label="Button 10"/>
        </s:VGroup>
    </s:Scroller>
</s:BorderContainer>
```

As you can see, the Spark approach to implementing functionality is a bolt-and-build approach because it enables you to only add in the elements you need, which is something that's carried through the entire Flex 4 framework.

Charting Components

The Charting components are perfect for dealing with visualizing data or report creation. I won't go into any detail about charts, because they are all quite obvious (see Figure 2.14). The good thing about the charts in Flash Builder 4, however, is that you also get the source code—something that wasn't present in earlier versions of Flash Builder. So, if you want to harness their power and functionality to create new, interesting ways of displaying data beyond just skinning this collection, you can have a good read through the code to give you an in-depth understanding of how they tick.

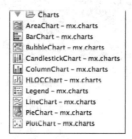

Figure 2.14   Charting components

As you can see, there is a diverse selection. Also, notice that there is a separate Legend component that can indicate to the end user what color represents which piece of information.

AIR-Specific Components

The AIR-specific components are extensions of those we have already seen, updated to enable interaction with the user's operating system. As you can see from Figure 2.15, there aren't that many—six. We're not going to dwell on most of these because their siblings have already been discussed.

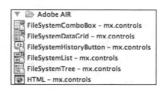

Figure 2.15   AIR components

Notice the HTML component, which enables you to load web content into your AIR applications. Don't get this confused with using HTML to create an AIR application or simply display HTML–formatted text. This is a Flex component that harnesses WebKit (a fully fledged web browser within the AIR architecture that loads web content, including embedded SWFs) directly into your Flex-based AIR application (see Figure 2.16). As obvious as it sounds, keep in mind that you can only use these components in an AIR project. If you are developing an application or component for the web (such as a native Flex project), you will get errors when you try to compile your application.

Figure 2.16   HTML component with my blog loaded into it.
(Note the AIR badge installer on the right.)

That's about it for the Flex 4 components. There are more of them in the entire framework, but the ones highlighted in this chapter are the ones you are likely to use the most. The components that have been omitted from this chapter are generally the base concrete component classes from which a lot of these are subclassed.

Summary

This chapter showed you all the components that come with Flash Builder. You have also seen those components specific to desktop application development through AIR.

You learned more about the hierarchy and origin of Flex components from a historical and programmatic standpoint.

Next, you get a better understanding of the core component methods and their purpose within the component framework, and an introduction to some special types of components. You also get a better understanding of which components to use as the foundations of your own components and why.

Anatomy of a Component

Now that you have seen all the components present within Flex 4.0, let's focus on what actually makes up the structure of a component and the core behaviors and functionality that you need to provide for it to operate within the Flex framework. In this chapter, you get a clear understanding of how to structure your components, both in ActionScript and MXML, and which component is most suitable as the base class for your own components. Finally, you get an overview of a unique type of component, but I'll save that surprise for you until later in this chapter.

Component Life Cycle

Regardless of how simple or complex you make your components, there is one constant: Your component needs to be instantiated and when it does, it needs to be able to initialize itself and create and display any assets it requires. If it is interacted with or data changes that it consumes or manages, it needs to notify not only external elements of your application that it has changed in some way, but also most likely itself and its own children. This is commonly referred to as the component life cycle. Figure 3.1 shows an illustration of the actual cycle.

As part of this cycle, various methods are invoked, events dispatched, and properties set, some only once during the initialization of the component and others numerous times depending on user, data, or state-driven influences. As Figure 3.1 shows, the `Constructor` and `createChildren()` methods are invoked only once during the entire life cycle of the component, whereas the `commitProperties()`, `measure()`, and `updateDisplayList()` methods can be invoked repeatedly, depending on the type of influence that has been placed on the component. Each of these core component framework methods has their access modifier set to *protected* to avoid unnecessary or accidental direct interaction from external sources, but at the same time, enables any subclasses to inherit and invoke them.

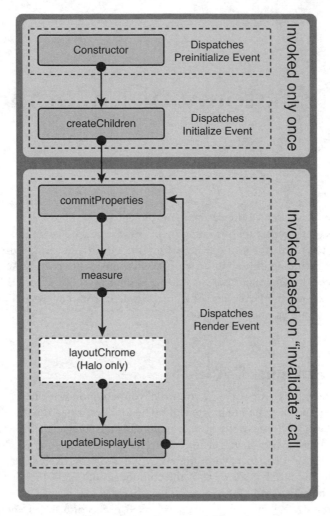

Figure 3.1   Component life cycle

Within your component, you can tailor all or none of these methods and any number in between; if you do need to alter one, you need to make sure you meet two requirements of inheritance:

- The method must invoke the super class or method, passing the relevant parameters if present.
- The method must use the override keyword to indicate that you want to add or alter the functionality of that method that already exists within the parent class method within your component.

The following code shows an overridden `updateDisplayList()` method:

```
// marked as override so we can change its functionality
override protected function updateDisplayList(unscaledWidth:Number,
unscaledHeight:Number):void
{
  /*
    Call the super.methodName so that additional functionality
    that is declared within it can be executed
  */
  super.updateDisplayList(unscaledWidth, unscaledHeight);

  // Your code for your component included here
  _myTextDisplay.setActualSize();
  ...
}
```

As you can see, it is fairly straightforward to override a component method ready to add the specific functionality that your component requires. Word to the wise, however: Don't override a method if you aren't going to add any additional functionality. Although it doesn't affect the component, it adds needless code that provides no benefit and reduces the legibility of your class when others look through it to see how it operates. For example, taking the previous code and just leaving it as illustrated in the following provides no inherent value beyond just bloating your code:

```
override protected function updateDisplayList(unscaledWidth:Number,
unscaledHeight:Number):void
{
  super.updateDisplayList(unscaledWidth,unscaledHeight);
}
```

With those points in mind, let's look at which method performs what role within this life cycle and how you can leverage this process to produce rich components without having to re-create functionality that is already there.

Understanding the Structure

Now, you have a clearer understanding of what the component life cycle consists of. The next step is to understand how it actually moves through these phases and what each of the component methods actually does. After you have a clear understanding of that, you can quickly create the core structure of your component without thinking about it. However, to avoid running before you can walk, you need to know what you can harness within each method, so you can place your component code in the correct place to avoid potential pitfalls.

The obvious place to start is the component constructor. Although not strictly part of the component life cycle, it is the initialization point of all classes—including components—by invoking the class's constructor via the new keyword. Don't skip the constructor section, though; you need to adhere to some specific rules that differ from a standard ActionScript class. That said, let's see what those differences are.

Component Constructor

The component constructor is slightly different from normal class constructors because you don't create it with any parameters. There are a few good reasons for this. First, your component is more likely to be declared in MXML, where you cannot pass parameters into the constructor of your component. Second, if another component instantiates your component purely by interface or by base class type (UIComponent, for example), there is no way for you to cleanly set those parameters. Although you could provide these parameters and simply give them all default values, as the following example shows, this is a poor design approach that's better handled within the constructor and associated component methods via the components properties and accessors/mutators (getter/setters).

```
private var _property1:Number;
private var _property2:Number;

// An incorrect implementation of the property
// variables within the component constructor.
public function MyComponent(property1:Number=100, property2:Number=100)
{
  _property1 = property1;
  _property2 = property2;
}

// The correct approach
public function MyComponent()
{
  _property1 = 100;
  _property2 = 100;
}
```

As you can see, the second example sets the values of two variables when the component is instantiated. This is the preferred method by which you would assign internal values to your "startup" variables. Now this may sound all well and good for internal values, but what if you want to provide external values and have those applied to your component during the startup phases? Well, again, the Flex component framework provides us with a method to achieve this, commitProperties(), which is covered in a bit. For now, remember that the constructor is where you instantiate your variables with internally defined values.

After you have these values assigned, you need to know that they can be accessed. The Component framework takes care of this by dispatching a *preinitialize* event when the constructor finishes processing. It also does a few things in the background: It calculates any style values that have been assigned to your component and adds a reference to its parent. For example, if you placed this directly into your main MXML file, it would set this property to be a reference to Application. If it were placed inside a Panel component, it would be a reference to that.

Now, even though you should assign your variables needed for the initial startup of your component in the constructor, a few items shouldn't be declared here—namely anything that needs to be added to the DisplayList at startup. These objects need to be instantiated and added in a method called createChildren().

createChildren()

The createChildren() method is invoked directly after the constructor, after the component is added to the parent container via the addChild() method, be that implicitly by declaring the component in MXML within a parent tag or explicitly by using the parents addChild() method in ActionScript. Note that, in the case of container components that inherit from Group, you need to use the addElement() method instead of addChild(), because Group and its subclasses don't support addChild(). This is because they also support the adding and displaying of graphical elements that have been declared in FXG and those components that inherit from UIComponent or one of its subclasses. We look at FXG in Chapter 10, "Skinning and Styling."

The createChildren() method is where you should instantiate and add all your display objects required to get your component up and running with its default values and views. Like the constructor, the createChildren() method is invoked only once during the entire life cycle of your component, so it is ideally suited for the creation and adding of display objects that persist because you need to worry about this process only once. A good approach to take with the createChildren() method is if you have to create drawn objects as part of the initialization process of your component, separate these into individual methods and just invoke these during the createChildren() phase. This has two benefits: It keeps your code clean, and it enables a level of separation, so if you want to draw or process something again after the initial setup phases, you can easily access these methods.

There are a few exceptions to this rule of using createChildren() to add all your display objects to your component. What if you need to add something to the display that exists only if the user clicks or rolls over a bit of your component? Do you create those elements here or is there an alternative? I tend to create only those display items needed and use additional methods to create items when required and add them to the DisplayList at that point; but, as I said, you can do that or instantiate the objects in createChildren(), but don't add them to the DisplayList until you need them. Either way, keep in mind that you need to take the stack index of your children into consideration to ensure that they aren't obscured or masked from input when they finally get added; each item added to a particular DisplayList is effectively placed above the previous one (like a stack of magazines, the oldest being at the bottom and the most recent addition at the top).

commitProperties()

The commitProperties() method deals with any updates or alterations to the values within your component that have been influenced by external means; for example, setting the value of an attribute in a component's MXML tag like this:

```
<mx:Button label="Hello World" />
```

Here, the button's default value for its label property of Button has been replaced with my Hello World (I know, not original). What actually happens is that the value gets set within the Button component, which then triggers a request to the component framework to recommit the properties of the button with the new value. To do this, the button invokes its invalidateProperties() method, flagging that it needs to be updated in the next render phase because something has changed. When the next render phase happens, the commitProperties() method is executed and the value of the label property is set to Hello World.

If any of the display objects have also been altered or resized, additional invalidation calls may be required, so each one is flagged and they are all batched up to be invoked in turn within subsequent render phases. In the previous example, Hello World is longer than Button, so after the Button has assigned the new label value, it also calls the invalidateSize() method because the component needs to make sure it is still the correct size. The invalidateSize() method in turn calls the measure() and/or updateDisplayList() method.

measure()

The measure() method is slightly different from most of the other methods within the components life cycle. By this, I mean that it is invoked only if the width and height of your component are not provided with an actual value. Therefore, if you provide a width and height for your component when you place it in your application, measure() is completely ignored by Flex, even if you invoke the invalidateSize() method because Flex doesn't need to work out what size your component is because it is already defined.

For those of you who want to know what it actually does, here is the deal: When the measure() method is invoked, it checks to see whether the explicitHeight and explicitWidth properties return NaN (Not a Number); if they do, it then executes whatever code it contains to calculate the actual width and height of your component. Now, you may be rereading the previous sentence at this point; where did this explicitHeight and explicitWidth stuff come from? Well, the Flex framework has an extended selection of height and width properties, and all of them perform slightly different roles. To help clarify what each does, they are all listed in Table 3.1.

Table 3.1   **Various Size Properties Within the Flex Framework**

Type	Description	Notes
explicitHeight explicitWidth explicitMaxHeight explicitMaxWidth explicitMinHeight explicitMinWidth explicitHeight explicitWidth	The *explicit* sizes are used by the components' containers, not the component, and they relate to various values, such as the actual, minimum, or maximum size of that component. Used by the parent container to calculate both the size and position of your component within itself.	The component's container uses these values to calculate its size. If the parent of your component is a container-based component, these values are unlikely to be factored. Also, all these values are based on the component's own coordinate system and are affected by scaling when applied in relation to their parent. Therefore, dimensions may not return identical values from the respective coordinate system.
maxHeight maxWidth minHeight minWidth	Used by the parent container to calculate both the size and position of your component within itself.	The max and min size values are similar in nature to the explicit values. These values are also affected by scaling when applied in relation to their parent and, as such, may return different values as calculated by their respective coordinate systems.
percentHeight percentWidth	Enable you to define a percentage value (0–100) for your component.	If you set the `height`, `width`, `explicitHeight`, or `explicitWidth`, these values are reset and ignored.
measuredHeight measuredWidth measuredMinHeight meaasuredMinWidth	The properties you use to define the default sizes for your component. They are the only properties to do with sizing you should use in your `measure()` method.	You do not need to set any of these externally because they are automatically set via the width and height properties.

Table 3.1   **Various Size Properties Within the Flex Framework**

Type	Description	Notes
height width	The properties that you use to dictate the size of your component externally. When either is set, it causes a resize event to be dispatched, which eventually results in your component recalculating its dimensions, if applicable.	Although you can place a percentage value in the MXML width (width="100%"), you cannot do this in ActionScript. You need to use the percentHeight or percentWidth if you want to achieve the same result.

As you can see, only a couple of them are actually used by your component as a basis for size calculation by the component itself. The others are part of the framework and, for the most part, happily trot alongside your component. I will point out the percentHeight and percentWidth attributes, however, because these are not exposed within MXML. This is because the width and height attributes of MXML are clever enough to work out the data type when it is applied and, therefore, enable you to set a percentage value for that property. After all, every attribute in MXML is basically a string. ActionScript, on the other hand, isn't as forgiving, so if you want to set percentage values for your components in ActionScript, you need to use the percentHeight and percentWidth properties as required. I know that was a bit of a slog, but you'd have come across all those different sizing options at some point if you hadn't already, so it was worth getting it out of the way where it has some relevance.

Given all that preceding information, how do you actually set the size of your component? Well, you have a few options. First, you can obviously set the default width and height of your component. If you don't supply a value for either or both of these, they default to 0, effectively making your component invisible. I personally wouldn't use this as a mechanism to set the visibility of your component because you are likely to have child components that may size incorrectly if they are relying on their parents' dimensions. The second thing you can do is set the *minimum* width and height of your component; this has the benefit of letting Flex know that you don't want your component to go below a certain size—this is especially useful if you have a complex layout that doesn't degrade gracefully or just becomes completely unusable if it goes below a certain size.

```
override protected function measure():void
{
  measuredHeight = 200;
  measuredWidth = 200;
  measuredMinHeight = 25;
  measuredMinWidth = 100;
}
```

Be warned: This isn't set in stone, and there are certain instances in which external factors can override and even ignore this.

For the most part, you are likely to set these properties to the same value, as the following code shows. Either way, the main use of the measure() method is to set the default dimensions of your component so that another developer doesn't need to provide initial values just to get your component to display in his application.

The upshot is that these values are used when you drop a component from the Component Panel within Flex Builder onto the design view. The vast majority of the control components display at a default size for that specific component type as defined in their respective measure() methods.

```
override protected function measure():void
{
  measuredHeight = measuredMinHeight = 200;
  measuredWidth = measuredMinWidth = 100;
}
```

Now that we looked at resizing our component with measure(), let's look at updating those visual elements that may have been altered by resizing your component through external influences, such as if a developer supplies a specific width and/or height or via its children.

layoutChrome()

It is worth pointing out that layoutChrome() is a Halo-specific method. It has no use or equivalent within the Spark framework because of the life cycle Spark components have for their skins—something that you'll get a better understanding of in Chapter 10. With that in mind, I included it in this chapter for completeness; if you are interested in only developing components based on the Spark framework, you can skip this section. For those who want to work with the older Halo component framework (and some components are still provided only as Halo versions), read on.

The concept behind the layoutChrome() method is that container styling and visuals should be kept separate from content. For the most part, there isn't a huge need to have them separated because you can manage their updating together and everything is fine. However, if the container's autoLayout property is set to false, you could have a problem because when autoLayout is set to true, recalculation of the size and position of your component, and all its children, is performed whenever a child component's position or dimensions change. So, if the container changes size, or its contents do, they can both expand or contract to accommodate the changes if that is how they've been configured. That's why this is the default value in the vast majority of Flex container components.

If autoLayout is set to false, Flex updates only the measurement and/or the position when a child is added or removed—not too helpful for our border if it were clumped in with all the other layout code because it could cause unforeseen layout issues if it updated itself only when this happened.

Fortunately, Flex continues to invoke the `layoutChrome()` method even if `autoLayout` is set to false. So, as long as you put all your container's chrome within the `layoutChrome()` method, it updates correctly whenever the position or size changes, regardless of whether the rest of the content is set to update. But don't be tempted to throw all your visual element controls into a `layoutChrome()` method just for the sake of it. Most components don't require this because they update themselves and their children all at once; however, if you create a container-style component that may or may not be based on a template component, this process comes into its own.

updateDisplayList()

You've seen how to apply values to your component's properties and set the size, and for Halo-based components, you know how to manage the chrome of a container. The last core component method makes sure everything is cleaned up and ready to go because it is in charge of updating the display status of your component: `updateDisplayList()`.

The `updateDisplayList()` method is the final step before your component actually appears within your application; it is responsible for setting any child component properties, sizing, and positioning elements as required. In addition, it is responsible for applying any graphical style elements, including any nonchrome skins. Also, at this point, the parent container calculates the component's final size, if it has been set externally and/or altered by its children, before setting its visibility to true.

For a method that does so much, it has a short description, I know. There is one more thing that you need to know about `updateDisplayList()`, and it may have already been sitting at the back of your mind while you were reading about `measure()`. If `measure()` is invoked only if you *don't* set the width and height, how do you set them after you have set your component's initial size? Well, it's probably no surprise that you do that here, within `updateDisplayList()`. Of all the core methods, `updateDisplayList()` is the only one that accepts parameters, as you can see in the following code line. But, like all the preceding methods, it shouldn't be directly invoked by you, the developer; this should be left to the Flex component framework via the relevant invalidation call.

```
updateDisplayList(unscaledWidth:Number, unscaledHeight:Number):void
```

These two values are passed to the component as part of the `invalidateDisplayList()` call and are set to the component's coordinate system, not the parents. The reason for this is that `unscaledWidth` and `unscaledHeight` values do not include any scaling, as the name implies, that may have been applied to the component. So, aim to use these values when performing update calculations that affect your component and its children, not `width` and `height`, as you might think as these do have the scaling modifiers applied.

Inherit, Composite, or Rolling Your Own

One thing that a lot of developers mull over is whether their components should use a pure inheritance chain from UIComponent or a subclass thereof. Is the sum of their components parts through composition, or do you just ignore the whole component framework because of its perceived file size overhead and just go it alone?

If you want to get the most out of component development for the Flex framework, use a combination of inheritance and composition utilizing those classes that already exist within the Flex and Component frameworks—these can include your own components as you develop them. However, if you want to make a component that will work in both Flex and Flash,[1] you will have issues from the outset. This is mainly because Flash and Flex use slightly different component models. Flash's is designed to be lightweight and simple to skin visually via the Flash Authoring tool. Flex's is more robust and contains more unified features that you would expect and need in rich application development; that is not to say that some of the classes you may create to be used by your component couldn't be shared between the two. I, for example, use utility classes that operate identically both within a pure Flash project and a Flex application. To be honest, you will create cleaner and more resilient components if you target only one format.

If you are interested in seeing how you can leverage Flash to create components for Flex, you can find out how in Chapter 11, "Creating Flex Components with Flash Professional CS5." If you feel that the component framework is too heavy and you'd rather "roll your own," go for it; however, before you decide whether that is the path for you, let's briefly look at what UIComponent has to offer, just so you can see what you might want to include in your own component if you do go it alone.

UIComponent

UIComponent contains the core functionality and properties that a component may need without the necessity of creating it on a per-component basis. Figure 3.2 shows the inheritance chain of UIComponent. Notice how only FlexSprite and UIComponent are part of the Flex framework, whereas the rest of the inheritance chain Sprite and above are actually part of the Flash Player architecture and, as such, are also available to ActionScript 3.0 in the Flash Authoring IDE.

Although this has little impact on development techniques or performance per se, it is handy to know because it will hopefully help you become accustomed to the class package hierarchy as you move through this book. The main benefit of knowing this is that you can't optimize player-based classes, like Sprite, but you can optimize code that is purely ActionScript, even to the point of ignoring UIComponent and "rolling your own" component framework.

---

[1] I use the term Flash to signify any ActionScript-based solution that doesn't require the Flex framework and uses the Flash Authoring components.

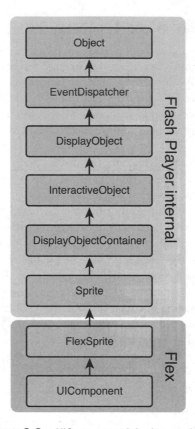

Figure 3.2   UIComponent inheritance chain

Something for Nothing

I'm not going to sugar coat this: Using the Component framework increases your application's overall file size. After all, there is a lot of functionality to include that you can hook into. Although, now that you can externalize the Flex framework (including the core component framework) from your main application, that hit isn't so bad. Plus, if you were to re-create all this functionality for your own framework, it wouldn't be that much smaller from a file-size perspective. If you want to pare the component framework right back, extending from UIComponent is probably a good place to start because it contains the core functionality that all components harness.

What does UIComponent actually give you, though? Well, it provides the vast majority of the core component functionality, like event management, low-level user interactions via the mouse and keyboard, including tabbing and focus management. It also manages the component life-cycle phases that you have just read about, as well as being responsible for managing style changes within the component framework, while the vast majority of this functionality is provided as stubbed methods and properties that, in some cases, need to be overridden to provide access to the functionality you require. A large proportion of it is based on class composition as opposed to class inheritance. By this, I mean that instances of other classes are accessed as if they are properties and methods of this particular class. Don't worry if this all sounds a bit alien at the moment; a lot of these classes and how to interact with them are covered in later chapters.

Although UIComponent is the basis for all the components within the Flex 4 framework (Halo or Spark), the major difference between the Halo and Spark components is that all the Spark components are actually extended from an additional set of base classes that extend UIComponent. Granted, you could argue that all the Halo components are extended from additional base classes. However, these were created to provide support for the new layout, grouping, and skinning models that the Spark components employ. The reason that Spark has additional classes, as shown in Figure 3.3, has to do with some of the shortcomings of the Halo component framework in these areas.

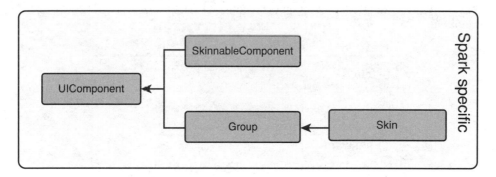

Figure 3.3   Spark UIComponent inheritance chain

I won't go into detail about these new Spark classes, because they are discussed in Chapter 9, "Manipulating Data," and Chapter 10. With that in mind, let's continue.

With all this, understanding which solution you ultimately adopt is up to you, but I recommend starting with either the Halo or Spark component frameworks so that you can see if you need to create your own components from scratch or if you just need to play around with the classes to understand what classes contain the functionality you need and where they are. Remember that nothing is stopping you from extending or creating any class to add in that missing piece of functionality.

UIComponent for MXML

Something that will become clearer as we start to explore the actual makeup of components is that, although you can subclass your ActionScript components from UIComponent, you cannot do the same with MXML. This is partly because a UIComponent has no visual elements and, therefore, is only suitable as a base class. It is also because, although ActionScript does not support the concept of abstract classes,[2] UIComponent is designed with that concept in mind, and therefore doesn't implement the vast majority of the properties it provides to its subclasses, making its use as a base for a component defined in MXML pointless. If this has you scratching your head over what sounds like a limitation of MXML for component development over ActionScript, think about how many components you may create that actually need to extend directly from UIComponent. The likelihood is that you will extend your components from one of the more functional subclasses than inherit directly from UIComponent.

That said, there is one problem that you may face while developing MXML components. If you decide to forego the Flex component framework as a basis for your MXML component, you run into issues when you try to initialize your component. This is because you cannot define a constructor for an MXML component. If you do, you will get a compiler error that your component has duplicate constructors. Don't get this confused with an ActionScript component instantiated via MXML, like the simple Login Panel example in the following listing (see Figure 3.4 for a visual representation of what it looks like).

Figure 3.4   MXML Login dialog component

```
<?xml version="1.0" encoding="utf-8"?>
<s:Panel xmlns:fx="http://ns.adobe.com/mxml/2009"
         xmlns:s="library://ns.adobe.com/flex/spark"
```

---

[2] A class that provides common functionality and behavior across subclasses but isn't designed to have instances. Think of this as a template where the subclasses are the implementations of that template.

```
        xmlns:mx="library://ns.adobe.com/flex/mx"
        title="Login">

  <s:layout>
    <s:VerticalLayout horizontalAlign="center" verticalAlign="middle" />
  </s:layout>

  <mx:Form id="formContainer" visible="true">
    <mx:FormItem id="emailLbl" label="Email:" required="true" >
      <s:TextInput id="email"/>
    </mx:FormItem>
    <mx:FormItem label="Password:" required="true" id="formitem1">
      <s:TextInput id="password" displayAsPassword="true"/>
    </mx:FormItem>
    <s:VGroup id="formButtonsContainer" width="100%"
              horizontalAlign="right" verticalAlign="middle">
      <s:HGroup id="formButtons">
        <s:Button id="registerBtn" label="Register"/>
        <s:Button id="submitCredentialsBtn"  label="Login"/>
      </s:HGroup>
      <mx:Label id="forgottenLbl" text="Forgotten your Details? Click here."/>
    </s:VGroup>
  </mx:Form>
</s:Panel>
```

What I'm specifically referring to is this: If you don't extend your MXML component from a subclass of UIComponent, you will find it difficult to create event listeners for the core component life-cycle events, like preinitialize, initialize, and creationComplete. Fortunately, Flex has a solution for this. It's called IMXMLObject, and it is an interface that you can implement on your MXML component to provide a hook for the compiler.

IMXMLObject

Having the component framework is well and good, but what if you want to base your components on something else and build the functionality from the ground up? In ActionScript, that isn't an issue, just a lot of work. For MXML components, it can be the equivalent of a brick wall. Luckily, that's where IMXMLObject comes in. This is an interface that you implement within your MXML component to allow pure MXML components to be created without subclassing from UIComponent. Like the majority of interfaces, you also need to implement the functions that are defined within it. In the case of IMXMLObject, there is only one: initialized().

I suspect you are now thinking, "Why would I want to create a component that does-n't inherit from the component framework and is in MXML?" Well, you may want to make a lightweight component that has only a specific function—the component frame-works do add in a lot of stuff that you may not necessarily want in your component. Or you may want to make some form of repository that is quicker to create in MXML as opposed to ActionScript. In the majority of component cases, you won't need to use this approach because you are more likely to extend your components from UIComponent and its subclasses or your own components that are derived from either the Halo or Spark component frameworks. However, for completeness, it is beneficial to know that it is there if you require that level of control in an MXML-based component.

The last aspect of the component framework is a unique form of component, even for Flex. These are the template components, and they provide a useful purpose when creat-ing components that can contain other components defined at author time by a devel-oper; think about all the container components, for example.

Template Components

Even though all the components within the Flex framework are descendants of UIComponent, and they perform a variety of functions, there is a super set of components that exhibit a particular style of creation and data management commonly referred to as the template components. Don't confuse them with the common definition of a template by thinking that these components are like blueprints and instances are made from them. No, these components define and manage what types of child components are declared by providing the flexibility for those component types to be determined at implementa-tion time, not as part of their actual code base.

This may sound too good to be true, but it is another example of the lateral-ness of component development. Yes, the ability to drop additional components onto a container component and have them all add themselves to the correct display lists and such is because of *templating*. Template components need not just be big containers; you can define aspects of your component to allow only certain types of components to be included. However, before you start to glaze over with information overload, let's go over how template components actually implement this *templating* functionality.

Deferring Instantiation

Template components employ a process known as *deferred instantiation*. Deferred instantia-tion enables you to define an aspect of your component as a marker that then creates its child assets from the class descriptors when required. That way, you can provide a general data type for your component that can then be replaced with a concrete version of it as required. The beauty of this is that you provide a real level of flexibility to your compo-nents, allowing a developer the ability to use any component that conforms to the general type that was initially defined. Deferred instantiation usually comes in two variants: by class or via the interface IDeferredInstance. The process by which you define your template areas is similar, as the following Halo example shows. I highlighted the key areas so that you can easily recognize them.

```
package com.developingcomponents.components
{
  import mx.core.UIComponent;

  import spark.components.Group;
  import spark.layouts.HorizontalLayout;
  import spark.layouts.supportClasses.LayoutBase;

  public class UIComponentTemplateExample extends UIComponent
  {
    private static const DEFAULT_WIDTH  :uint = 200;
    private static const DEFAULT_HEIGHT :uint = 30;

    private var _controlBar      :Group;
    private var _layout             :LayoutBase;

    [Bindable]
    [ArrayElementType("spark.components.Button")]
    public var controlBar        :Array;

    public function UIComponentTemplateExample()
    {
      super();
      _layout = new HorizontalLayout();
    }

    override protected function createChildren():void
    {
      super.createChildren();
      _controlBar = new Group();
      _controlBar.layout = _layout;
      addChild(_controlBar);
    }

    override protected function commitProperties():void
    {
      super.commitProperties();
      createDeferredItems();
    }

    override protected function measure():void
    {
      super.measure()
```

```
    measuredWidth = measuredMinWidth = DEFAULT_WIDTH;
    measuredHeight = measuredMinHeight = DEFAULT_HEIGHT;
    _controlBar.setActualSize(DEFAULT_WIDTH, DEFAULT_HEIGHT);
}

override protected function updateDisplayList(unscaledWidth:Number,
                                    unscaledHeight:Number):void
{
    super.updateDisplayList(unscaledWidth, unscaledHeight);

    width = unscaledWidth;
    height = unscaledHeight;
    _controlBar.setActualSize(width, height);
}

private function createDeferredItems():void
{
    for (var i :int = 0; i < controlBar.length; i++)
    {
        _controlBar.addElement(controlBar[i]);
    }
}

public function get layout():LayoutBase
{
    return _layout;
}

public function set layout(value:LayoutBase):void
{
    _layout = value;
    _controlBar.layout = value;
}
}
}
```

As you can see, this component uses an array that has some metadata applied to it. (If you have not used metadata before, don't worry; you can find out more about it in Chapter 7, "Working with Metadata.") This particular metadata sets the `ArrayElementType` to `spark.components.Button`. Although we cannot type arrays, we can make sure that, if external data is provided, it is of the type we require via the use of the `ArrayElementType` metadata block; in this case, it is typed to Spark Button components.

After we have our array of Button components, we need to process them so that they can be added to the relevant display list. Most of the time, you want to do this either via `commitProperties()` or `creationComplete()`, depending on whether you are creating an ActionScript or MXML-based component. In the case of the previous code example, we are adding it to a control bar called _controlBar (original name!) via the commitProperties() method. One thing to remember is that, although this example is fairly explicit in the type of child asset that can be supplied to the control bar, you can be more general. For example, there is nothing stopping me from changing the ArrayElementType to mx.core.UIComponent if I wanted. Although, from a functional point of view, you wouldn't want to give a developer the ability to place a Panel component inside your control bar—or would you?

Implementing interfaces as a form of deferred instantiation is almost identical. Again, there is an ArrayElementType block over the array used for our child elements. However, as you have probably noticed, instead of a concrete class, we now instead have an interface declared. If you look further down, you see that it uses the same loop to add our buttons as in the previous example. Instead of having the ArrayElementType defined as spark.components.Button, it is defined as mx.core.IDeferredInstance, and the loop to add them as children of the control bar is initially cast as Button, which subsequently calls the getInstance() method to create the child asset. For brevity, I included only the main changes in the previous example when implemented via IDeferredInstance.

```
package com.developingcomponents.components
{
  ...

  import spark.components.Button;

  [Bindable]
  [ArrayElementType("mx.core.IDeferredInstance")]
  public var controlBar        :Array;

  ...

  private function createDeferredItems():void
  {
    for (var i :int = 0; i < controlBar.length; i++)
    {
      _controlBar.addElement(Button(
                          IDeferredInstance(
                          controlBar[i]).getInstance())));
    }
  }
  ...
}
```

The same result can be achieved from either option. IDeferredInstance provides far more flexibility because you can instantiate any class that implements the IDeferredInstance interface; although to achieve this, you need to either make sure you cast your class to the lowest common denominator or, in the case of the example code, explicitly cast it to the type of element you require (a Spark Button, in this case). The only caveat to using `IDeferredInstance` is that the constructor for the class being instantiated (such as the Button components that are passed in) cannot have any parameters passed as part of the constructor signature, which, as you have already seen, is a requirement for constructors in components. So, no worries there.

Before we move on, you may be wondering why we use arrays for our deferred elements instead of using a vector? If you were assigning concrete class instances to your template component, then yes, you can remove the metadata and the array and replace it with a vector. Unfortunately, if you try this for the `IDeferredInstance` version, you get an error when assigning the Button elements via MXML because, as far as the compiler is concerned, these are Spark Button components and, as such, they don't provide a hook to the `IDeferredInstance` interface.

Summary

This chapter looked at the core methods used within the component framework: `createChildren()`, `commitProperties()`, `measure`, `updateDisplayList()`, and `layoutChrome()`. You also learned how to tell your component to update itself when values are set externally via `invalidateProperties()`, `invalidateSize()`, and `invalidateDisplayList()`.

You now better understand the advantages and disadvantages of straight inheritance, composition, and starting from scratch when it comes to choosing what (or what not) to extend your component from initially. This chapter also covered how to create an MXML component that doesn't extend from a subclass of the component framework but uses an interface called `IMXMLObject`.

Finally, you learned about deferred instantiation through a general class type or the use of `IDeferredInstance` and template components, which enable you to provide a greater level of flexibility in aspects of your components without compromising the overall structure or functionality.

You're almost done with the majority of the theory. We ramp up the code in the majority of the chapters from now on, so get your coding gloves on.

Onward....

II

Developing Components

Creating Your First Component

The previous chapters gave you a slew of information about what a component is actually constructed of, the methods that it provides for creating its content and child assets; and what the process is when you want to update elements of your component.

This is the first chapter where you're actually "doing" something. From here on, you get knee deep in code and create your first components, building up to finally "wrapping" it all up and distributing it (which is Part III, "Distribution"). However, to avoid the "don't run before you can walk" adage, you start off slowly by creating your first simple component. Then, we revise it.

MyFirstComponent

If you've ever read any technical manual before, this is the point at which you are normally presented with the "Hello World" example. Honestly, you could do the same here, but I don't think they really give you much value, and I'm sure they are there more for filler than function. With that in mind, we will create something more visual: a red square (see Figure 4.1). (Okay, it's a gray square in the book, but you know what I mean.) It may not sound impressive, but this gives you a good overview of the core component methods that you will use day in and day out.

Figure 4.1   In case you had any doubt what
a red (gray) square looks like

The first thing we need to do is open Flash Builder, and you're going to use the Flex project you created in Chapter 1, "Getting Started." If you didn't create it or want to create a new project, do it now. I'll wait....

Don't be tempted to create your components within a project that you are using to build your actual application in because it makes debugging and separating the codebase harder as the project progresses. Also, if the application is large, the automatic build times in Flash Builder can get lengthy, which gets annoying after a while.

OK, we need to create the ActionScript class for our component, so select New > ActionScript Class from the File menu, or right-click your src folder and do the same. This opens the New ActionScript Class dialog (see Figure 4.2). In the package field, place a period-delimited path that our class will be placed within. The accepted approach is to use your own URL (or your company's) in reverse as the base, so in my case, I use com.flashgen. This prevents classes with the same name from clashing; if you were to use a selection of class libraries from various sources without the unique prefix for your package path, there would be a high risk of classes having identical names. Using a package path helps prevent this, as the following example shows:

```
// Without the package path the MyFirstComponent classes
// would clash and cause issues within your application.

import com.developingcomponents.MyFirstComponent;
import com.someotherdomain.MyFirstComponent;
```

Figure 4.2   New ActionScript Class dialog

Creating the Class

Having established the base prefix of your package path, you can run free with any additional nested packages. Be aware, however, that you don't want to nest your classes too deeply or in a single flat format. Think of it as a folder structure (because that is what it is) and organize your classes based on type or functionality. In the case of components, the common package names are `components` or more specific package names, such as `media` or `buttons`. Just keep it short and on topic.

For this component, and throughout this book, I use `com.developingcomponents.components`, but feel free to replace this with your domain if you want. In the Name field, supply the class name. We're going to name the component `MyFirstComponent`, so put that in there and leave the modifiers as they are.

Last, you need to set the superclass and, because you are starting from scratch with this component, you need to extend your class from `UIComponent`. This enables you to create a component that is compatible with both the Halo and Spark component frameworks. You have a couple of options here: You can either just type `UIComponent` in the Superclass field and click Finish, or you can browse for the class via the Browse button.

Later on, we look at the functionality that the new Spark base classes `SkinnableComponent` and `Group` provide when it comes to skinning and styling; if you can't wait, feel free to skip to Chapter 10, "Skinning and Styling." However, because this is about the basic building blocks of Flex 4 components in general, let's start at the lowest common denominator.

As you start out, you'll probably use the Browse button until you are more familiar with the Flex classes. Either way, after you have the required information in the Superclass field, you can leave the code generation options with their default settings. Click Finish to create your class.

Flash Builder automatically creates the folder structure in your `src` folder based on the package information you provided with your class. It also opens the class ready for you to start coding. Your class should look something like this:

```
package com.developingcomponents.components
{
    import mx.core.UIComponent;

    public class MyFirstComponent extends UIComponent
    {
        public function MyFirstComponent()
        {
            super();
        }
    }
}
```

Core Component Methods

At the moment, there is not much to separate this class from any other ActionScript class, but you can sort that out by adding the createChildren(), measure(), and updateDisplayList() methods. After these methods are in place, your class will start to look more like a component (from a code point of view). I tend to keep my classes organized in blocks, so I keep all the core component methods together right under the constructor, like so:

```
public class MyFirstComponent extends UIComponent
{
  public function MyFirstComponent()
  {
    super();
  }

  override protected function createChildren():void
  {
    super.createChildren();
  }

  override protected function measure():void
  {
    super.measure();
  }

  override protected function updateDisplayList(unscaledWidth:Number,
                                               unscaledHeight:Number):void
  {
    super.updateDisplayList(unscaledWidth, unscaledHeight);
  }
}
```

Because these are inherited methods you are implementing, don't forget to use the override keyword to mark them correctly; otherwise, the compiler will complain. Also, be sure to include the call to the relevant super method for each of them; if you don't, your components will cough and splutter because they will be missing additional function calls that you haven't implemented in your overridden methods.

Adding Some Form

At this point, your component is nothing more than bare stub methods, so let's start by adding some form to it. If you remember from Chapter 3, "Anatomy of a Component," I mentioned that you use the measure() method to define the default size of your component, and I gave a simple example where I set the relevant size properties with values assigned within the measure() method. Well, I'm going to show you how to do it properly now.

We need a couple of variables first—one for the width and one for the height—but we're not going to use instance variables. We're going to use static constants. If you've never used static constants, they are class-based variables, so they can be accessed only through the class itself, and they are immutable, which means that their values cannot be changed. They are perfect for defining the default values for our component. Of course, the other benefit is that, like all variables, they keep magic values[1] out of your methods. Add the two static constants highlighted to the top of your class, as shown:

```
public class MyFirstComponent extends UIComponent
{
  private static const DEFAULT_HEIGHT :Number = 200;
  private static const DEFAULT_WIDTH  :Number = 200;

  public function MyFirstComponent()
  {
    super();
  }
  ...
}
```

Now, you need to add these values to your `measure()` method, and because we don't want the size to ever drop below this, set both the `measuredMinHeight/Width` and `measuredHeight/Width` properties to the same value. Place the following code inside your `measure()` method just below the call to `super.measure()`:

```
override protected function measure():void
{
  super.measure();
  measuredMinHeight = measuredHeight = DEFAULT_HEIGHT;
  measuredMinWidth = measuredWidth = DEFAULT_WIDTH;
}
```

Notice that I have short-circuited the variable assignment. This allows you to assign a value to more than one variable in the same statement as opposed to repeating the same code over subsequent lines. The main thing to note from this is that you have now set your components' default size and its minimum size. I could get you to test this at this point, but we have no displayObjects, so you won't see anything. Worry not, though; that's next on the agenda.

---

[1] A magic value is a value that is hard-coded into a statement of a class or program that provides no indication of its purpose or meaning.

Showing Yourself Off

Drawing with components is easy, because they all have a graphics object for you to hook into. When it comes to drawing primitives, like rectangles and ellipses, you don't even have to try and work out the line placement anymore. There are methods that do it all for you—just provide the relevant parameters and away you go. You have a couple of options as to where you put the code to access and manipulate the graphics object of your component, but the one constant is that, at some point, `updateDisplayList()` will be invoked. As you saw in Chapter 3, the `updateDisplayList()` method deals with updating all the child assets and any other visual elements of your component prior to making it visible or updating it as part of a render phase, so it is an ideal candidate for your drawing code. And for your first component, we just place the graphics code straight into the `updateDisplayList()`.

A word about the following code: I created a function variable called g that holds a reference to your component's graphics object. You don't need to use this. You could just put `this.graphics` in place of g. However, it makes the code easier to read and obviously takes less time to write. If you do use the code as shown, you need to import the `flash.display.Graphics` package into your component; otherwise, you'll get a compiler error. Flash Builder should do this automatically for you, but in case it doesn't, you know where the package lives so you can add it manually.

```
override protected function updateDisplayList(unscaledWidth:Number,
                                              unscaledHeight:Number):void
{
  super.updateDisplayList(unscaledWidth, unscaledHeight);

  height = unscaledHeight;
  width = unscaledWidth;

  var g       :Graphics  = this.graphics;

  g.clear();
  g.beginFill(0xff0000, 1);
  g.drawRect(0, 0, unscaledWidth, unscaledHeight);
  g.endFill();
}
```

If you've never used the drawing API before, let's go over it so that you know what it actually does. As mentioned, the first thing that happens is that the component's graphics object[2] is stored in a local variable called g; then, we get into the actual drawing process.

---

[2] In case you are wondering, the graphics property of UIComponent is inherited from Sprite and gives you access to the drawing API. Therefore, it doesn't need to be instantiated or declared, or even added as a child of a component because it is automatically created when a descendant of Sprite is instantiated.

If the component's size is altered, this code redraws the red rectangle to reflect this. However, if the size is smaller than its previous size, the graphics object needs to be cleared before it draws the new rectangle; otherwise, the new smaller rectangle would be lost in the previous larger version. This gives the impression that the rectangle hadn't actually been drawn to the smaller, correct size.

The first step the Graphics object needs to do is clear its content by using the `clear()` method. Next, it starts a fill process, which in this case, is set to the color red with no alpha transparency. As part of the fill process, it then draws the rectangle, starting at 0,0—our component's natural registration point—and then sets the width and height to that of the `unscaled` values that were passed in by the invalidation call to `updateDisplayList()`. Finally, it ends the fill process, and—bingo—you have a red rectangle with the correct dimensions.

Tip

If you paste code from one class to another, you more than likely will miss an import or two. To rectify this, locate the variable declaration that is causing the issue, place your cursor at the end of the type declaration (for example, `:Sprite`), and just press Ctrl+Space. Flash Builder automatically imports the class for you.

This is also helpful if you have no idea what package a particular class belongs to.

Testing It Out

That's it for your first component. It may not seem like much, but you've actually achieved quite a bit—well done. All you have left to do is test it. So, save the class and open the main application MXML file for your project. (This is `DFC_DevelopingComponents.mxml` if you are using the project you created in Chapter 1).

Adding your component to the MXML is exactly the same as adding any other component. In Flash Builder's code view, put your cursor between the opening and closing application tags and type `<MyFirst`, and the code hinting should spring into action and offer you your component (see Figure 4.3).

Figure 4.3   Adding MyFirstComponent to your default MXML file

Select `MyFirstComponent` from the drop-down list, and Flash Builder inserts it in the MXML document; it also adds an additional namespace to the application tag: `xmlns:components="com.developingcomponents.components.*"`. This is the namespace that points to the folder in which your component resides. As you add more components to that folder, they all automatically show up in the code hinting under `<components:>`.

Your `MyFirstComponent` tag is probably still open. To close it, you can either just place a `>` after the component type to create a complimentary closed tag below it, or you can short-circuit it with a `/>` instead. After you close it, save the MXML file and test it. If everything went according to plan, you should be looking at a red rectangle that probably doesn't look dissimilar to the one shown in Figure 4.1.

Did you notice how you didn't supply any values for width and height, but it still sized itself correctly to 200x200 pixels? That is the `measure()` method in full effect. However, we are always going to be stuck with a red rectangle. Suppose someone wants you to create a blue rectangle? At this point, you have two choices: change the code so it makes the rectangle blue and save it as a new class, or subclass your blue rectangle from the red one and override the `updateDisplayList()` to change the color value that way. Now, neither of those are particularly useful, so let's approach this from a third, more flexible way.

This Belongs to Me

To allow properties to be set externally, you must add some form of mechanism to allow this to happen. This is generally referred to as the public API or Interface. (API stands for Application Programming Interface.) I prefer API, because there are already different interpretations of Interface and that leads to confusion.

To provide access to our properties, we need to first create a **private** variable (in this case, to hold the color value). I said private, because you shouldn't let your variables be accessed directly; you have no control over how they are processed if you do. Of course, by making the variable private, it cannot be accessed externally. To fix that, you need to create an accessor and mutator (or getter/setter, as they are more commonly known). The following code block shows the basic structure:

```
private var _backgroundColor    :uint = 0xff0000;


public function set backgroundColor(val:uint):void
{
  _backgroundColor = val;
}


public function get backgroundColor():uint
{
  return _backgroundColor;
}
```

Add this code below your updateDisplayList() method and, after it is in place, you need to update your beginFill() method within the updateDisplayList() method so that it no longer uses 0xff0000 as the color parameter but uses _backgroundColor instead. Your updated beginFill() code should now look like this:

```
g.beginFill(_backgroundColor, 1);
```

Now, you can set the color of your rectangle (in this case, green) externally, like this:

```
<components:MyFirstComponent id="mfc" backgroundColor="0x00ff00" />
```

That's great, but if you tried to change the color through a user gesture, such as the result of a button click, nothing will happen (as the following code demonstrates):

```
<?xml version="1.0" encoding="utf-8"?>
<s:Application xmlns:fx="http://ns.adobe.com/mxml/2009"
               xmlns:s="library://ns.adobe.com/flex/spark"
               xmlns:mx="library://ns.adobe.com/flex/mx"
               xmlns:components="com.developingcomponents.components.*"
               minWidth="1024" minHeight="768">

  <s:layout>
    <s:BasicLayout/>
  </s:layout>

  <components:MyFirstComponent id="mfc" x="10" y="10"/>

  <s:Button x="10" y="220" width="200"
            label="Click to set the color to green"
            click="mfc.backgroundColor=0x00ff00"/>
</s:Application>
```

Your component receives the color change request but, while the property has changed, your component needs to be told that this has happened so that it can respond to the update and reflect the change by setting the color to the new value. To do this, we need to add an invalidation call to the setter method, but which one?

In more complex components, where the setting of a single value could potentially result in various methods being invoked, it's best practice to call the invalidateProperties() method and update the component from within commitProperties(). This component doesn't need to process the data change, but it is good form to wire it up in the same way. To achieve this, add the following code to your component:

```
override protected function commitProperties():void
{
  super.commitProperties();
  invalidateDisplayList();
}
```

> **Tip**
>
> I put the core component methods in execution order, so by that token, the
> `commitProperties()` method would go between the `createChildren()` and `measure()`
> methods.

As you can see, we don't have anything in the `commitProperties()` method at all
apart from a call to the superclass's `commitProperties()` implementation and the
`invalidateDisplayList()` call. However, it is now following the correct flow, which is
the important thing. But, you are still missing one more element. As it stands, the
`commitProperties()` method won't be invoked when we change the color of our component. To do that, we need to include an `invalidateProperties()` call in our color setter, like so:

```
public function set backgroundColor(val:uint):void
{
  _backgroundColor = val;
  invalidateProperties();
}
```

This flags that your component needs to call its `commitProperties()` method during
the next render phase. The method doesn't get called immediately, because other elements
within your component may also need updating, so it allows them to be batched together.
By marking your component ready for an update at a given point, it is more efficient than
having it call `commitProperties()` every time an individual element changes.

Now that you have updated your code to reflect these changes, save your class again
and update the main MXML file to include a button that, when clicked, updates the component's color. The code included in the click event of the button in the following
MXML just creates a random color, so you can click away and see your component
update based on the mouse click:

```
<?xml version="1.0" encoding="utf-8"?>
<s:Application xmlns:fx="http://ns.adobe.com/mxml/2009"
                xmlns:s="library://ns.adobe.com/flex/spark"
                xmlns:mx="library://ns.adobe.com/flex/mx"
                xmlns:components="com.developingcomponents.components.*"
                minWidth="1024" minHeight="768">

  <s:layout>
    <s:BasicLayout/>
  </s:layout>

  <components:MyFirstComponent id="mfc" x="10" y="10"/>

  <s:Button x="10" y="220" width="200"
            label="Click to set random color"
            click="mfc.backgroundColor=Math.round(Math.random()*
                  0xffffff)"/>
</s:Application>
```

So far, we have been dealing only with drawing basic content that is displayed as part of the component and, although that is a start, at some point, you're going to want to add additional display elements. This is where the `createChildren()` method comes into play.

Sibling Rivalry

Until this point, you have just been manipulating the drawing API of your actual component; it has no other assets or children. In this section, we add some children to your component. To start, let's add another display object so we can do more drawing.

Create a new private `Sprite` variable within your component and call it `_ellipse`:

```
private var _ellipse  :Sprite;
```

Now, you need create a new instance of it. Because it's a display object that is created as part of the component's instantiation, you need to create it in the `createChildren()` method. After it is instantiated, you need to add it to your components own display list.

```
override protected function createChildren():void
{
  super.createChildren();
  _ellipse = new Sprite();
  addChild(_ellipse);
}
```

Next, update the `updateDisplay()` method and do a bit of drawing in this new child. Below the code that draws the rectangle, paste the following code. This draws a blue ellipse the same dimensions as the component.

```
var eg        :Graphics = _ellipse.graphics;

eg.clear()
eg.beginFill(0x0000ff, 1);
eg.drawEllipse(0, 0, unscaledWidth, unscaledHeight);
eg.endFill()
```

Save the file and test your main MXML file again. Now, you should have a red rectangle with a blue circle in the middle of it. Clicking the button updates only the rectangle because the code for the ellipse is hard-coded.

Challenge

Why don't you extend your component further so that you can update the color of the ellipse with a different color to the rectangle? Use the structure you created to update the rectangle's color as a guide.

Congratulations! You are now truly on the path to component development bliss. No, really! Oh, OK, so there is still a lot to learn, but you made a good start. Let's move on to extend this component with a few more elements so that you can begin to grasp the layout within the component hierarchy.

MyFirstComponent (Revised)

I'm now probably going to annoy a lot of you by pointing out that what you have just created can be produced with less code and less time. However, there's a method to my madness. You needed to create a component that extends from UIComponent to give you a feel of how much additional work you need to provide just to get it to size, draw, and render correctly, which isn't necessarily a bad thing, as you'll see later in this chapter.

Distilling MyFirstComponent (Halo)

Now, you've done the hard work. Let's look at how to create the same result by using UIComponent's subclasses—namely Container, which if you have never used it before, is the base class for Canvas and the majority of the other Halo container components. Let's go back to the drawing board with your first component and look at how you can update it to leverage the functionality in Container to achieve the same results with less code. First, let's look at how to optimize your component in ActionScript. As you can see, although there is still a fair amount of code, it doesn't need to draw the red rectangle any more. This is handled via the setStyle() method called in the component's constructor, saving a few additional lines of code.

```
package com.developingcomponents.components
{
  import flash.display.Graphics;

  import mx.core.Container;
  import mx.core.UIComponent;

  public class MyFirstComponent extends Container
  {
    private static const DEFAULT_HEIGHT :Number = 200;
    private static const DEFAULT_WIDTH  :Number = 200;

    private var _ellipse        :UIComponent;

    public function MyFirstComponent()
    {
      super();
      setStyle("backgroundColor", 0xff0000);
    }

    override protected function createChildren():void
    {
      super.createChildren();
```

```
    _ellipse = new UIComponent();
    addChild(_ellipse);
}

override protected function measure():void
{
    super.measure();
    measuredMinHeight = measuredHeight = DEFAULT_HEIGHT;
    measuredMinWidth = measuredWidth = DEFAULT_WIDTH;
}

override protected function updateDisplayList(unscaledWidth:Number,
                                        unscaledHeight:Number):void
{
    super.updateDisplayList(unscaledWidth, unscaledHeight);

    var eg   :Graphics = _ellipse.graphics;

    eg.clear();
    eg.beginFill(0x0000ff, 1);
    eg.drawEllipse(0, 0, unscaledWidth, unscaledHeight);
    eg.endFill();
    }
  }
}
```

The second alteration is that our _ellipse Sprite is now a UIComponent instance. This is partly because the addChild() method on Halo components allow only instances that implement the IUIComponent interface. This may seem strange as the code complete in Flash Builder and the supporting documentation both indicate that addChild() should just accept any class that inherits from DisplayObject. This, of course, flies in the face of your MyFirstComponent example because UIComponent itself adheres to the DisplayObjectContainer definition of addChild(), which is why you could add a Sprite to its display list.

The final difference between the revised version of MyFirstComponent and your original MyFirstComponent class is in the updateDisplayList() method. Because you can use the StyleManager to set the Constainer's background color via setStyle(), there is no need to manipulate the component's built-in graphics object to draw the red background—you did that in the constructor. Instead, all you need to do is draw a blue circle in the _ellipse instance, exactly like you did in the original component. As you can see in the previous code listing, you've gone from 34 lines of code in the first version of MyFirstComponent to 21 lines in the revised version. Now that this is all done, let's test it out.

If you open DFC_DevelopingComponents.mxml and either replace or add your new component next to your first component and export the file, you should see an identical red rectangle with a blue circle in it. If you replaced your first component, you need to update your Button click event so that it uses the `setStyle()` method of your new component as opposed to just setting a property called `backgroundColor`. If you're not sure how to go about updating the code, I've included it here:

```
<?xml version="1.0" encoding="utf-8"?>
<s:Application xmlns:fx="http://ns.adobe.com/mxml/2009"
               xmlns:s="library://ns.adobe.com/flex/spark"
               xmlns:mx="library://ns.adobe.com/flex/mx"
               xmlns:components="com.developingcomponents.components.*"
               minWidth="1024" minHeight="768">

  <s:layout>
    <s:BasicLayout/>
  </s:layout>

  <components:MyFirstComponent id="mfc" x="10" y="10"/>
  <s:Button x="10" y="237" width="200"
            label=" Click to set random color"
            click="mfc.setStyle('backgroundColor',
                                 Math.round(Math.random()*0xffffff))"/>
</s:Application>
```

Wait, there's more....

Slimming Down with MXML (Halo)

After all my comments about using only MXML for components that have simple functionality or act as facets of a greater whole, it's only right to show you how you can distill your original component down even further through the mystical power of—ta da!—MXML. Seriously, MXML can be beneficial in component development, and this is a good case in point.

The first thing you need to do is create a new MXML component file based on Container. First, make sure you have your component package selected (if you're using the same structure as me, this will likely be called `com.developingcomponents.components`), and now either right-click that folder, or from the main menu, select `File > New MXML Component` (see Figure 4.4).

If you didn't initially select the components folder, you can navigate to it via the Browse button next to the Package text field in the dialog or just type it into that field. In the Name field, give the MXML component a name; in this case, I opted for `MyFirstComponent_Redux` and in the Based On text field, you can type the component class this MXML component inherits from. If you know the package location, just type it in this field; if not, browse to the relevant component entry via the Browse button. (I suggest that you just use the Browse button.) After clicking the Browse button, a dialog appears. In the top field, type *Container*, and all the relevant results appear in the lower portion of the dialog, as shown in Figure 4.5.

Figure 4.4   New MXML Component dialog

Figure 4.5   Selecting the component you want to base
your component on

Select **Container - mx.core** and click OK. After you do that, your New MXML
Component dialog should look like Figure 4.4; all that is left to do is set the width and
height properties to 200 and click Finish to create your new MXML component.

As soon as you do this, the MXML editor opens with your new MXML-based component. If all went well, and I'd be surprised if it didn't, your code should look something
like this:

```
<?xml version="1.0" encoding="utf-8"?>
<mx:Container xmlns:fx="http://ns.adobe.com/mxml/2009"
              xmlns:s="library://ns.adobe.com/flex/spark"
              xmlns:mx="library://ns.adobe.com/flex/mx"
              width="200" height="200">
  <fx:Declarations>
    <!-- Place non-visual elements (e.g., services, value objects) here -->
  </fx:Declarations>
</mx:Container>
```

Notice that our container component has a default width and height of 200, which
we set as part of the creation process. So, you don't need to implement a measure()
method or a DEFAULT_WIDTH or DEFAULT_HEIGHT. Moving on, the first thing that you
need to do is set the color of the container—again, you don't need to write any Action-
Script because the MXML exposes the relevant attributes for you. So, if you place your
mouse cursor after height="200" and insert a space, the code hinting will kick in; either
start to type backgroundColor or select it from the code hint drop-down and set its value
to 0xff0000. The last bit of code is an <mx:Script></mx:Script> block that contains
the _ellipse declaration and a method to draw it, as the following code shows:

```
<?xml version="1.0" encoding="utf-8"?>
<mx:Container xmlns:fx="http://ns.adobe.com/mxml/2009"
              xmlns:s="library://ns.adobe.com/flex/spark"
              xmlns:mx="library://ns.adobe.com/flex/mx"
              width="200" height="200"
              backgroundColor="0xff0000">

  <fx:Script>
    <![CDATA[
      import mx.core.UIComponent;

      private var _ellipse    :UIComponent = new UIComponent();

      protected function createCircle():void
      {
        var eg  :Graphics = _ellipse.graphics;
        eg.clear();
        eg.beginFill(0x0000ff, 1);
        eg.drawEllipse(0, 0, width, height);
        eg.endFill();
```

```
        addChild(_ellipse);
      }
    ]]>
  </fx:Script>
</mx:Container>
```

The last thing to do is get this new component to automatically invoke the `createCircle()` method. Now, you have a few options here. You could do it during the component's `initialize`, `preinitialize`, or `creationComplete` phase, based on where in the component's life cycle you want to execute this new code block. Realistically, though, these types of methods are usually called on `creationComplete`. You are then safe in the knowledge that the component has initialized all its properties, added any child assets it may have, and run through its `updateDisplayList()` method at least once. To achieve this, you need to make a couple of minor alterations and you're done. The first change you need to make is to the `createCircle()` method signature: Update it so that it takes one parameter of type `Event`:

```
protected function createCircle(e:Event):void
```

The final bit of code will actually call this method when the component finishes its creation process. You can achieve this by adding the `creationComplete` attribute to your base `Container` tag and setting its value to the `createCircle()` method. Don't forget to include the event parameter in the call. If you're not sure what I mean, here's the code:

```
<mx:Container xmlns:mx="http://www.adobe.com/2006/mxml" width="200"
height="200" backgroundColor="0xff0000" creationComplete="createCircle(event)">
```

I go into more detail about events in Chapter 8, "Events and Event Handling," but for now, just alter your code as indicated, and I'll discuss the reasons for doing it in that chapter. After you add that last piece of code, your component should look like this:

```
<?xml version="1.0" encoding="utf-8"?>
<mx:Container xmlns:fx="http://ns.adobe.com/mxml/2009"
              xmlns:s="library://ns.adobe.com/flex/spark"
              xmlns:mx="library://ns.adobe.com/flex/mx"
              width="200" height="200"
              backgroundColor="0xff0000"
              creationComplete="createCircle(event)">

  <fx:Script>
    <![CDATA[
      import mx.core.UIComponent;

      private var _ellipse  :UIComponent = new UIComponent();

      protected function createCircle(e:Event):void
      {
```

```
        var eg   :Graphics = _ellipse.graphics;
        eg.clear();
        eg.beginFill(0x0000ff, 1);
        eg.drawEllipse(0, 0, width, height);
        eg.endFill();

        addChild(_ellipse);
      }
    ]]>
  </fx:Script>
</mx:Container>
```

That's it. If you update the DFC_DevelopingComponents.mxml file to use this component as opposed to the revised version of MyFirstComponent, export it again, and you'll
see that this looks exactly the same but with far fewer lines of code.

Distilling MyFirstComponent Down (Spark)

Although Halo provides a few variants when it comes to optimizing MyFirstComponent,
Spark deals with it in a slightly different manner. You may recall from Chapter 3 that the
Spark framework extends the UIComponent class to add support for a more logical and
separated approach to functionality, layout, and display. To that end, we can take the original MyFirstComponent and extend it by using Spark classes. The major difference is that
you need two classes: the component and its associate skin.

Here is the ActionScript version. As you can see, there isn't anything to it, so it makes
more sense to declare it in MXML, which isn't much more complex either:

```
package com.developingcomponents.components
{
  import com.developingcomponents.skins.MyFirstComponentSkin;

  import spark.components.supportClasses.SkinnableComponent;

  public class MyFirstComponent extends SkinnableComponent
  {
    private static const DEFAULT_HEIGHT :Number = 200;
    private static const DEFAULT_WIDTH  :Number = 200;

    public function MyFirstComponent()
    {
      super();
      setStyle("skinClass",
               com.developingcomponents.skins.MyFirstComponentSkin);
    }

    override protected function measure():void
    {
```

```
            super.measure();
            measuredMinHeight = measuredHeight = DEFAULT_HEIGHT;
            measuredMinWidth = measuredWidth = DEFAULT_WIDTH;
        }
    }
}
```

As you can see, like the Halo `Container` version of `MyFirstComponent`, you use the `setStyle()` property to provide the `skinClass` reference. Note that, unlike most `setStyle()` calls, the skin path is declared as an absolute reference to the skin itself. This is required because the component needs to have a reference to the skin so that it can actually create an instance of it.

Although we have to create two classes to achieve the same result as the Halo examples, notice that there is an obvious separation of the user interface and the actual component, which makes it easier in the long run to update and manage. Here is the MXML equivalent of the previous ActionScript example:

```
<?xml version="1.0" encoding="utf-8"?>
<s:SkinnableComponent xmlns:fx="http://ns.adobe.com/mxml/2009"
                      xmlns:s="library://ns.adobe.com/flex/spark"
                      xmlns:mx="library://ns.adobe.com/flex/mx"
                      width="200" height="200"
        skinClass="com.developingcomponents.skins.MyFirstComponentSkin">

    <fx:Declarations>
        <!-- Place non-visual elements (e.g., services, value objects) here -->
    </fx:Declarations>
</s:SkinnableComponent>
```

Like the ActionScript version, there is no style information or drawing happening within the component. This is because, as previously mentioned, Spark components separate their styling and skinning to a skin file assigned to the component through the `skinClass` attribute, which I highlighted in the previous code. Don't worry with the details at this point; as mentioned earlier, we'll look at the Spark styling classes in Chapter 10. For now, just look through the skin file.

```
<?xml version="1.0" encoding="utf-8"?>
<s:Skin xmlns:fx="http://ns.adobe.com/mxml/2009"
        xmlns:s="library://ns.adobe.com/flex/spark"
        xmlns:mx="library://ns.adobe.com/flex/mx">
    <!-- host component -->
    <fx:Metadata>
        [HostComponent("com.developingcomponents.components.MyFirstComponent")]
    </fx:Metadata>

    <s:Rect width="100%" height="100%" x="0" y="0">
        <s:fill>
```

```
      <s:SolidColor color="0xff0000" />
    </s:fill>
  </s:Rect>

  <s:Ellipse width="100%" height="100%" x="0" y="0">
    <s:fill>
      <s:SolidColor color="0x0000ff" />
    </s:fill>
  </s:Ellipse>

  <s:Group id="contentGroup" />
</s:Skin>
```

Notice that, instead of using ActionScript to access the drawing API, like the Halo examples, all we do is declare the relevant primitives and color fills as required. Simple and to the point.

Weapon of Choice

With a little forethought and knowledge, you can condense the amount of time and code needed to create your components. However, this isn't an exercise in making single-line components. It's more about recognizing when and where you can optimize your code and capitalizing on those benefits that MXML or ActionScript have to offer, regardless of whether you stick to pure ActionScript, pure MXML, or mix it up.

Summary

In this chapter, you created your first component in ActionScript by extending UIComponent. By overriding the measure() and updateDisplayList() methods, you learned how to extend and implement the default size of a component. You also got a feel for the process of adding child assets to your component's display list and manipulating the graphics object to programmatically draw content.

You also learned how you can reduce the amount of code within your component by picking the best base component class for your requirements, which culminated in converting the component from ActionScript to MXML. You also were briefly introduced to the differences between the Halo and Spark components when declaring graphical objects.

Congratulations! You've covered a lot of ground in this chapter. Next, we look at how to manipulate the visual elements of our fledging component.

Managing States

This chapter gives you a better idea of how to manage the states within your components, how to update the display, how to add and remove children, and how the layout of your application is manipulated to reflect this.

What Are States?

From a conceptual standpoint, the terms *state* and *states* can refer to a few different things. However, within the Flex world, state usually describes the various visual views that a user may access through user interaction or external influence. To be completely correct, states are generally referred to as **view states**, although don't confuse this term with the `ViewStack` component or skin states; they refer to different things.

The vast majority of you probably have dealt with states without even thinking about it. The most common form of state management is controlling the visibility of an object that is displayed to the user (see Figure 5.1).

This fairly basic example illustrates how important state management is to allowing an application or component to respond in a visual way by providing relevant functionality only when it's required. However, Flex's view states provide additional functionality that is generally transparent in implementation. Although it is simple to make something invisible when it's not in use, in most cases, that element remains a part of the UI layout and, therefore, affects how the associated elements are displayed. Take the two images in Figure 5.2 as an example.

The view on the left is of three panels side by side, whereas the image on the right shows the same panels with the central one's visibility set to false. However, as you can see, it still affects the layout of the two other panels, which is not generally the wanted effect.

This is caused because that although the central panel is invisible, it is still included within the layout of the applications. Therefore, you would not only have to set the visibility of an item, but also make sure it is excluded from the layout as well by setting `includeInLayout="false"`. Now, multiply that by all the elements that you may want to alter, and you are heading for a lot of additional overhead for a simple thing, like updating the current view state. Obviously, you could just remove your content from the relevant display list, but when you want to add it back in, you may need to be explicit in respect to where it sits within the display list Z order. Either way, it is something that you can get Flex to deal with so that you can concentrate on the rest of your component.

Figure 5.1   Simple example of a dual-state image selection component; clicking the button changes the image displayed and updates the button text and functionality.

Figure 5.2   Comparison of the same view where the central container has been hidden. The actual layout isn't affected, which results in an odd void between the outer panels.

Flex's View States

The Flex framework has a more methodical approach for dealing with view states. It provides a selection of container and navigation components that enable the manipulation of the display. This gives you the ability to hide and show these individual views as required and removes them from the layout when it is recalculated. When this happens, it dispatches events that enable you to easily listen and respond to the changing state before, during, and after the state changes, and its resulting content events (creationComplete, show, hide, and so on) and any custom events that you may have defined. We look at events in detail in Chapter 8, "Events and Event Handling."

The Flex framework also enables you to incorporate a states block within any component; however, you are likely to use it most from within container style components. Either way, the process is the same, as shown in the following example:

```xml
<?xml version="1.0" encoding="utf-8"?>
<s:Application xmlns:fx="http://ns.adobe.com/mxml/2009"
               xmlns:s="library://ns.adobe.com/flex/spark"
               xmlns:mx="library://ns.adobe.com/flex/mx"
               minWidth="150" minHeight="180" >

   <s:layout>
     <s:VerticalLayout horizontalAlign="center"
                       paddingTop="5" paddingBottom="5"
                       paddingLeft="5" paddingRight="5"/>
   </s:layout>

   <s:states>
     <s:State name="normal" />
     <s:State name="author" />
   </s:states>

   <mx:Image id="imageHolder" width="140" height="140"
             horizontalAlign="center" verticalAlign="middle"
             source="@Embed(source='assets/images/flashgen_com.png')"
             source.author="@Embed(source='assets/images/mikejones.jpg')"/>

   <s:Button id="selectorBtn" width="140"
             label="Show Mike"
             label.author="Show FlashGen"
             click="currentState='author'"
             click.author="currentState=''"/>
</s:Application>
```

This is actually the code that created the views in Figure 5.1. I highlighted the states information so it is easy to see what is happening. As you can see, it is made up of two distinct sections. First, you have the <s:states/> block. This is where you declare the individual states using the <s:State /> tag. There are two in the example: normal (the default view state) and author. The second section discusses attribute overrides, which we'll get to in a moment.

> **Note**
>
> If you declare a state change within an eventHandler attribute, shown in the previous code as click="currentState='author'", make sure you use single quotes within the handler and omit the binding braces. Otherwise, you'll get errors.

If you are coming from Flex 3, you'll immediately spot a change here. Previously, the `<s:states />` block declared and managed all the changes that would be applied to each individual view state. In Flex 4, this has been moved to the actual component itself when declaring them in MXML. This provides a cleaner and more transparent declaration of the components that are present within a state and any attributes that may need to be updated for that particular view state.

As you can see in the Button in the previous code, duplicate entries exist for the `label` and `click` attributes. If you look closer, you see that, for each attribute, the second entry has the view state suffixed to it (`label.author="Show FlashGen"`). This is how you declare value changes based on a view state. So, the Button sets a new label value and a new click handler when the view state is set to author:

```
<s:Button id="selectorBtn" width="140"
        label="Show Mike"
        label.author="Show FlashGen"
        click="currentState='author'"
        click.author="currentState=''"/>
```

Creating States in MXML

The `<s:states />` tag is nothing more than an array. It is exposed in MXML to make it easy to add instances of `<s:State />` objects for processing at a undetermined point in time. The `<s:State />` tag handles the real work; this is where you actually declare your new state and provide it with a relevant name. Before we jump ahead, let's look at the properties of the `State` class (see Table 5.1). Note that in MXML 4 (Flex 4) you cannot use the majority of these properties beyond declaring the tag itself. The rest are for ActionScript, as you'll see in a bit.

Table 5.1 **Attributes of `<s:State>`**

Attribute	Description
name	Name of the view state. This actually references the view state when switching from one state to another via the `currentState="[view state name]"` (for example, `currentState="myNewState"`).
basedOn	Allows reference of another state as a basis for a new state. This is used only in ActionScript. Deprecated from use in MXML in Flex 4.
overrides	An array of objects and properties specific to a particular state. This is used only via ActionScript. Overrides are discussed in the next section. Deprecated from use in MXML in Flex 4.
stateGroups	Name of the groups to which this state belongs. Returned as an array of strings.
enterState	Event dispatched when the view state is entered.
exitState	Event dispatched when the view state is exited.

For the most part, you will likely use view states in their basic format:

```
<s:State name="myNewState" />
```

Assigning States

Within a component, you can declare whether it is present in a particular view through the use of the `includeIn` and `excludeFrom` attributes. `includeIn` enables you to define the view states that a particular component is in via a set of comma-separated state names. So, if I had an application with four view states—`normal`, `state1`, `state2`, and `state3`— the following code would include this Button component in the `normal` and `state3` view states only:

```
<s:Button id="btn" label="My Button" includeIn="normal, state3"/>
```

`excludeFrom` performs the exact opposite by enabling you to define the view states that you don't want a particular component to be present in; given the four states, this would give you the exact same result as the `includeIn` example:

```
<s:Button id="btn" label="My Button" excludeFrom="state1, state2"/>
```

Attributes are handled slightly differently. To provide an attribute change within a component based on a particular state, you need to suffix the attribute with the state name (as the first code sample demonstrated). If you want to override the Button component label attribute based on the view state, you need to suffix the label with the view state's name and provide a new value, as the following sample illustrates:

```
<s:Button id="btn"
          label="My Button"
          label.state1="State 1"
          label.state2="State 2"/>
```

For the record, `includeIn`, `excludeFrom`, and state-suffixed attributes (for example, `label.myViewState=""`) are all language extensions within MXML and, therefore, don't have a direct equivalent in ActionScript.

Warning

If you declare an `<s:states />` block in an MXML component, it can be declared only in the base component. If you try to redeclare it in a subclass of that particular component, you get an error. This makes updating and altering individual view states painful in MXML components that are subclassed by other MXML-based components.

stateGroups

To save you from having to repeat display elements in an additional component view state, you can use the `stateGroups` attribute to provide an identifier that easily groups common consistent elements within various states. The basic syntax for declaring a `stateGroup` is as follows:

```
<s:State name="myNewState" stateGroups="group1, group2" />
```

By looking at the following code, you can see that trying to include or exclude the various view states from each element soon escalates out of control, and this has only three items:

```xml
<?xml version="1.0" encoding="utf-8"?>
<s:Application xmlns:fx="http://ns.adobe.com/mxml/2009"
               xmlns:s="library://ns.adobe.com/flex/spark"
               xmlns:mx="library://ns.adobe.com/flex/mx"
               minWidth="1024" minHeight="768">

  <fx:Script>
    <![CDATA[
      import mx.events.ListEvent;
      import mx.events.FlexEvent;

      protected function cBox_changeHandler(event:ListEvent):void
      {
        currentState = cBox.selectedLabel;
      }
    ]]>
  </fx:Script>

  <s:layout>
    <s:VerticalLayout horizontalAlign="center" paddingTop="20"/>
  </s:layout>

  <s:states>
    <s:State name="normal" />
    <s:State name="state1" />
    <s:State name="state2" />
    <s:State name="state3" />
    <s:State name="state4" />
    <s:State name="state5" />
  </s:states>

  <s:Button id="btn1" label="Button 1"
            includeIn="normal, state1, state2, state4"/>
  <s:Button id="btn2" label="Button 2"
            excludeFrom="normal, state3"/>
  <s:Button id="btn3" label="Button 3"
            includeIn="normal, state3, state5"/>

  <s:ComboBox id="cBox"
              dataProvider="{['normal', 'state1', 'state2', 'state3', 'state4',
                             'state5']}"
              selectedIndex="0"
              change="cBox_changeHandler(event)"/>
</s:Application>
```

As you can see, the three buttons appear in various states, but for most of the time, one or more of them is present in the majority of the views. As it currently stands, all the states are declared in various permutations within the Button components `includeIn` or `excludeFrom` attributes. Now, although we are setting only their presence in a given state in this example, you can see that if any of the attributes were also updated, it would start to bloat. By adding `statesGroups`, you reduce the amount of view-state inclusions within each of your components, as this revised code demonstrates:

```
<?xml version="1.0" encoding="utf-8"?>
<s:Application xmlns:fx="http://ns.adobe.com/mxml/2009"
               xmlns:s="library://ns.adobe.com/flex/spark"
               xmlns:mx="library://ns.adobe.com/flex/mx"
               minWidth="1024" minHeight="768">

  <fx:Script>
    <![CDATA[
      import mx.events.ListEvent;
      import mx.events.FlexEvent;

      protected function cBox_changeHandler(event:ListEvent):void
      {
        currentState = cBox.selectedLabel;
      }

    ]]>
  </fx:Script>

  <s:layout>
    <s:VerticalLayout horizontalAlign="center" paddingTop="20"/>
  </s:layout>

  <s:states>
    <s:State name="normal" stateGroups="g1, g2, g3"/>
    <s:State name="state1" stateGroups="g2" />
    <s:State name="state2" stateGroups="g2" />
    <s:State name="state3" stateGroups="g1, g3" />
    <s:State name="state4" stateGroups="g2" />
    <s:State name="state5" stateGroups="g3" />
  </s:states>

  <s:Button id="btn1" label="Button 1" includeIn="g2"/>
  <s:Button id="btn2" label="Button 2" excludeFrom="g1"/>
  <s:Button id="btn3" label="Button 3" includeIn="g3"/>

  <mx:ComboBox id="cBox"
               dataProvider="{['normal', 'state1', 'state2', 'state3', 'state4',
                            'state5']}"
```

```
                    selectedIndex="0"
                    change="cBox_changeHandler(event)"/>
</s:Application>
```

You aren't limited by how many `stateGroups` a particular state can belong to, so as you add functionality or additional assets to a view, you can easily update the `stateGroups` to refine which asset appears in what view state.

That's pretty much all you need to know about view states for MXML. When you want to declare a view state in ActionScript, there are a few differences—mainly because, in Flex 3, MXML mirrored ActionScript in an almost identical manner—attribute for property. This means that declaring states in ActionScript can be slightly more verbose when you compare it to the MXML version in Flex 4.

Working with States in ActionScript

As mentioned earlier, the `<s:states>` tag is nothing more that an array, and as long as your component extends from `UIComponent`, you don't have to declare it. (By default, the `states` variable has a value of `null`.) You do have to declare your `State()` instances, however, and add some basic information to them. At the minimum, you need to provide a value for the `name` property of your `State()` instance.

You may recall that the `State` class has a few additional properties that aren't used when declaring view states in MXML. The handiest of these is the `basedOn` property. In the following example, you can see that the `_mySecondState` view state sets its `basedOn` property to that of `myFirstState`, which is the `name` value of `_state1`, not its instance name:

```
<?xml version="1.0" encoding="utf-8"?>
<s:Application xmlns:fx="http://ns.adobe.com/mxml/2009"
               xmlns:s="library://ns.adobe.com/flex/spark"
               xmlns:mx="library://ns.adobe.com/flex/mx"
               creationComplete="creationCompleteHandler(event)">

   <fx:Script>
     <![CDATA[
       import mx.events.FlexEvent;
       import mx.states.State;

       protected function creationCompleteHandler(event:FlexEvent):void
       {
         var _state1 :State = new State();
         _state1.name = "myFirstState";

         var _state2      :State = new State();
         _state2.name = "mySecondState";
         _state2.basedOn = "myFirstState";
         states.push(_state1, _state2);
       }
```

```
    ]]>
  </fx:Script>
```

`</s:Application>`

basedOn enables you to use the referenced view state as a basis for your new view state, as the highlighted code illustrates. Don't worry if you have no idea what else the code is creating; we look at that next because that has to do with view state overrides.

Overrides

In ActionScript, an override, in the context of view states, is a term that refers to an object that deals with the manipulation of a particular view–state element, be that adding a component, setting a component's property, style, or event handler (or all the above). Although it may appear that declaring and manipulating views may seem restricted by this somewhat sparse set of options, it is actually powerful. However, as the complexities of your view states grow, it requires some lateral thinking and optimizing what is being overridden to avoid needless repetition or instantiation of objects. As briefly mentioned in the last section, view states have four override classes that you can declare to alter the default view state based on which ones are present in a particular State block: AddItems, SetProperty, SetStyle, and SetEventHandler . Notice that Table 5.2 has two additional properties listed: AddChild and RemoveChild. These are no longer used with Flex 4, but they are included for completeness (avoid accidental use).

Table 5.2 **View State-Specific Tags**

Tag	Description
AddChild	Adds additional Flex components (or any class that is a subclass of UIComponent) to a new specific view state beyond the default view. This is deprecated in Flex 4 and should be used only if you are creating a Flex 3 Halo-specific application. For a Spark/Halo application, use the AddItems class.
AddItems	Similar in functionality to AddChild. However, it provides additional features used by the Spark component framework and Flex 4 view states when declared in ActionScript.
RemoveChild	The opposite of AddChild. It removes elements that are not required in a particular state. Again, this has no use in a Flex 4 application and should be used only in Flex 3 applications.
SetProperty	Enables you to change the value of a single property on a specific object. You need to use additional SetProperty tags if you want to update numerous properties on an individual object.
SetEventHandler	Use SetEventHandler to alter, add, or remove event handlers of a component.
SetStyle	Enables you to apply alternative styling values to an object. (Obviously, the component needs to have style support to achieve this.)

AddItems

To make the inclusion of this updated functionality and bring everything inline with the new process by which you declare view states in MXML, a new class now enables you to manage the adding of items to a view state: AddItems.

The reason for this is that the new Spark containers support the addition of FXG and components that inherit from UIComponent, but to achieve this, the old addChild property has been superseded by the new addElement property. (However, the basic theory behind both addChild and addElement is the same.)

To bring the new view state model inline with these changes, you now use the AddItems class instead of AddChild. The AddItems class has a selection of properties and methods that can be used when declaring content for a particular view state, as Table 5.3 shows.

Table 5.3 **AddItems Properties**

Property	Description
creationPolicy	The creation policy of the items "auto", "all", or "none". The default value is "auto". This is the ActionScript alternative to itemCreationPolicy.
destination	The object to which the item is being added.
destructionPolicy	The destruction policy of the items "auto or "never". The default value is "never". This is the ActionScript alternative to itemDestructionPolicy.
isArray	Denotes whether the collection represented by the target property is to be a single array instance or a collection of items (which is the default).
isStyle	Denotes whether the collection represented by the target property is a style.
items	The view state items to be added. (Note: You cannot declare items and itemsFactory on the same AddItems instance.)
itemsFactory	The factory used to create the items. (Note: You cannot declare items and itemsFactory on the same AddItems instance.)
position	The position of the child item in the display list in relation to the object declared in the relativeTo property.
propertyName	The name of the array property to be altered
relativeTo	The object to which the item is being added.

Declaring and assigning an AddItems object to a view state is straightforward, but the part that initially tends to trip up most people is forgetting to add it to the relevant view state's overrides property. Take the following updated basedOn code; now that I have added an AddItems instance, this adds a HGroup that contains two Buttons. However, a lot is going on, so let's break it down and go over each part:

```
<?xml version="1.0" encoding="utf-8"?>
<!--Example of using "basedOn" to assign the same items to two different states -->
<s:WindowedApplication xmlns:fx="http://ns.adobe.com/mxml/2009"
                       xmlns:s="library://ns.adobe.com/flex/spark"
                       xmlns:mx="library://ns.adobe.com/flex/mx"
                       creationComplete="creationCompleteHandler(event)">

  <fx:Script>
    <![CDATA[
      import mx.events.FlexEvent;
      import mx.states.AddItems;
      import mx.states.SetProperty;
      import mx.states.State;

      import spark.components.HGroup;

      protected function creationCompleteHandler(event:FlexEvent):void
      {
        var _state1 :State = new State();
        _state1.name = "myFirstState";
        var _item       :AddItems = new AddItems();
        _item.itemsFactory = new DeferredInstanceFromFunction(createButtonGroup);
        _state.overrides.push(_item);

        var _state2       :State = new State();
        _state2.name = "mySecondState";
        _state2.basedOn = "myFirstState";
        states.push(_state1, _state2);
      }

      protected function createButtonGroup():HGroup
      {
        var _group       :HGroup = new HGroup();
        _group.percentWidth = 100;
        _group.height = 50;
        _group.verticalAlign = VerticalAlign.MIDDLE;

        var _array       :Array = ["Button A", "Button B"];

        for(var i:int = 0; i < _array.length; ++i)
        {
          var _btn          :Button = new Button();
          _btn.name = "btn" + String(_array[i]);
          _btn.label = _array[i];
          _group.addElement(_btn);
        }
```

```
      return _group;
   }

   protected function btn0_clickHandler(event:MouseEvent):void
   {
     currentState = "normal";
   }

   protected function btn1_clickHandler(event:MouseEvent):void
   {
     currentState = "myFirstState";
   }

   protected function btn2_clickHandler(event:MouseEvent):void
   {
     currentState = "mySecondState";
   }

  ]]>
</fx:Script>

<s:layout>
  <s:VerticalLayout />
</s:layout>

<s:states>
  <s:State name="normal"/>
</s:states>

<!--
<s:Button id="btn0" label="Show Normal State"
         click="btn0_clickHandler(event)" />
-->
<s:Button id="btn1" label="Show myState"
         click="btn1_clickHandler(event)" />
<s:Button id="btn2" label="Show mySecondState"
         click="btn2_clickHandler(event)" />

</s:WindowedApplication>
```

When you instantiate a new instance of an AddItems class, you must provide, at the very least, a value for its itemsFactory property. This property, as the name implies, is part of a factory process whereby the content passed to it is created and, in this case, displayed, based on particular requirements:

```
protected function creationCompleteHandler(event:FlexEvent):void
{
  var _state1 :State = new State();
  _state1.name = "myFirstState";
  var _item        :AddItems = new AddItems();
  _item.itemsFactory = new DeferredInstanceFromFunction(createButtonGroup);
  _state1.overrides.push(_item);

  var _state2      :State = new State();
  _state2.name = "mySecondState";
  _state2.basedOn = "myFirstState";
  states.push(_state1, _state2);
}
```

By default, view state elements added to an `AddItems` instance are created only when the view state is viewed for the first time, so when you assign view items to the `AddItems.itemsFactory` property, you must use one of two special classes: `DeferredInstanceFromFunction` and `DeferredInstanceFromClass`. Both classes create a deferred instance of the reference that is passed to it. So, in the following code snippet, the reference would be the `createButtonGroup()` method, because we are using the `DeferredInstanceFromFunction` class:

```
_item.itemsFactory = new DeferredInstanceFromFunction(createButtonGroup);
```

If you want to create a deferred instance of a particular component, you could use the `DeferredInstanceFromClass` class instead:

```
_item.itemsFactory = new DeferredInstanceFromClass(MyComponent);
```

However, if you use this approach, be aware that configuring the generated instance isn't going to be as easy as using a helper method that creates all the components and assigns the relevant properties, event handlers, layout, and so on. Personally, I find `DeferredInstanceFromClass` more useful if you have a prebuilt view (in MXML, for example), and all you need to do is assign it to a view state because it is already preconfigured.

If you want to have your view state create its content immediately on initialization, when your application starts up, for instance, you can use the `AddItems.items` property. This is the same as using `itemsFactory` and setting `AddItems.creationPolicy = "all"`.

For items and `itemsFactory`, note that you can declare only one of them. If you use `itemsFactory`, you cannot declare items on the same `AddItems` instance. Likewise, if you set `creationPolicy` to `auto` and use the items property, the initialization of the `AddItems` instance would be treated as if `creationPolicy` were set to `all` because the items property automatically overrides the `creationPolicy` setting, as these two examples illustrate:

```
var _item        :AddItems = new AddItems();
_item.itemsFactory = new DeferredInstanceFromFunction(createButtonGroup);
_items.creationPolicy = "all"
```

This code snippet is identical to the following code and, if you need to create your view items at application startup, this is a far more succinct approach to take:

```
var _item        :AddItems = new AddItems();
_item.items = createButtonGroup(); // calls the method directly
```

SetProperty

The remaining three view-state overrides operate in a similar manner and provide the ActionScript equivalent of `attribute.state=""` in MXML. `SetProperty`, as the name implies, deals with the setting and updating of a single property of a component. Table 5.4 lists its properties.

Table 5.4   **SetProperty Properties**

Property	Description
id	Name of the `SetProperty` instance in MXML (Flex 3 only)
name	Name of the property you want to alter
target	Object on which the property exists
Value	Value you want to set on the object property

`SetProperty()` also inherits the `prototype` property; however, you are generally going to use only the properties listed in Table 5.4.

```
//Implemented in MXML
<s:Button id="myButton" width="50" width.myFirstState="100" />
```

The MXML equivalent is the use of attribute suffixes, so the following code examples result in identical output:

```
// Implemented in ActionSCript
var _setButtonWidth    :SetProperty;

_setButtonWidth = new SetProperty(myButton, "width", 100);

_myFirstState.overrides = new Array();
_myFirstState.overrides.push(_setButtonWidth);
```

SetEventHandler

Like `SetProperty`, `SetEventHandler` is used when you want to update a specific event handler of an object. This can be extremely useful if you want to reuse a button in a particular view state by renaming it and updating the method it invokes when it is interacted with.

Table 5.5 **SetEventHandler Properties**

Property	Description
id	Name of the `SetEventHandler` instance in MXML (Flex 3)
name	Name of the event type
handler	Object or method that will handle the event (only used in MXML, Flex 3)
target	Object or component that will dispatch the event
handlerFunction	Object or method that will handle the event (only used in ActionScript)

In the following example, when the view state is set to `myFirstState`, clicking the `Button` instance `myButton` results in the method `updateView()` being called, and the buttons event object being passed to it.

Like previous comparisons, the attribute overrides in MXML are inline within the component instance itself, whereas, in the ActionScript version, they are added to the actual view state's overrides array.

Again, the following MXML and ActionScript implementations result in identical results. The MXML implementation:

```
//Implemented in MXML
<s:Button id="myButton" click.myFirstState="updateView(event)" />
```

The ActionScript implementation:

```
// Implemented in ActionScript
var _setMyButtonHandler        :SetEventHandler
_setMyButtonHandler = new SetEventHandler(myButton, "click");

_setMyButtonHandler.handlerFunction = updateView;

_myFirstState.overrides = new Array();
_myFirstState.overrides.push(_setMyButtonHandler);
```

As with all overrides, you need to push your `SetEventHandler` instances into the relevant view-state overrides array to apply them.

SetStyle

`SetStyle()` operates in a similar manner to the `setStyle()` method on all display objects that support Flex styles. Therefore, this property is completely useless on a component that doesn't have any style values—`Group`, for example—but you don't need to worry about your component not having that because Chapter 10, "Skinning and Styling," covers styling components.

Like `SetProperty()`, `SetStyle()` only has a few properties, as Table 5.6 and the following code examples illustrate.

Table 5.6   **SetStyle Properties**

Property	Description
id	Name of the `SetStyle` instance in MXML (no longer applicable in Flex 4)
name	Name of the style property you want to alter
target	Object on which the style exists
value	New value you want to set the object's style to

Like `SetProperty()`, the ActionScript implementation is straightforward, but don't forget to add it to your view states overrides array. (I'll stop droning on about that now.) As with the other overrides, the following code snippet shows both the MXML and ActionScript equivalent.

As with most comparisons between MXML and ActionScript, the ActionScript version is slightly more verbose.

MXML:

```
// Implemented in MXML
<s:Button id="myButton" color.myFirstState="#FF0000" />
```

ActionScript:

```
// Implemented in ActionScript
var _setButtonFill    :SetStyle;

_setButtonFill = new SetStyle(myButton, "color", #FF0000);

_myFirstState.overrides = new Array();
myFirstState.overrides.push(_setButtonFill);
```

Creating and Destroying View States

Creation policies enable you to determine when the items associated with a particular view state are actually created in MXML. This is handled by the attribute `itemCreationPolicy`, which (by default) has a value of `deferred`. Therefore, all elements assigned to a particular view state beyond the default one are created when required and not before. There are a few reasons for this. First, why slow the startup time of your application[1] by creating all the view states when it starts up? The second, and more important, factor is that, if this happened, your application would use additional memory on states that the user may or may not actually require.

---

[1] By application, I use it as a literal example because the procedure can equally be applied to components that support custom view states.

However, there are instances in which you do want to create a state and its assets when the application initializes. To achieve this, explicitly set the itemCreationPolicy to immediate. By doing this, the item is created as soon as the document in which it resides is initialized. The following code shows both the implicit deferred creation of button1 and the explicit immediate creation of button2. Notice how both are included only in their respective states and do not exist in the default normal state.

```
<?xml version="1.0" encoding="utf-8"?>
<s:Application xmlns:fx="http://ns.adobe.com/mxml/2009"
               xmlns:s="library://ns.adobe.com/flex/spark"
               xmlns:mx="library://ns.adobe.com/flex/mx"
               minWidth="1024" minHeight="768">

  <fx:Script>
    <![CDATA[
      import mx.events.ListEvent;

      protected function cBox_changeHandler(event:ListEvent):void
      {
        currentState = cBox.selectedLabel;
      }

    ]]>
  </fx:Script>

  <s:layout>
    <s:VerticalLayout horizontalAlign="center" paddingTop="20"/>
  </s:layout>

  <s:states>
    <s:State name="normal"/>
    <s:State name="state1"/>
    <s:State name="state2"/>
  </s:states>

  <s:Button id="button1" label="Button 1" includeIn="state1"/>
  <s:Button id="button2" label="Button 2" includeIn="state2"
           itemCreationPolicy="immediate" />


  <mx:ComboBox id="cBox"
               selectedIndex="0"
               dataProvider="{['normal','state1','state2']}"
               change="cBox_changeHandler(event)"/>
</s:Application>
```

If you ran this example with the debugger running, you see that `button2` exists regardless of whether you have switched to its view state (`state2`), whereas `button1` shows up only in the debugger after you switch to its specific view state at least once. This is useful if you have a particularly complex layout that may stagger the transition between view states as it is initializing when left to the default deferred instantiation of that state and its elements.

Having the ability to create your assets either when the application first starts up or when their parent view state is first viewed, it would be handy if you could choose when to dispose of them. After all, you may not want to have the assets of a particular state persisting within your application.

Although you can destroy a view state, you are still at the behest of the automatic garbage collection routines that the Flash Player provides. By default, all view state items are cached indefinitely, even when accessing another view state where those items are excluded. Just like `itemCreationPolicy`, when it comes to marking your assets for garbage collection, you now have access to an `itemDestructionPolicy` attribute, which is set to `never` by default. If you do want to mark elements for garbage collection, just set their `itemDestructionPolicy` to `auto` and, when marked, they will get collected on the next garbage collection cycle where they are no longer being displayed/referenced. The following code snippet illustrates how you do this:

```
<s:Button id="button1" label="Button 1" includeIn="state1"/>
<s:Button id="button2" label="Button 2" includeIn="state2"
          itemDestructionPolicy="auto" />
```

In most instances, however, the default setting should suffice, but it is helpful to know that you can mark your elements for garbage collection if they are part of a view state that is no longer required.

> **Note**
>
> `itemCreationPolicy` and `itemDestructionPolicy`, like `includeIn` and `excludeFrom`, are language extensions and are present only within MXML. In ActionScript, you need to use the `creationPolicy` and `destructionPolicy` properties of the `AddItems` class.

As indicated in the Note, in ActionScript, you don't have access to `itemCreationPolicy` or `itemDestructionPolicy`. Instead, if you want to control the creation and destruction of view state content, you need to use `AddItems`. `creationPolicy` and `AddItems.destructionPolicy`. You would assume that because these properties are used instead of `itemCreationPolicy` and `itemDestructionPolicy`, they'd accept the same values. That is true for `destructionPolicy`, but `creationPolicy` accepts the values `auto`, `all`, and `none`.

As mentioned earlier, setting the `creationPolicy` property of an `AddItems` instance to `all` when using the `itemsFactory` is functionally equivalent to using the

AddItems.items property. If you set the creationPolicy to none, you must call
createInstance() method of the AddItems instance before you switch to the target
view state. Take the alteration I made to the basedOn example; selecting either
myFirstState or mySecondState results in a runtime error, because
_items.createInstance() hasn't been called first and created the deferred items.

```
protected function creationCompleteHandler(event:FlexEvent):void
{
  var _state1 :State = new State();
  _state1.name = "myFirstState";
  var _item        :AddItems = new AddItems();
  _item.itemsFactory = new DeferredInstanceFromFunction(createButtonGroup);

  // This will throw an RTE if you don't call _items.createInstance()
  // prior to switching to either "myFirstState" or "mySecondState"
  _items.creationPolicy - "none";
  _state.overrides.push(_item);

  var _state2      :State = new State();
  _state2.name = "mySecondState";
  _state2.basedOn = "myFirstState";
  states.push(_state1, _state2);
}
```

In my mind, this is counter-intuitive because you would assume that setting the
creationPolicy to none would enable you to switch to the relevant view state and create the content manually as required. This is not how it currently operates. I have a nag-
ging feeling this may be a bug; if it is, I'm sure it will be fixed in future updates to the
Flex framework. Regardless, at least you know how it functions, so you hopefully won't
get caught trying to figure out why it doesn't function as expected.

The last thing to cover is working with view states in your components because most
examples in this chapter have been based around MXML and script blocks. Although
that's perfectly valid when it comes to component development, you may be wondering
how you implement them in a pure ActionScript component.

Adding States to Components

Adding view states to your components follows exactly the same process as the samples
throughout this chapter. Here is a simple component that has three view states; like the
examples earlier, they are normal, myFirstState, and mySecondState.

Notice that the actual process of creating the view states and their content is the same
as previous examples. The main difference is that I have created a method called
createStates() that deals with the actual view state creation. This method is, in turn,
invoked from within the components createChildren() method.

```
package com.developingcomponents.components
{
  import mx.core.DeferredInstanceFromFunction;
  import mx.states.AddItems;
  import mx.states.State;

  import spark.components.Button;
  import spark.components.Group;

  public class BasicStateComponent extends Group
  {
    private static const DEFAULT_WIDTH              :uint = 320;
    private static const DEFAULT_HEIGHT             :uint = 200;

    private var _stateNames            :Array = ["normal",
                                                 "myFirstState",
                                                 "mySecondState"];
    private var _count                 :int;

    override protected function createChildren():void
    {
      super.createChildren();

      createStates();
    }

    protected function createStates():void
    {

      for(var i:int = 0; i < _stateNames.length; ++i)
      {
        _count = i;

        var _state        :State = new State();
        _state.name = _stateNames[i];
        var _items        :AddItems = new AddItems();
        _items.itemsFactory = new DeferredInstanceFromFunction(createButtonGroup);
        _state.overrides.push(_items);
        states.push(_state);
      }
    }

    protected function createButtonGroup():Button
    {
      var _btn          :Button = new Button();
      _btn.label = _stateNames[_count];
```

```
        return _btn;
    }
  }
}
```

The advantages of doing it within the `createStates()` method means that the view states and their content are created as your component is initialized and therefore are accessible if the `currentState` attribute is set in MXML. This is particularly useful when using the `AddItems.items` property or if you have set your view state(s) creation policy to `all`.

Worth Noting

Before moving to the next chapter, let's recap a couple of key points about view states. Specifically, ones that can be easily overlooked after you start using them in ActionScript because of the nonlinear approach object-orientated programming has compared to the more opaque processes that MXML enables by its structure and formatting:

- View-state overrides are processed in order (first in, first out).
- Feel free to use various creation policies to optimize view content creation.
- Use the `basedOn` property to keep persisting components separate and reusable across related views/subviews.

Summary

This chapter showed you how the Flex framework can take out a lot of the heavy lifting when it comes to updating and altering the visual layout and process management within your components.

You also saw how you can manage states within ActionScript and learned about a particular quirk of states when inherited from one MXML component to another.

With some forethought, you saw how you can easily update and manipulate multiple view layouts so that their addition and subsequent removal have no awkward visual impacts on your components.

Finally, you saw the new Flex 4 state implementation within MXML and how it provides a simpler approach to state management compared the ActionScript equivalent.

Next, we look at how we can take these processes and add more zing to them. With that in mind, let us move onward.

Effects and Transitions

In Chapter 5, "Managing States," you saw how the Flex framework provides a simple solution to updating and altering the visual layout of your component. However, as you probably also noticed, it wasn't the most graceful or engaging process from a user perspective because the user interface just flicks from one state to the other. This sort of interaction, or lack thereof, isn't something that I'd be happy unleashing on the world, and I'm sure you feel the same.

Fortunately, the Flex framework and underlying ActionScript libraries nip those types of user-experience nightmares in the bud and enable you to be proactive and reactive when it comes to user interaction and updating the visuals of your components.

Effects

Like most things in Flex, effects are usually declared in MXML. (But as with everything else in the Flex framework, they can be instantiated in ActionScript as well.) As component developers, you are likely to opt for the ActionScript route for the majority of your components. That said, it is worth understanding how to implement and interact with effects in MXML before you see how to perform the same process in ActionScript.

Flex effects can be as simple or as complex as you want; however, the more complexity, the more effects you need to combine. This is both the strength and weakness of effects in the Flex framework. The reason for this is to easily cut effects into core types, which provides a simple process to declare a solitary effect type or combine it with additional effects to create more complex interactions. This can, unfortunately, result in a lot of code for what appears to be a simple interaction.

Effect Types

If you look in the language reference for Flex 4, you see that there are a few effects packages/subpackages. Within each of these is a gamut of effects that you can use. However, listing all of them in this chapter won't benefit you; that's what the documentation is for. A better approach is to talk about effects in terms of their semantic grouping, allowing some effects to be present in one or more of these groups.

In those terms, effects can be broken into four distinct groups: effects that affect the targets' properties, those that transform the targets, those that work with the filters on a target, and those that use Pixel-shaders.

Property Effects

Property effects, as the name implies, work by interacting directly with the target's properties. This may be by fading the target (manipulating the alpha property), resizing it by adjusting the width and height values, or setting a color value for the backGroundColor of the target, to name a few. Of course, you can use them individually or combined to create more elaborate effects. (We look at combining effects later.)

For common property effect manipulation, there are dedicated effect types, like Resize, Fade, Move, and AnimateColor. Here is a simple example where you can choose two colors and then interpolate between them via the AnimateColor effect. This may seem like a simple task, but color interpolation prior to Flex 4 was a calculation headache if you wanted to do it over time, as the new AnimateColor effect does.

```xml
<?xml version="1.0" encoding="utf-8"?>
<s:Application xmlns:fx="http://ns.adobe.com/mxml/2009"
               xmlns:s="library://ns.adobe.com/flex/spark"
               xmlns:mx="library://ns.adobe.com/flex/mx"
               width="330" height="330">

    <fx:Declarations>
      <s:AnimateColor id="aniCol"
                      colorFrom="{fromCol.selectedColor}"
                      colorTo="{toCol.selectedColor}"
                      duration="5000"
                      target="{col}" />
    </fx:Declarations>

    <s:VGroup width="100%" height="100%">
      <s:HGroup width="100%" height="40"
                verticalAlign="middle">

        <s:Label text="From Color:"/>
        <mx:ColorPicker id="fromCol"
                        selectColor="0xffcc00" />
        <s:Label text="To Color:"/>
        <mx:ColorPicker id="toCol"
                        selectColor="0x00fcfc"/>
        <s:Button id="playBtn" label="Play Color Transition"
                  click="aniCol.play()" />
      </s:HGroup>

      <s:Rect width="100%" height="100%">
        <s:fill>
```

```
        <s:SolidColor id="col" color="{fromCol.selectedColor}" />
      </s:fill>
    </s:Rect>
    </s:VGroup>
</s:Application>
```

If you want more flexibility, you can just use the default `Animate` effect and provide the required parameters for the target's properties that you want to manipulate during the effect. To achieve this, combine `SimpleMotionPath` entries for each property to be animated. The `SimpleMotionPath` effect enables you to define the starting value of a property and the value that property will finish with. It is a more concise version of the `MotionPath`/`Keyframe` effect process, which is discussed later in this chapter.

```
<?xml version="1.0" encoding="utf-8"?>
<s:Application xmlns:fx="http://ns.adobe.com/mxml/2009"
               xmlns:s="library://ns.adobe.com/flex/spark"
               xmlns:mx="library://ns.adobe.com/flex/mx">

  <fx:Declarations>
    <s:Animate id="moveSquare" target="{square}">
      <s:SimpleMotionPath property="x" valueFrom="100" valueTo="200"/>
      <s:SimpleMotionPath property="y" valueFrom="100" valueTo="300"/>
    </s:Animate>
  </fx:Declarations>

  <s:BorderContainer id="square"
                     x="100" y="100"
                     width="100" height="100"
                     backgroundColor="0xff0000" />

<s:Button label="Click Me!"
          click="moveSquare.play()"/>
</s:Application>
```

Transformation Effects

When applying transformation effects (`move`, `scaleX`, `scaleY`, `rotate`, and so on) to a target when used in parallel, they are combined into a single transformation. This negates any risk, whereas uncombined transformations running in parallel might result in erroneous playback when applied.

> **Note**
>
> This means that transformation effects cannot be used in repeating effect blocks, where the effect is repeated numerous times, or use the properties `repeatBehavior`, `repeatCount` or `repeatDelay` when combined together.

Rotating targets has always been hit-or-miss in the past (Flex 3 and earlier), mainly because Flex employs a top-left coordinate system and, for the vast majority of cases, we, as developers, usually want to rotate visual assets based on a central reference point. With Flex 4, this is simple enough to achieve by setting the `autoCenterTransform` value to true in the relevant effect. This is especially useful if you apply the effect to multiple targets; in which case, Flex calculates the transform center for each item independently.

If, on the other hand, you want to rotate the target from a specific point, be that 2D (x/y-axis) or in 3D space (z-axis), set the required values for x, y, and z coordinates of your transform by assigning values to one or more of the `transformX`, `transformY`, and `transformZ` properties of that effect.

When rotating in 2D or 3D space, depending on the target's container, you may encounter some layout issues. For example, take Figure 6.1. If you had three boxes in an `HGroup` and you rotated the central box, the other two boxes get knocked out of alignment, as shown. This is because the width of the central box (corner to corner) is greater than that of its sides.

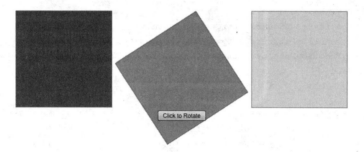

Figure 6.1   Rotating targets within a container
can have undesirable effects.

To fix this, set the `disableLayout` property of the effect to disable the parent container's layout for the duration of the effect, as shown in the following code:

```
<?xml version="1.0" encoding="utf-8"?>
<s:Application xmlns:fx="http://ns.adobe.com/mxml/2009"
          xmlns:s="library://ns.adobe.com/flex/spark"
          xmlns:mx="library://ns.adobe.com/flex/mx"
          minWidth="955" minHeight="600">

  <fx:Declarations>
    <s:Rotate id="rotationEffect" target="{redSquare}"
          autoCenterTransform="true"
          angleFrom="0" angleTo="360"
          disableLayout="true"/>
  </fx:Declarations>
```

```
  <s:layout>
    <s:VerticalLayout horizontalAlign="center" verticalAlign="middle"/>
  </s:layout>

  <s:HGroup height="200">
    <s:BorderContainer id="blueSquare"
                       width="200" height="200"
                       backgroundColor="0x0000ff"/>
    <s:BorderContainer id="redSquare"
                       width="200" height="200"
                       backgroundColor="0xff0000"/>
    <s:BorderContainer id="GreenSquare"
                       width="200" height="200"
                       backgroundColor="0x00ff00"/>
  </s:HGroup>
  <s:Button label="Click to Rotate" click="rotationEffect.play()" />
</s:Application>
```

Note that if you do disable the layout of the container during the effect, it plays as expected, but depending on the stack order of the visual items within the parent container, your target may appear on top and/or underneath the other display item within the container as the effect runs. So, in the previous example, the HGroup stacks the display items lowest first, from left to right. The red square, in this case, would appear above the blue square (positioned on the left) and below the green square (positioned on the right) during some points of its rotation.

In most cases, however, you don't want to disable the layout of the parent container entirely. If you run the previous code, you notice that there is a slight wobble of the items in the HGroup as the red square rotates. Instead, consider using the applyChangesPostLayout property of the effect. (For 3D transformations, this is set to true by default.) This allows the effect to be applied to the target, but the parent ignores any change to layout during the effect. Wobble fixed.

Filter Effects

Filter effects are slightly different from the normal effect because they target the filters of a target and not the target itself. This enables you to alter the visual appearance of the target without modifying any of its properties. The following example animates a DropShadowFilter that is applied to the BorderContainer:

```
<?xml version="1.0" encoding="utf-8"?>
<s:Application xmlns:fx="http://ns.adobe.com/mxml/2009"
               xmlns:s="library://ns.adobe.com/flex/spark"
               xmlns:mx="library://ns.adobe.com/flex/mx"
               minWidth="955" minHeight="600">
  <fx:Script>
    <![CDATA[
      import spark.filters.DropShadowFilter;
```

```
      ]]>
    </fx:Script>

    <fx:Declarations>
      <s:AnimateFilter id="dropShadowFilterEffect"
                         target="{square}"
                         repeatCount="0"
                         repeatBehavior="reverse"
                         bitmapFilter="{new spark.filters.DropShadowFilter()}">
        <s:SimpleMotionPath property="color"
                            valueFrom="0xff0000" valueTo="0xff0000"/>
        <s:SimpleMotionPath property="distance"
                            valueFrom="0" valueTo="10"/>
        <s:SimpleMotionPath property="angle"
                            valueFrom="0" valueTo="360"/>
      </s:AnimateFilter>
    </fx:Declarations>

    <s:layout>
      <s:VerticalLayout horizontalAlign="center" verticalAlign="middle"/>
    </s:layout>

    <s:BorderContainer id="square"
                        width="200" height="200"
                        backgroundColor="0xffffff"
                        borderColor="0x000000"/>
    <s:Button label="Run Filter" click="dropShadowFilterEffect.play()" />
</s:Application>
```

Note that you don't have to have already applied a filter to the target before declaring an effect. Here the filter is instantiated as part of the overall `Animate` effect.

Pixel-Shader Effects

Like filter effects, Pixel-shader effects don't modify a target's property. Instead, they apply an animation to the target where the before and after are represented by bitmaps. To achieve this, the effect captures a before bitmap and an after bitmap of the target and then applies the animation between the two snapshots.

To create Pixel-shader effects, you can use Pixel-Bender Toolkit to define your .pbj files so that you can run custom Pixel-shaders. Alternatively, effects like `Wipe` and `CrossFade` use their own built-in Pixel-shaders. Although you can use Pixel-shader effects on their own in the same manner as Move or Resize, because they require a before-and-after bitmap, they are more commonly used as part of a transition.

Working with Effects

Having discussed the various effect groups and looked at numerous examples, you may be suffering from sensory overload. So, let's take a step back and look at what constitutes an effect and how you implement and assign them to your components.

Declaring Effects

The basic structure of a single effect type is as follows. (For those who have used the Flex 3 framework, notice that Flex 4 effects are declared within the new `<fx:Declarations/>` block.)

```
<fx:Declarations>
<s:EffectName id="effectID" target="effectTarget" [additional attributes] />
</fx:Declarations>
```

As you can see, it is pretty much the same structure as any other MXML tag. You have the type of effect it is, the id of the effect so you can easily reference it, and the object to which it is applied. Beyond that, each effect has its own set of attributes that you can bind to, which enables you to set bound values for their various properties, as the following example shows:

```
<s:Move id="moveButton" target="{myButton}" xTo="200" yTo="200" />
```

This Move effect is assigned to a component called myButton, and it will move it from its initial position to an x and y position of 200. In ActionScript, declaring an effect requires a few more lines, but it performs exactly the same functionality. This example is identical to the MXML version:

```
private var _moveButton :Move = new Move();
_moveButtom.target = myButton;
_moveButton.xTo = 200;
_moveButton.yTo = 200;
```

Are there any advantages to using ActionScript over MXML? Not really; it depends on how you implement your components. I usually create my effects in ActionScript, but that's because I create almost all of my components in ActionScript. If I were creating a component in MXML, I would leverage the power of MXML and create my effects by using it. My preference for creating components in ActionScript is purely because I have used ActionScript for so long that I tend to default to it, but apart from a few quirks—see Chapter 5 about declaring states within an MXML component—creating components in ActionScript has no performance difference compared to creating them in MXML.

Triggering Effects

After you declare your effect(s), you have a few options on how to trigger the effect within a component. Although this can be subjective, there are generally only two main ways: manually (active) or automatically (passive).

Active Triggers

Active triggers require the effect to be invoked directly, by calling the `play()` or `stop()` methods of the target effect. In the following example, the button click actively triggers the `moveButton` effect by calling its `play()` method directly, starting the effect process:

```
<s:Button id="playMoveEffectBtn"
        label="Click to move myButton"
        click="moveButton.play()" />
```

Obviously, you aren't required to assign the effect call within the event attribute in MXML. By leveraging the event handler generation in Flash Builder, it makes more sense to put the call inside a handler method because you have more flexibility if you need to perform additional functions prior to calling the effect; it also creates a unified approach should you want to reuse it via ActionScript. In this next code example, I highlighted the event attribute in the Button component and the handler that Flash Builder has generated for me. That way, you can see the difference between the two versions:

```
<?xml version="1.0" encoding="utf-8"?>
<s:VGroup xmlns:fx="http://ns.adobe.com/mxml/2009"
        xmlns:s="library://ns.adobe.com/flex/spark"
        xmlns:mx="library://ns.adobe.com/flex/mx"
        width="400" height="300">

  <fx:Script>
    <![CDATA[
      protected function playMoveEffectBtn_clickHandler(event:MouseEvent):void
      {
        // perform any functions before the effect is triggered
        // now play the effect...
        moveButton.play()

        // Perform any functions after the effect is triggered
      }
    ]]>
  </fx:Script>

  <s:Button id=" playMoveEffectBtn"
          label="Click to move myButton" click="
          playMoveEffectBtn_clickHandler(event)" />

</s:VGroup>
```

Passive Triggers

A passive trigger is one that happens without the need to explicitly invoke it. A common way to achieve this is to assign your effect to the relevant `eventEffect` property of your component.

Passive triggers don't call the effects `play()`, (or `stop()`) methods directly. Instead, the effect is assigned to a reciprocal effect handler on the target components associated event.

So, if you want to use an effect whenever the target component is shown or hidden, you just need to make sure that the target component had a `showEffect` and/or `hideEffect` attribute so you could pass a reference to your effect. Most components have a selection of `eventEffect` attributes—`addEffect`, `creationCompleteEffect`, `hideEffect`, `showEffect`, `resizeEffect`, to list a few of the common ones. Check out the Adobe Flex language guide to see which `eventEffects` are supported by each component.

The following example shows a `ViewStack` component that contains three `Canvas` components. On each canvas, the `hideEffect` and `showEffect` are associated with the two `<s:Move/>` effects that are defined within the `<fx:Declarations/>` tag. When the `ViewStack` updates its `selectedIndex` (via a `ButtonBar` component), the current target triggers the `moveOff` effect as it is associated with the `hideEffect` attribute and then the new target (based on the newly selected `ViewStack.selectedIndex`) fires off its `showEffect` and triggers the `moveOn` effect moving from outside the application area.

```
<?xml version="1.0" encoding="utf-8"?>
<s:Application xmlns:fx="http://ns.adobe.com/mxml/2009"
               xmlns:s="library://ns.adobe.com/flex/spark"
               xmlns:mx="library://ns.adobe.com/flex/mx"
               minWidth="400" minHeight="400"
               creationComplete="creationCompleteHandler(event)">

    <fx:Script>
      <![CDATA[
        import mx.collections.ArrayCollection;
        import mx.events.FlexEvent;

        [Bindable]
        private var _dpColl        :ArrayCollection;

        protected function creationCompleteHandler(event:FlexEvent):void
        {
          _dpColl = new ArrayCollection([{label:'View 1', data:0},
                                         {label:'View 2', data:1},
                                         {label:'View 3', data:2}]);

        }
      ]]>
    </fx:Script>

    <fx:Declarations>
      <s:Move id="moveOn" xFrom="{this.width}" xTo="0" />
      <s:Move id="moveOff" xFrom="0" xTo="{-this.width}" />
    </fx:Declarations>
```

```
<mx:ViewStack id="vStack" selectedIndex="{tbar.selectedIndex}"
              left="0" right="0" top="0" bottom="0">
  <mx:Canvas backgroundColor="0xff0000"
             showEffect="{moveOn}" hideEffect="{moveOff}" />
  <mx:Canvas backgroundColor="0x00ff00"
             showEffect="{moveOn}" hideEffect="{moveOff}" />
  <mx:Canvas backgroundColor="0x0000ff"
             showEffect="{moveOn}" hideEffect="{moveOff}" />
</mx:ViewStack>

<s:ButtonBar id="tbar" dataProvider="{_dpColl}"  />
</s:Application>
```

This is useful, but suppose you want a combination of active and passive effect management or you want to know when one effect ends and another starts. Well, luckily, Effects support a selection of events that also dispatch as they run.

All the effects in the Flex framework dispatch the following events. (For example, when an effect starts to play, it dispatches the `effectStart` event and when the effect ends, it dispatches the `effectEnd` event.) The Spark effects also support the `effectRepeat` event, which is dispatched when an effect that is set to repeat starts a new repetition. Spark effects also support the `effectUpdate` event, which is dispatched every time the effect updates the target.

Orchestrating Effects

So far, we've only discussed effects in a singular instance; however, you can combine effects to create all manners of visual displays. To achieve this, the Effects classes include a set of classes that deal with the combining and processing of grouped effects. They are Parallel, Sequence, and Pause. You can even combine these to create pseudo logic or flow within your composite effect.

If you want a panel to grow to a specific size and then move, you can easily do this by using a `<s:Sequence/>` tag to wrap a `<s:Resize/>` and a `<s:Move/>` effect together, as shown here. Sequences, as the name implies, process their contents in sequence, so when the sequence block is triggered, the target is resized first and, after that effect finishes, the component can then be moved.

```
<s:Sequence id="resizeThenMove" target="{myPanel}">
  <s:Resize widthTo="400" heightTo="400" />
  <s:Move xTo="200" yTo="200" />
</s:Sequence>
```

If, on the other hand, you want to combine the `<s:Resize/>` and `<s:Move/>` so they happen simultaneously, you just need to swap out the `<s:Sequence/>` for a `<s:Parallel/>`. This executes any effects that it encapsulates simultaneously.

```
<s:Parallel id="resizeAndMove" target="{myPanel}">
  <s:Resize widthTo="400" heightTo="400" />
  <s:Move xTo="200" yTo="200" />
</s:Parallel>
```

At the beginning of this chapter, we looked at how to instantiate a single effect in ActionScript, but what does the ActionScript equivalent look like when you have something like the previous Parallel effect block? Here is a simple example of a Parallel effect written solely in ActionScript. You can see that you need to declare and instantiate your effects and then push them in to the Parallel instance.

Because this is a Parallel effect, it doesn't matter in which order they are added. However, when using the Sequence effect in ActionScript, pay careful attention to the order that you add them to the Sequence instance, because this determines the order that they are run when the Sequence is triggered—the first effect added is the first one executed.

```
<?xml version="1.0" encoding="utf-8"?>
<s:Application xmlns:fx="http://ns.adobe.com/mxml/2009"
               xmlns:s="library://ns.adobe.com/flex/spark"
               xmlns:mx="library://ns.adobe.com/flex/mx"
               creationComplete="creationCompleteHandler(event)">

  <s:layout>
    <s:VerticalLayout horizontalAlign="center" verticalAlign="middle" />
  </s:layout>

  <fx:Script>
    <![CDATA[
      import mx.effects.Glow;
      import mx.effects.Parallel;

      import spark.components.BorderContainer;
      import spark.components.Button;
      import spark.effects.Fade;

      private var _demoContainer :BorderContainer = new BorderContainer();
      private var _showBtn        :Button = new Button();
      private var _parallel       :Parallel = new Parallel(demoContainer);
      private var _visible        :Boolean = true;

      private function creationCompleteHandler(e:Event):void
      {
        // Define our container
        _demoContainer.setStyle("backgroundColor", 0x000000);
        _demoContainer.width = 250;
        _demoContainer.height = 250;
```

```
        // Set up the button values and the handler
        _showBtn.label = "Hide";
        _showBtn.addEventListener(MouseEvent.CLICK, updateDisplay);

        // Define our Fade effect here
        var _fade      :Fade = new Fade();
        _fade.alphaFrom = 0;
        _fade.alphaTo = 1;
        _fade.duration = 1000;

        // Define our Glow effect here
        var _glow      :Glow = new Glow();
        _glow.alphaFrom = 1;
        _glow.alphaTo = 0;
        _glow.blurXFrom = 0;
        _glow.blurXTo = 30;
        _glow.blurYFrom = 0;
        _glow.blurYTo = 30;
        _glow.color = 0xff0000;

        // OK here we add our fade and glow to the Parallel object
        _parallel.addChild(_fade);
        _parallel.addChild(_glow);
        // Finally add it all to the display list.
        addElement(_demoContainer);
        addElement(_showBtn);
    }

    private function updateDisplay(e:MouseEvent):void
    {
      if (_visible)
      {
        _parallel.play(null, true);
        _visible = false;
        _showBtn.label = "Show";
      }
      else
      {
        _parallel.play();
        _visible = true;
        _showBtn.label = "Hide";
      }
    }
  }
  ]]>
 </fx:Script>
</s:Application>
```

Note that if you set the duration property of these tags, they are applied slightly differently. Sequences apply the duration value for each effect they contain. So, an effect sequence with duration of 5000ms (5 seconds) plays each effect it contains for 5 seconds. The Parallel effect, on the other hand, runs all the effects it contains for 5 seconds in total.

That just leaves `<s:Pause/>`. Use this to add a delay in your sequence blocks by either setting a duration of time to elapse before continuing to the next effect in the sequence or until a specified event is dispatched by the target.

```
<s:Sequence>
  <s:Move target="{loginPanel}" yFrom="100" yTo="300"/>
  <s:Pause duration="5000" />
  <s:Move target="{}loginPanel" yFrom="300" yTo="100"/>
</s:Sequence>
```

Although Parallel and Sequence effects offer a clear and concise way to combine various effects together, enabling the creation of new and more elaborate effect types, note that they are still bound by the same restrictions that any other display object has.

For example, if you were to create a Parallel effect block and place a wipe up effect and a wipe left effect within it, you would naturally assume that the result would be an effect that, when invoked played a wipe from the bottom right to the top left. Unfortunately, that's not the case. This is because quite a few of the effects are based on masking and, therefore, negate each other on the basis of a first in, first out process.

Working with MotionPath and Keyframe

You may be wondering how the transformation effects are combined into a single transformation. Well, in the background, all the properties and their relative values are converted in to key frames. (Yes, all you old-school Flash developers, I just said key frames.) The Flex 4 framework has a set of animation classes that certain effects use for the creation and playback of properties based on key frames.

The following code example shows a simple effect that moves the target component around the screen by altering its x and y position.

> **Note**
>
> When dealing with the x and y position of a target, make sure to include a key frame that has a time value of zero and no value set.
>
> This gives the effect a hook into calculating its initial key frame value prior to triggering the effect. When omitted, this can cause animating the position of the target fail.

It is built around the `Animate` effect class, similar in nature to the one shown at the beginning of this chapter, but instead of using `SimpleMotionPath`, it uses `MotionPath` and `Keyframe`. Within it, there are three `<s:MotionPath/>` blocks, and you can see that these contain numerous `<s:Keyframe/>` nodes. Each key frame entry accepts two values: `time` and `value`. To target a particular property, you need to list it in the property attribute of the `MotionPath` instance.

```
<?xml version="1.0" encoding="utf-8"?>
<s:Application xmlns:fx="http://ns.adobe.com/mxml/2009"
               xmlns:s="library://ns.adobe.com/flex/spark"
               xmlns:mx="library://ns.adobe.com/flex/mx">
  <fx:Declarations>
    <s:Animate id="moveSquare" target="{square}">
      <s:MotionPath property="x">
        <s:Keyframe time="0" />
        <s:Keyframe time="300" value="100" />
        <s:Keyframe time="600" value="0" />
        <s:Keyframe time="900" value="100" />
        <s:Keyframe time="1200" value="0" />
        <s:Keyframe time="1500" value="100" />
      </s:MotionPath>
      <s:MotionPath property="y">
        <s:Keyframe time="0"/>
        <s:Keyframe time="300" value="100" />
        <s:Keyframe time="600" value="0" />
        <s:Keyframe time="900" value="100" />
        <s:Keyframe time="1200" value="0" />
        <s:Keyframe time="1500" value="100" />
      </s:MotionPath>
      <s:MotionPath property="backgroundColor">
        <s:interpolator>
          <s:HSBInterpolator />
        </s:interpolator>
        <s:Keyframe time="100" value="0xFF0000" />
        <s:Keyframe time="1500" value="{Math.random() * 0xFFFFFF}" />
      </s:MotionPath>
    </s:Animate>
  </fx:Declarations>

  <s:BorderContainer id="square"
                     x="100" y="100"
                     width="100" height="100"
                     backgroundColor="0xff0000" />
  <s:Button label="Click Me!"
            click="moveSquare.play()"/>
</s:Application>
```

The other item that is highlighted in the code is the backgroundColor MotionPath. This includes an interpolator to enable the interpolation of HSB from RGB uint start and end values. The beauty of MotionPath and Keyframe is that, if the target has a property, you can create a MotionPath / Keyframe block to apply effects to it.

Transitions

After you have the basic layout of your component created and you have added in the various view states that your component may require, it's time to think about how you move between one state and the next, whether that be automatically via some external data binding or through user interaction. One thing is certain: At some point, you need to handle the transition between the two view states. The most common form of transition is that of the screen flick, where one of your views is immediately replaced by the next. Although this may be fine for, say, an admin system or application that won't be seen by the general public, it doesn't make for a good user experience because a result can often be jarring. (And, even if it isn't for public consumption, that's not an excuse to leave it like that.)

Fortunately for us, the Flex framework deals with transitions with the same aplomb as it does with view states, which makes it easy to apply various types of effects so that the switch between one view state and the next is more visually pleasing and user friendly.

The majority of the time, you are likely to be using Move, Wipe, or Resize transitions, which enable you to alter the visual layout of your application or, in the case of switching between view states, move the current state so that the new state is revealed. Declaring transitions in MXML is simple, as the following snippet illustrates. One interesting point is that, although effects have to be declared within the `<fx:Declarations/>` tags when used as part of a transition, they can just be placed within the transition block. This is illustrated in the following MXML-based component:

```
<?xml version="1.0" encoding="utf-8"?>
<s:BorderContainer xmlns:fx="http://ns.adobe.com/mxml/2009"
                   xmlns:s="library://ns.adobe.com/flex/spark"
                   xmlns:mx="library://ns.adobe.com/flex/mx"
                   width="320" height="240"
                   mask="{mask}">
  <fx:Declarations>
    <!-- Place non-visual elements (e.g., services, value objects) here -->
  </fx:Declarations>

  <s:states>
    <s:State name="normal" />
    <s:State name="panelView" />
  </s:states>

  <s:transitions>
    <s:Transition fromState="*" toState="panelView">
      <s:Move target="{panel}"
              yFrom="{this.height}"
              yTo="{this.height - panel.height}"/>
    </s:Transition>
  </s:transitions>
```

```
<s:Group id="mask" width="100%" height="{this.height}">
  <s:Rect width="100%" height="100%">
    <s:fill>
      <s:SolidColor color="0xff0000" />
    </s:fill>
  </s:Rect>
</s:Group>

<s:BorderContainer id="panel" backgroundColor="0x333333"
                   width="100%" height="100"
                   y="{this.height}"
                   y.panelView="{this.height - panel.height}"/>
</s:BorderContainer>
```

Declaring transitions in ActionScript is a similar process to declaring view states. Like view states, all classes that inherit from UIComponent have an array called transitions. This is where you push your transition objects after they are created.

```
package com.developingcomponents.components
{
  import mx.graphics.SolidColor;
  import mx.states.AddItems;
  import mx.states.SetProperty;
  import mx.states.State;
  import mx.states.Transition;

  import spark.components.BorderContainer;
  import spark.components.Group;
  import spark.effects.Move;
  import spark.primitives.Rect;

  public class TransitionComponent extends BorderContainer
  {
    private static const DEFAULT_WIDTH  :uint = 320;
    private static const DEFAULT_HEIGHT :uint = 200;
    private var _move                   :Move;
    private var _defaultTransition      :Transition;

    private var _defaultState           :State;
    private var _panelState             :State;

    private var _defaultItems           :AddItems;
    private var _updatePanel            :SetProperty;
    private var _panel                  :BorderContainer;

    private var _panelHeight            :int = 100;
```

```
private var _mask                :Group;

public function TransitionComponent()
{
  super();
}

override protected function createChildren():void
{
  super.createChildren();

  createMask();
  createPanel();
  createEffects();
  createStates();
  createTransitions();
}

override protected function measure():void
{
  super.measure();

  this.measuredWidth = this.measuredMinWidth = DEFAULT_WIDTH;
  this.measuredHeight = this.measuredMinHeight = DEFAULT_HEIGHT;
}

override protected function updateDisplayList(unscaledWidth:Number,
                                    unscaledHeight:Number):void
{
  super.updateDisplayList(unscaledWidth, unscaledHeight);

  this.setActualSize(unscaledWidth, unscaledHeight);
}

protected function createPanel():void
{
  _panel = new BorderContainer();
  _panel.setStyle("backgroundColor", 0x333333);
  _panel.percentWidth - 100;
  _panel.height = _panelHeight;
  _panel.y = this.height + _panelHeight*2;
  addElement(_panel);
}

protected function createMask():void
{
  var _rect     :Rect = new Rect();
```

```
  _rect.fill = new SolidColor(0xff0000);
  _rect.width = DEFAULT_WIDTH;
  _rect.height = DEFAULT_HEIGHT;

  _mask = new Group();
  _mask.addElement(_rect);
  _mask.width = DEFAULT_WIDTH;
  _mask.height = DEFAULT_HEIGHT;
  addElement(_mask);
  this.mask = _mask;
}

protected function createEffects():void
{
  _move = new Move();
  _move.yBy = -_panelHeight;
  _move.target = _panel;
}

protected function createStates():void
{
  _defaultState = new State();
  _defaultState.name = "normal";
  _defaultItems = new AddItems();
  _defaultState.overrides.push(_defaultItems);

  _panelState = new State();
  _panelState.name = "panelView"
  _panelState.basedOn = "normal"

  _updatePanel = new SetProperty();
  _updatePanel.target = _panel;
  _updatePanel.name = "y";
  _updatePanel.value = this.height + _panelHeight;

  _panelState.overrides.push(_updatePanel);

  states.push(_defaultState, _panelState);
}

protected function createTransitions():void
{
  _defaultTransition = new Transition();
  _defaultTransition.fromState = "*";
  _defaultTransition.toState = "panelView";
  _defaultTransition.effect = _move;
```

```
        transitions.push(_defaultTransition);
    }
  }
}
```

As with most ActionScript examples, when compared to the MXML equivalent, they tend to be verbose.

Most of a transition's power comes from the effects that you associate with them. There's one thing I suggest you do when it comes to effects and transitions within your components: Create them in MXML first because they are easier to tweak and quicker to test.

After you have the desired effect and your transitions work as you expect, integrate them within your component and convert them to ActionScript, if required. Hopefully, seeing the same functionality side by side, so to speak, gives you a better understanding of how you can work with effects, transitions, and view states in both MXML and ActionScript.

Summary

In this chapter, you saw how to use effects, individually or as part of a sequence.

We looked at `MotionPath` and `Keyframe`, which enable us to animate a target in a more configurable manner to enable for easy creation of an expressive animation effect.

Finally, you saw how to integrate effects into transitions to provide a visually richer experience when switching from view state to view state.

Working with Metadata

In previous chapters, you saw how to add view states to your component, create transitions, and harness the effects classes within the Flex framework. Before we start working with data, let's pause and look at the third language within the Flex framework: metadata.

Although it's not actually a language, without metadata, you would need to write an awful lot more code to achieve the same results. The funny thing about `metadata` is that we've all used it, but I doubt we've ever paused for more than a second to contemplate how it works and how you can create your own tags. Well, this chapter looks at that whole process.

What Is Metadata?

If you've been building applications using the Flex framework, you are probably already familiar with metadata tags, but what are they exactly? In the loosest terms, metadata is data that describes other data, generally through descriptive labels. So, what does that actually mean in relation to developing components?

Metadata within the Flex framework (and specifically, component development) can be divided in to three distinct groups: those that integrate with Flash Builder, those that act as compilation markers, and those that provide validation. Of these three groups, the majority of metadata tags fall into the initial group: those that integrate with Flash Builder. Now, if you already looked at this book's Table of Contents, you probably noticed that there's an entire chapter on integrating your components with Flash Builder, so why didn't I just put this information in there and remove this chapter?

Well, the truth is that there's more to metadata than just integration, and I thought it would be beneficial to understand how to create your own custom metadata should you need to for use within your own components.

One caveat I raise is that, although you are free to put your own custom metadata within your components that allow for the processing of data, be careful not to place too many constraints on the developer who is going to implement them and the associated objects that need to be tagged. The more hoops they have to jump through, the less likely they will be to use your components in the future. The idea of using standard data types, especially when passing datasets to your components, is covered in Chapter 9, "Manipulating Data," so don't worry too much about this if it sounds confusing.

That said, if you are the "component guy" within a development team, and you already have custom metadata, feel free to provide additional integration points. It's a fine balance to take between risking coupling your components too tightly to a specific framework or data requirement or going completely "vanilla." If in doubt, think about what, and who, your components are aimed at. If the answer is everyone, consider the standard data type route—using renderers to provide the flexibility needed to display the data passed in. If, on the other hand, it's a sealed project, add in hooks and markers that make the development and reusability of your components beneficial to the entire team and the application design.

How Do I Use Metadata?

This is probably a moot point, but in case you've never used metadata before, let me quickly discuss how you actually go about using it in your components. Metadata within Flex is represented by the use of textual identifiers enclosed within square braces that in turn are placed above relevant data types, marking them for later inspection based on the tag type applied.

In Flex, metadata tags come in two varieties: those associated with the entire object or class and those associated only with a single class element. Therefore, declaring a metadata tag varies between metadata types; some are placed on a variable or method, and others are place before the actual class declaration, but the implementation is the same:

```
[MetadataTag] Affector
```

Table 7.1 lists all the current metadata tags that ship with version 4.0 of the Flex framework. Some of you have already seen them, others are likely to have already used them, and some you may never have realized they were present. You may never use some of these tags, and they might not be suitable for use within components that are aimed at a widespread audience because they place additional requirements on your component that may turn other developers off, as mentioned earlier. Again, if you want to declare a specific tag, don't feel that you can't because I said so; after all, for every standard approach, there are often a myriad of alternatives.

Table 7.1 **Metadata Tags**

Tag	Description
[AlternativeClass]	Provides you with a way to mark the component with an alternative class, indicating a change has occurred from a certain version moving forward.
[ArrayElementType]	Enables you to define the object type in an array. Don't confuse this with the new Vector class. From a component development perspective, this is usually used in Template components.

Table 7.1   **Metadata Tags Continued**

Tag	Description
[Bindable]	Provides you with a marker to indicate that a property can be the source of a data-binding expression.
[DefaultProperty]	Provides an indicator of a default property that can be used when declaring your component in MXML.
[Deprecated]	Lets you mark a class or class attribute as deprecated so the compiler can issue a warning when that element is used in your application.
[Effect]	Provides a hook to Flash Builder that enables you to indicate the effects present in your component when declared in MXML.
[Embed]	Provides a marker for embedding various asset types.
[Event]	Provides a hook to Flash Builder, which enables you to indicate the events present in your component when declared in MXML.
[Exclude]	Removes the class element from the Flash Builder's tag inspector.
[ExcludeClass]	Removes the class from the Flash Builder's tag inspector. This is equivalent to the @private tag in ASDoc when applied to a class.
[HostComponent]	When using Spark skins, this tag indicates that it is mapped to a certain component type.
[IconFile]	Enables you to define an icon for your component for use when displayed in the Component panel within Flash Builder.
[Inspectable]	Exposes attributes of a component when declared in MXML. Can be used to limit property values from within Flash Builder.
[InstanceType]	When using instances of IDeferredInstance, it enables you to specify the actual object type.
[NonCommittingChangeEvent]	Marks an event as an interim trigger.
[RemoteClass]	Tag to map an ActionScript class with a complimentary server object. Commonly used with the ActionScript Messaging Format (AMF).
[RichTextContent]	Notifies the compiler that when this property is declared in MXML it should always be treated as a string. Data binding and embedding supported by associated property.

Table 7.1   **Metadata Tags Continued**

Tag	Description
[SkinPart]	Defines a property within a component as a corresponding skin part.
[SkinState]	Defines the required view states that this component's skin must support.
[Style]	Exposes style attributes when a component is declared in MXML within Flash Builder.
[SWF]	Enables attributes of the actual SWF to be defined within an ActionScript application file.
[Transient]	Indicates that a property should be ignored when the object is sent to the server (used in conjunction with [RemoteClass]).

Depending on your outlook, that may be a fairly long or rather short list of tags. Personally, I'm pleased that additional tags have been added in version 4.0 of the Flex framework. In my experience, however, you generally use only some of these within specific component archetypes—one that immediately comes to mind are template components and their use of the [ArrayElementType] and [InstanceType] tags.

Working with Metadata

We've covered what metadata is, how it relates to Flex, and to which metadata tags you have access. All that is left to discuss is how you go about declaring individual tags and what benefits they offer beyond their basic implementation. Before we get into detail, note that you don't have to use any of these tags if you don't want. Although some are hard to avoid ([Bindable], for example), your components will generally function as expected if metadata is omitted.

That said, here is a list of the ones I use on a regular basis when creating my components: Inspectable, Bindable, Event, Style, Effect, ExcludeClass, Exclude, DefaultProperty, HostComponent, SkinPart, SkinState, and IconFile. Obviously, the likes of Event and Bindable are probably used more than the others, but on the whole, a well-designed and well-thought out visual component will likely include almost all these tags.

Exposing Information About Your Component

Generally speaking, if you are distributing your components, even within your own team, your components should provide as much automated support as possible. This is for two good reasons: One, you don't want to keep getting interrupted by other developers wanting to know what attributes your component has, which are the defaults and how they access them; two, easy to implement equals more likely to be used. Ease of implementation doesn't mean simple, however; it means making the process of getting the component to run as smooth and quick as possible by providing the relevant pointers and hooks. This leads nicely to the first tag that we're going to look at, which is probably the most powerful integration tag of all because it provides the vast majority of author time support: `[Inspectable]`.

Inspectable Tag

By default, all public class elements, properties, and getter/setters are exposed to the code-hinting engine in Flash Builder. In most cases, that is fine; however, there are certain cases where it would be beneficial to do provide more guidance. This is especially useful when you are developing components that you want to publically distribute. Fortunately, that is where the `[Inspectable]` tag steps in.

In its simplest form, it just precedes the relevant class element. Unfortunately, this doesn't provide any more benefit over just declaring your class elements as public. After you start defining values for the attributes it provides, it becomes useful.

```
// No more beneficial than not having the tag present
[Inspectable]
public var myVar            :String;
```

By providing various attributes with relevant values, you can determine the default value for your property, provide a list of options, place it within the relevant category in the Property panel, and more.

I discuss the `[Inspectable]` attributes in frequency order. By that, I mean those you're likely to use most often to those that are rarely used. So, the first couple of attributes are the `defaultValue` and `enumeration` properties. `defaultValue` enables you to assign, as you would expect, a default value to the class element with which the `[Inspectable]` tag is associated. So, for example, the following code declares a Boolean variable, and the `[Inspectable]` tag provides a default value of true. Therefore, if the developer omits the value, the component will use this automatically. The value for this attribute can be either a `String` or a `Number`.

One thing to point out here is that the `defaultValue` attribute functions only if the component has been compiled into a SWC; otherwise, it is ignored. I've also found it to be temperamental, so I tend to declare a default value for my variables instead of solely relying on the `defaultValue` attribute in the `[Inspectable]` tag.

```
[Inspectable(defaultValue="true")]
public var showMessage     :Boolean;
```

With the default value set, let's look at how to give our developers some guidance for what are valid values for our property. This is where `enumeration` comes in. This attribute enables you to define a comma-separated list of values that displays when the developer activates code complete within the MXML editor in Flash Builder. This enables you to provide them with a default list that indicates what the accepted values are for that particular property. Obviously, this doesn't preclude them from assigning a different value, nor does it prevent them from using bound variables.

When using the enumeration attribute, be careful not to accidentally put any spaces between values; otherwise, it won't function as expected. So, this is correct:

```
[Inspectable(enumeration="true,false")]
```

However, this use of enumeration will fail because of the additional space before the value false:

```
[Inspectable(enumeration="true, false")]
```

Even if you don't need to provide extended attributes to your entire public API, it is worth at least organizing those exposed class elements into relevant groups within the main Properties panel in Flash Builder. By default, all public class elements are placed in the *Other* category. However, some of your properties might be ones that a developer will access every time he configures an instance of one of your components, so placing them in a pertinent group is advantageous. This is easy to do by defining the category attribute in the [Inspectable] tag. You can choose from Common, Effects, Events, Size, Styles and, of course, Other.

```
[Inspectable(category="Common")]
public var showMessage      :Boolean;
```

The [Inspectable] tag also enables you to define where within the Properties panel that property naturally sits. I use the term naturally, because the grouping of items into collections is a human thing to do, and Flash Builder doesn't care one way or the other. But, because other developers will probably be using your components, it seems logical to put similar items in associated groups.

Unfortunately, you can't alter the default Properties panel with the [Inspectable] tag because this is coded based on each individual component type and requires a different approach to achieve this. (We look at this in Chapter 13, "Component Integration in Flash Builder 4.")

Sometimes, you may have a variable that represents something beyond its data type. For example, properties that take numeric values may not necessarily be just for performing calculations. They may be for determining time or representative of a color.

```
[Inspectable(format="Color")]
```

In this case, you can provide a format value. When using format attributes, be careful because they are ignored if you place them on a noncompatible data type by mistake.

Acceptable format values are Color, EmbeddedFile, File, Length, and Time.

Under the hood, this changes the editor used when setting the properties value through the Properties panel. Therefore, if you have a variable used to set the background color of your component, setting the associated [Inspectable] tag's format attribute to Color launches the color picker as opposed to the default property editor for the actual data type (which, in most cases, is just an input text field).

One of the lesser-used attributes is the `name` property. This enables you to define a more user-friendly term to use instead of the variable name, which is used by default.

```
[Inspectable(name="showDialog")]
public var myShowDialogVariable    :Boolean;
```

Although you can put spaces in a `name` property, I advise against it for a few reasons. First, it breaks with the accepted naming convention used within all the standard components that come with Flash Builder; and second, just because it looks nice in the Properties panel doesn't mean it will be useful for a developer when she is actually coding up your components. I have never had any real requirements to use the `name` tag; if you name your public properties in a sensible manner, you shouldn't have to either.

I clump together the last few, because they are rarely used. (By that, I mean I've never had a need to use them, so they are likely to be used in rare cases). They are `environment`, `listOffset`, `type`, `variable`, and `verbose`. These all smell of legacy support; I could be wrong, but they aren't documented beyond a cursory reference in the documentation, so these can probably be ignored.

Describing Events

Events are handled in a different way than the `[Inspectable]` tag, mainly because they are declared on the actual class and not a property or method. Another difference is that you can declare an `[Event]` tag on your component without actually providing any mechanism within it to dispatch the actual event. The reason why you can do this is purely because the Event metadata tag is a marker tag in the purist sense. It just informs Flash Builder that, when you declare the component in MXML, it will dispatch the relevant event. It doesn't place any explicit contract on your class to actually fulfill that requirement, however. So, if you were to place the following code on your class, it marks it as dispatching the `showControlBar` event of the `VideoControlBarEvent` (whether it does is another thing):

```
[Event(name="showControlBar",
       type="com.developingcomponents.events.VideoControlBarEvent")]
```

Unfortunately, because you can't use constants in the `name` attribute, you run the risk of event name typos, so be on the look out if your event handlers don't fire correctly. (We're going to look at the event model in relation to components and how to create, dispatch, and mark them within your component in Chapter 8, "Events and Event Handling.") However, note that your class won't break if you add the metadata for an event to it. It'll just infuriate other developers when they use the attribute in MXML to hook in to a nonfiring event.

If you have an internal event that is an interim step in your validation chain, you can use the `[NonCommittingChangeEvent]`. This enables you to declare events that don't trigger any associated validators every time they fire. This is useful when dealing with user-generated events, like text input, where you'd normally have listeners set to fire on keyDown and keyUp. Normally, these types of interactions would fire every time the user inputs a value. However, you might only want this to validate on a particular key press (when the user presses the Tab or Return key, for example). The [NonCommittingChangeEvent] requires the name of the event you want to exclude from the validation routine. In the example just described, you could omit the change event from your text input routine, like so:

```
[NonCommittingChangeEvent("change")]
```

Although the tag is called [NonCommittingChangeEvent], you aren't limited to just omitting change events. However, because these are the most common form of events to be dispatched the most often, it makes sense to omit those when needed. If you don't use validators, this tag is a moot point, but it keeps validation from being run needlessly and risking the performance of not only your components, but the applications they inhabit.

Exposing Styles and Effects

Like the [Event] metadata tag, [Style] and [Effect] tags are class markers. And, like [Event], they too only form a loose contract with the classes they are placed upon, regardless of whether the actual elements exist.

The basic structure is the same except with [Effects], you define not only the effect itself, but also the event type that when fired triggers this effect. So, in the following code, the class effect showControlBarEffect is triggered by the showControlBar event:

```
[Effect(name="showControlBarEffect", type="showControlBar")]
```

You may have noticed that I used the event name suffixed with Effect as the name for this effect. This is the commonly accepted standard for declaring effect metadata. If you think about it, it makes sense. Although you may place the actual event metadata next to the effect, having them use the same name makes it easier to confirm that the complimentary [Event] tag is actually present.

Style tags, on the other hand, define numerous facets of an individual style defined within your component. In its most basic form, a [Style] metadata tag must include a name attribute. Beyond that, all other attributes are optional. However, the most common format for a [Style] tag is generally formatted like the following example, indicating not only the name, but also the type, format, and whether this is an inherit-ing style:

```
[Style(name="cornerRadius", type="uint", format="Color", inherit="no")]
```

The type attribute defines the data type of this style, and the format attribute operates in an identical manner to the [Inspectable] tag format attribute. If you use data types that aren't standard ActionScript types, such as Date, String, and so on, you need to use the fully qualified name of the class (for example, com.developingcomponents.className).

The inherit attribute refers to inheritance of CSS properties, not object inheritance, and you can set it to yes or no. If you define a parent component with an inheriting style, all its children inherit that style (if they implement it), unless any of them override it themselves. Within the Spark and Halo component frameworks, `color` and `fontFamily` are two common styles that are inherited. Obviously, if you mark a style as noninheriting, only that component will implement them, and it won't be passed to any of its children.

You also have access to an enumerated list of possible values for your style, through the `enumeration` attribute, again in a similar fashion to the `[Inspectable]` tag (both in implementation and its effect on the `format` attribute).

```
[Style(name="cornerRadius", enumeration="2,4,6,8,12,16")]
```

With Flex 4.0, you have access to themes and, if you want to define a set of styles that are defined only when a particular theme is applied, you can via the `theme` attribute. Just provide the name of the theme in question as the value of the theme property.

```
[Style(name="cornerRadius", theme="Wooden")]
```

When dealing with a stateful component, you may want to assign a `[Style]` tag to specific skin states. Like most attributes, you just need to provide a comma-separated list of the states in which your style should be applied. So, if you had a Button component with up, over, down, disabled, and wanted to apply a specific style to only the over and down states, you just need to include those state names within the states attribute.

```
[Style(name="MyButtonSkin", type="class" states="down,over")]
```

Omitting this attribute assigns the style to all states within the component.

Embedding Assets

Asset embedding, like bitmaps, audio, video, SWFs, and so on, tends not to be that important when developing components beyond the occasional icon. On the other hand, font embedding is important. Not just because the developer using your components may not have the font in question (be careful not to inadvertently distribute a copyrighted font), but you may be using transforms, fades, and such on textual elements within your component that won't render correctly if you haven't embedded the font face in question.

Embedding assets is fairly consistent across the board, but a few "gotchas" exist with font embedding. One that tends to catch people is this: When using the `[Embed]` tag in ActionScript, you need to declare individual glyphs or ranges in Unicode. The following example is a freely distributable Helvetica variant (Coolvetica) that is used in the time display in a media player, so the only values required are the numbers 0–9 (U+0030–U+0039) and a colon (U+003A) for the separator.

```
[Embed(source='/assets/fonts/coolvetica.ttf', fontName='timerFont',
      mimeType='application/x-font', advancedAntiAliasing='true',
      unicodeRange='U+0030-U+0039,U+003A')]
private var _timerFont    :Class;
```

As you can see, I declared the font face and included the Unicode IDs for the glyphs I want to include. Unfortunately, at this point, there isn't an easy way to embed fonts within Flex beyond using Flash Professional to create a font SWF and loading that in, which is off topic and doesn't embed the fonts within your component anyway—but just be aware of it.

The process of embedding assets differs from most of the other tags detailed in this chapter because the Embed keyword crops up in other places within the Flex framework lexicon. For example, you can place an embed in the src attribute of an Image component:

```
<mx:Image src="@Embed(source='myImage.png')" />
```

Or you can embed assets through an associated CSS file:

```
Embed(source='myImage.png');
```

I won't explain the differences between the three different embed implementations any further because it is not that relevant to this chapter. But, ultimately, under the hood, the compiler is performing the same function.

Binding Data

The [Bindable] tag is probably one of the most familiar of all the metadata tags in the Flex framework. As you already know, it enables you to mark a property or method so that it can fire off a notification when its value changes. To do this, it associates itself with an event type and, when that event is dispatched, it notifies all the associated variables in its binding chain that its value has changed.

In its most compact form, you just need to precede your class element with the tag, and you are good to go. However, you may not be aware that [Bindable] is the equivalent of [Bindable(event="propertyChange")]. This is because if you omit an event attribute, Flex automatically creates an event attribute associated with propertyChange event. This is because it needs to be associated with an event, so it does this in the background; otherwise, it wouldn't function. The [Bindable] tag can be placed on the class itself or a class element. If you place it on the class, it triggers whenever a public class element is changed.

This is helpful, but times may arise when you might want to only notify the associated items in the binding chain when certain criteria are fulfilled. This gives you greater flexibility and precision, but it means that you need to make sure that you dispatch that particular event at some point; otherwise, the binding never fires.

Here, you can see we have a variable that is bound to the event mediaPlayerUpdated; however, the binding gets triggered only after the setter assigns the new value to the actual internal property. At this point, it dispatches the associated event.

```
[Bindable(event="mediaPlayerUpdated"]
public var isPlaying :Boolean;

public function set stopMediaPlayer(value:Boolean):void
{
  isPlaying = value;
  dispatchEvent(new MediaPlayerEvent("mediaPlayerUpdated"));
}
```

There are times when the [Bindable] tag won't trigger. For example, if you change an item within a dataProvider for a new item, the data binding does not execute. Nor will it if you change the value of a subelement on an item that has been marked as [Bindable] where that subelement is no longer valid. The initial assignment of the new value would fire, but the change of value on the subelement wouldn't. The following code fails for the subelement because the variable mediaBar—in this case an instance of CompactMediaBar—is bindable, but the fullscreen property on the CompactMediaBar instance isn't. To fix this, you need to make either the CompactMediaBar class or the fullscreen property bindable.

```
[Bindable]
public var mediaBar            :IMediaController;

// Binding executes
mediaBar = new CompactMediaBar(); // Implements IMediaController
// Binding fails
mediaBar.fullscreen = true;
```

Binding also fails to automatically execute if you assign it to something that the Flash Player updates automatically, such as mouse positions.

Setting Defaults

Setting a default property on a component is not the same as setting the defaultValue attribute on an [Inspectable] tag. The metadata tag [DefaultProperty] refers to the single default property of the component that can just be declared within the opening and closing tags of the component when declared in MXML without the need to define what it relates to. For example, although the word "Hello" is declared within the opening and closing tags of our DefaultPropertyComponent, it is actually being assigned to the "text" property (via the public setter method).

```
<?xml version="1.0" encoding="utf-8"?>
<s:Application xmlns:fx="http://ns.adobe.com/mxml/2009"
               xmlns:s="library://ns.adobe.com/flex/spark"
               xmlns:mx="library://ns.adobe.com/flex/mx"
               xmlns:components="com.developingcomponents.components.*">

    <components:DefaultPropertyComponent>
      Hello
    </components:DefaultPropertyComponent>
</s:Application>
```

To implement this, place your [DefaultProperty] tag on the class itself and provide it with the name of the class element to which it relates. In the previous example, the string between the opening and closing component tags relates to a property called text; you can see that, in the following code sample, this is actually a getter/setter pair, but it could just be a public variable—the choice is yours. I highlighted the important code elements so you can see how it all ties together.

```
package com.developingcomponents.components
{
  import flash.text.TextField;

  import mx.core.UIComponent;

  [DefaultProperty("text")]
  public class DefaultPropertyComponent extends UIComponent
  {

    private static const DEFAULT_WIDTH     :uint = 320;
    private static const DEFAULT_HEIGHT    :uint = 200;

    private var _defaultText    :String;
    private var _textField      :TextField;

    public function DefaultPropertyComponent()
    {
      super();
    }

    override protected function createChildren():void
    {
      super.createChildren();
      _textField = new TextField();
      addChild(_textField);
    }

    override protected function measure():void
    {
      super.measure();

      this.measuredWidth = this.measuredMinWidth = DEFAULT_WIDTH;
      this.measuredHeight = this.measuredMinHeight = DEFAULT_HEIGHT;
    }

    override protected function updateDisplayList(unscaledWidth:Number,
                                                  unscaledHeight:Number):void
    {
      super.updateDisplayList(unscaledWidth, unscaledHeight);

      this.setActualSize(unscaledWidth, unscaledHeight);
      _textField.text = _defaultText;
    }
```

```
public function get text():String
{
  return _defaultText;
}

public function set text(value:String):void
{
  if(value)
    _defaultText = value;
}
  }
}
```

Obviously, you can declare only one default property. If you try and add additional tags, you get an error. You can use bound variables within the MXML declaration of your component so that you aren't limited to hard-coded strings when implementing a default property in this manner.

Working with Skins

One of the big changes between the Spark architecture and that of the more established Halo components within Flex 4 is the introduction of UI separation. This is where the skin is completely separate from the logic and functionality of the component itself. We look at skinning and styling your components in Chapter 10, "Skinning and Styling," but let's look at what metadata you have access to when it comes to integrating and applying skins to your components.

First, we have the [HostComponent] tag. This enables you within your skin to define what component or component family that particular skin can be used with. This is particularly useful if you want to access properties of the host components because under the hood, Flex takes this tag and converts it in to a property within your skin class that point the references to the component type you defined.

```
[HostComponent("com.developingcomponents.components.RoundedRectangleComponent")]
```

All you need to do is provide the fully qualified class name of the component you want to assign to the [HostComponent] tag, as the previous code snippet shows, and the compiler does the rest. You see how you hook into this in Chapter 10 when we get into the process of actually creating, implementing, and accessing skins and styles within your components. The next two metadata tags provide markers for your skin classes and are applied directly to your component: [SkinPart] and [SkinState].

Within Spark components, the various aspects of the UI are defined as skin "parts," some are required and others are optional. To expose these, place the relevant class element and precede it with a [SkinPart] tag. Even though you declare the skin parts within your component, they are not set directly but are set via the skin class you associate with that particular component. You can use the [SkinPart] tag as is; however, it has two attributes that can be defined to add more refinement: type and required.

The `type` attribute enables you to define a data type for the skin part and thus dictates whether the part is static or dynamic. (Chapter 10 covers static and dynamic skin parts.) If you omit the `type` attribute, the `[SkinPart]` tag defaults to the property type it precedes.

Here are a few examples that illustrate a static and dynamic skin part. Note the use of `IFactory` for the actual class element type is mandatory for dynamic skin parts, although the actual type attribute within the `[SkinPart]` can represent any fully qualified class.

```
// A static skin part of type spark.controls.Button
[SkinPart]
public var playButton        :Button;


// A dynamic skin part that will accept any class type that implements
IVisualElement
[SkinPart(type="mx.core.IVisualElement"]
public var pauseButton       :IFactory;
```

The `required` attribute enables you to indicate whether the skin part is mandatory or optional, which is indicated by the use of `true` or `false`; by default, the value is `false`.

```
[SkinPart(required="true")]
```

The last metadata tag that provides skin support is the `[SkinState]` tag. This enables you to declare the various skin states that your component supports. You declare your skin states on the class in a similar way to `[Style]`, `[Event]`, and `[Effect]`, as the following code shows.

Don't confuse these with view states. These states are solely to do with skinning your component—think up state, down state, over state, and so on.

```
[SkinState("normal")]
[SkinState("compact")]
[SkinState("disabled")]
function StatefulComponent
{
       ...
}
```

Like `[HostComponent]` and `[SkinPart]`, we look at how you actually fully implement `[SkinStates]` in Chapter 10.

Excluding Component Attributes

One useful thing omitting properties or entire classes from Flash Builders code hinting. This may sound reasonable for properties because there are times when you inherit from a class and you just don't want to expose certain properties because they are redundant within your component or are empty, and you have no intention of implementing any additional functionality.

Implementing [Exclude] and [ExcludeClass] is a simple process; place the [Exclude] tag above the property of method you want to omit. In the case of [ExcludeClass], you just place it above the class declaration. I included a few examples here:

```
// Excluding a class from Flash Builder's code hinting
package
{
  [ExcludeClass]
  class MyExcludedClass{}
}

// Excluding a property from a class
package
{
  class MyClass
  {
    [Exclude]
    public var excludedProperty           :Boolean = true;
  }
}
```

Why do it for classes, though? Usually, this is done to stop people from accidentally implementing the wrong class when the code hinting kicks in.

Altering and Deprecating Properties and Classes

One tag that becomes more useful over time is the [Deprecated] tag. As it implies, this tag enables you to indicate to the end user that the specific property or method is now deprecated and that he should use an alternative. This one comes into its own when you are releasing updates to your component and need to "jiggle" the structure a bit as part of a refactoring process.

A good rule of thumb is to deprecate a property or method for a minimum of one major version and, on the subsequent major version release, remove the code from your component; that way, you give developers who use your components the opportunity to change the affected API call with the newly revised version without it entirely breaking their application. That said, it is always a hard decision when it comes to refactoring and deprecating properties or methods that are exposed through a class's public API, but this way, it will at least notify them if they are using Flash Builder.

If you are updating just the class of a component so that it uses a new base class instead of the original one, don't use the [Deprecated] tag; instead, use the [Alternative] tag. The reason for this is that deprecating a class or one of its elements indicates that, at some point in the future, it will no longer be accessible. However, you may be making a change to your component that provides additional functionality or changes how it fits within your own component hierarchy due to a refactoring process. If that is the case, use the [Alternative] tag to indicate this.

Providing an Icon

After you add all your metadata tags to your component that tie it into Flash Builder, you may think that's all you can do. Actually, you can add one more polished thing to your component, but it requires more work than those you've implemented so far.

The `[IconFile]` tag enables you to replace the default blue blob that you see in the Component panel next to your components when in Design View for something more conducive to your component. It takes more work than the other integration tags because you have to compile your components into a SWC to correctly display the icon. Don't worry if you don't know how to create SWC from your components; we cover that in Chapter 12, "The Flex Library Project."

The basic syntax for including a icon with your component is as follows:

```
[IconFile("path/to/icon")]
class MyClass{}
```

The icon file can be a PNG, GIF, or JPG, and you need to provide the absolute path to it from the root of the projects `src` directory. Therefore, if I had a folder in the root of my `src` directory called assets, and within this I placed my icons in a suitably named icons folder, I could assign an icon (`FGTableIcon.png`, for example) to my component like so:

```
[IconFile("assets/icons/FGTableIcon.png")]
class MyClass{}
```

When assigning icons to your components, watch out for this: If you get the path wrong, when you attempt to create a SWC, the process will fail, and it will fail silently! So, if you can't get your library project to create a SWC, comment out the `[IconFile]` metadata tag to see if that resolves it.

And the Rest

The rest of the metadata tags listed in Table 7.1 are either niche in their use (`[SWF]`), not directly relevant to component development (`[RemoteClass]`, `[Transcient]`), or self-explanatory in nature (`[RichTextContent]`), so I will not elaborate on them beyond their description. If you want to know more about these tags, see the Flex documentation.

Metadata in MXML

So far, you've seen how to implement metadata within ActionScript, so for completeness, I want to show you how you do it within MXML. There aren't any differences between ActionScript and MXML when it comes to declaring the actual metadata tags, except that only some of the tags you have already seen can be declared within an MXML `<fx:Metadata/>` block. The rest must be declared within an `<fx:Script/>` block. The reason for this is obvious after it is explained, but it initially can appear a little odd.

Recall that metadata in ActionScript classes can be assigned to two distinct aspects of your component class; before a class element—property, method, and such—or upon the class itself. This is where the split happens in MXML. If you define metadata that is to

be assigned to the MXML component class itself, it is placed within the
`<fx:Metadata/>` tags:

```
<fx:Metadata>[Metadata Tag]</fx:Metadata>
```

If, on the other hand, you are assigning metadata to a class element—for example, an
`[Event]` or `[Embed]` tag—it needs to precede the class element in the `<fx:Script/>` block:

```
<fx:Script>
  <![CDATA[
    [Bindable]
    public function get dataProvider():Object
    {
      ...
    }

    public function set dataProvider(value:Object):void
    {
      ...
    }
  ]]>
</fx:Script>
```

Creating Your Own Metadata Tags

One thing that a lot of people want to know about metadata is this: Can you create your
own metadata? The answer is, of course, yes. The process is a little convoluted, but it is
worth capitalizing on if you develop components for use in a specific framework or application because it provides you with an easy way in which to mark objects, even if they are
not from the same inheritance tree. On the other hand, if you produce components that
you plan to just distribute to the general developer community, custom metadata tags may
not hold much value at all. Either way, you can make that decision when you get to that
particular juncture.

Be aware that, although you can create your own metadata tags, some of the more
advanced built-in tags, like `[Embed]` and `[Bindable]`, hook into the compiler and perform some niche tasks, which is something to which as of this version you and I cannot
gain access. Don't be put off, however, because you can still do a lot of stuff with your
own metadata tags.

Are Metadata Tags Classes?

No, metadata tags are not classes; actually, they're not anything at all. I know that sounds
daft, but let me explain. If I were to create a custom metadata tag and place it on a class
and compile and run my application, Flash Builder does two things. First, it ignores the
metadata entirely because it doesn't know what to do with it; second, as the compilation

proceeds, it actually completely dumps the tags from the class—if they're not required, why keep them?

Let's tackle part two of that problem: How do you stop Flash Builder from removing the metadata from your class on compilation? Well, you need to tell the compiler to explicitly leave it in your application. To do this, open your Flex project's Properties panel and select the entry for the Flex Compiler. Within the additional compiler arguments field (see Figure 7.1), add the following code:

```
-keep-as3-metadata+=FGMetaDataExample
```

Figure 7.1   Keeping your custom metadata when compiled

You need to add your metadata tag names after the +=[1] In this case, I have a metadata tag called FGMetaDataExample. Note that it's "plus equals," not "equals." If you use just equals, it won't include the built-in metadata tags, which is not ideal. Now that you have your metadata tag in your application, how do you access it?

This is where reflection comes in. If you never heard of reflection before, it is a process by which an object describes itself detailing its public properties and methods without the

---

[1] To add further custom metadata entries, just separate them with additional += (for example, -keep-as3-metadata+=myMetaData,myOtherMetadata).

need for prior knowledge of that object. To achieve this in ActionScript 3.0, you need to use the utility class `flash.utils.describeType()`, which enables you to pass it an object instance and have it output the properties and methods it exposes as an XML structure.

```
<?xml version="1.0" encoding="utf-8"?>
<s:Application xmlns:fx="http://ns.adobe.com/mxml/2009"
               xmlns:s="library://ns.adobe.com/flex/spark"
               xmlns:mx="library://ns.adobe.com/flex/mx"
               minWidth="955" minHeight="600"
               creationComplete="init(event)">

  <fx:Script>
    <![CDATA[
      import com.developingcomponents.MetaDataDemo;
      import flash.utils.describeType;
      import mx.events.FlexEvent;

      protected function init(event:FlexEvent):void
      {
        trace(flash.utils.describeType(new MetaDataDemo()));
      }
    ]]>
  </fx:Script>
</s:Application>
```

Take the previous simple example. I have an application that, after it has completed its setup and fired off the `creationComplete()` event, I just pass a new instance of `MetaDataDemo` to `flash.utils.describeType()` and trace out the results. Looking at the following code block, you can see the custom metadata in place and below this, you have the structure of the class, as gleaned by reflection through `describeType()`.

```
package com.developingcomponents
{
  import mx.collections.ArrayCollection;

  [FGMetaDataExample]
  public class MetaDataDemo
  {
    private var _active     :Boolean;

    [Status]
    public var currentStatus    :String;

    [Content]
    public var currentContent     :ArrayCollection;
```

```
    public function MetaDataDemo()
    {
    }

    [SystemActive]
    public function get active():Boolean
    {
      return _active;
    }

    public function set active(value:Boolean):void
    {
      _active = value;
    }
  }
}
```

The class itself was marked with the tag [FGMetadataExample] and within it, I added property specific tags named [Status], [Content], and [SystemActive]—I marked these in bold so that you can see how they relate when the class is processed and the output is converted to XML by describeType(). Notice that the main metadata tag, [FGMetaDataExample], is located at the bottom, after all the class elements are listed. (Note that I condensed the output for brevity because the output contains information that isn't relevant to the current topic.)

```
<type name="com.developingcomponents::MetaDataDemo" base="Object"
      isDynamic="false" isFinal="false" isStatic="false">
  <extendsClass type="Object"/>
  <variable name="currentStatus" type="String">
    <metadata name="Status"/>
  </variable>
  <variable name="currentContent" type="ArrayCollection">
    <metadata name="Content"/>
  </variable>
  <accessor name="active" access="readwrite" type="Boolean"
declaredBy="com.developingcomponents::MetaDataDemo">
    <metadata name="SystemActive"/>
  </accessor>
  <metadata name="FGMetaDataExample"/>
</type>
```

Now you have an XML description of this class, you can check for the actual metadata tags using E4X. You may wonder why we just don't target the actual properties instead of the metadata. Well, until we passed our object through flash.utils.desdcribeType(), we had no idea what the properties are called, but we do know what metadata we are looking for, so we can target the metadata nodes and grab the relevant class element that it's contained within.

If you're wondering how you can do this in a flexible manner, look at how a lot of the Flex/ActionScript Inversion of Control (IoC) frameworks[2] manage reflection. They tend to use a mapping table, so class instances that contain custom metadata are mapped and therefore are easily reflected against during application initialization. This avoids unnecessarily iterating over *every* class in the application looking for those that implement the relevant metadata. Obviously, within a component, that might be more complex and excessive, but at least you have that option should you choose to implement your own metadata.

To recap with custom metadata tags: They are not compiled into your application by default, so if your class instance doesn't appear to be returning your metadata correctly when you process it, make sure that you have included the compiler flag, as shown in Figure 7.1.

Summary

This chapter looked at the various metadata tags that you have at your disposal for use within your component. Although the vast majority are hooks or markers for integrating into Flash Builder, they are all equally valuable in their own unique ways.

We discussed how to implement metadata tags in both ActionScript and MXML and where the two differed in their implementations and support.

Finally, you also saw how to create your own metadata tags and what actually goes on under the hood.

---

[2] If you want to find out more information about these frameworks, you can find links to them in Appendix A, "Flex Resources."

Events and Event Handling

The event model present in ActionScript and, by definition, the Flex framework, is far more robust than the old event model employed in ActionScript 2. For some, the concept of relying on events to manage and direct the flow of your application is a hard one to grasp and accept at first. In this chapter, you see how the event model applies to components and how to shield and dispatch events from your components and their children.

Why Events?

When it comes to component development, events form an important part of the Flex component fabric. Not only because the component framework is built to make extensive use of them, but also because it provides both an internal and external process by which your components can notify your applications of any changes.

Subscribers Versus Watchers

With that in mind, why use events in the first place? After all, isn't it easier to add a reference to the component and poll it to see when it changes? Well, yes, you could do that and just call methods on the component every time a user did something that would influence it. However, as more and more parts of your application weave together, you would find that so many external objects were polling your component that it would start to have not only performance issues, but it could start providing erroneous data to one or more objects if between one objects polling your component, another of those external objects updated that value within that component.

Recall from Chapter 3, "Anatomy of a Component," that the component invalidation routines are all event driven; they have to fire only once based on a flagging system. It would be far too inefficient to invalidate a component every time that the invalidation routine was called, given the diverse range and number of contributing factors that can call one of the invalidators within the component architecture. If this process used polling, it would bring the framework to its knees. (Well, it probably wouldn't, but it isn't particularly streamlined, so it would definitely hurt performance.)

Asynchronicity

Another benefit of event-based systems is that not all events (in fact almost no events in the Flex framework) are synchronous, and there is a good reason for this.

Working asynchronously can be a tricky concept to grasp, and when applied to component development, it can have the knock-on effect of managing the flow of your component, both internally and through external influences, seem that much harder.

The key advantage of an asynchronous system is that your component/application won't halt while the recipient of the event waits for it to arrive. How frustrating would it be if every time you clicked a button you had to wait for the event it dispatched to resolve before you could do anything else?

Event Flow

To understand how events affect your components, you need to understand the actual event flow. The event flow is broken up in to three distinct phases, and they all use the initiator of the event as the basis for each phase. These three phases are Capture, Target, and Bubbling. Generally speaking, usually only class extends `DisplayObject` that supports the `capture` and `bubbling` phases.

Capture

The Capture phase is the initial phase that any event first enters into. For an event to be monitored in this phase, you need to explicitly tell the event listener that it should act on the event in this phase, as the following code illustrates. As you can see, the Panel instance has an event listener assigned to it, which not only contains the event type it is listening for and the method that should be invoked when that event is broadcast, but also, it is set to trigger during the Capture phase (the third parameter, which is set to `true`).

```
<?xml version="1.0" encoding="utf-8"?>
<s:Application xmlns:fx="http://ns.adobe.com/mxml/2009"
               xmlns:s="library://ns.adobe.com/flex/spark"
               xmlns:mx="library://ns.adobe.com/flex/mx"
               minWidth="955" minHeight="600"
               initialize="init(event)">

   <fx:Script>
     <![CDATA[
       import flash.events.Event;
       import flash.events.MouseEvent;

       import mx.controls.Alert;

       public function init(e:Event):void
       {
         panel.addEventListener(MouseEvent.MOUSE_DOWN,
                             displayInfoAlert, true);
       }
```

```
   public function displayInfoAlert(e:Event):void
   {
     Alert.show("This an alert from the " + e.currentTarget.id,
               e.currentTarget.id );
   }
 ]]>
</fx:Script>

<s:layout>
  <s:HorizontalLayout horizontalAlign="center" verticalAlign="middle" />
</s:layout>

<s:Panel id="panel" title="Capture Example" width="250" />
</s:Application>
```

While in the Capture phase, the event passes from the root of the application passing through all subsequent objects until it reaches the parent container of the initiator (or target).

If any subscribers have been registered to capture the event in this phase, it will do so and, when processed, the event continues its journey. After it arrives at the initiator's parent container, it enters the next phase of the event flow—the Target phase.

Target

The Target phase is the default phase to which all event subscribers respond. Here, the event has reached the initiator that broadcast the event that is currently in the active event flow. The event arrives here and continues until it reaches the inner-most object of the application. After all subscribers process the event, it moves on to the final phase of the event flow—the Bubbling phase.

Bubbling

The Bubbling phase is basically the inverse of the Capture phase. Whereas the Capture phase worked from the root of the application down to the initiator's parent container, bubbling starts at the initiator's parent container and heads back toward the root of the application. This allows those subscribers, who are outside the scope of the initiator, to actually capture the event as it bubbles up. Generally, this is when you have a subscriber who is outside of the initiator's Target phase and, therefore, will never hear the event. To accomplish this, the event must be bubbled up to them so that they can respond to it.

A note of caution: Although bubbling events has its place, it isn't a cheap trick to get your events to the subscribers in your application. Bubbling takes up many resources and can cause system slow down in extreme cases (specifically if you're bubbling common event types). Of all the events within the Flex framework, few bubble by default. Generally, it is only the low-level events, such as keyboard and mouse events, that use this. That's not to say you can't bubble events, but just be sure you do it for the right reason and not as a fix for an architectural design flaw.

Dispatching Events

When it comes to components, you generally have two types of events: those that are used internally and those that are dispatched for external consumption. This may sound like overkill, but numerous occasions occur where you need to load, update, respond to, or remove something within your component, and the easiest and most efficient way to do this is through events.

The key difference between the two types is that, internally, the events are usually common Flex framework events, such as FlexEvent.CREATION_COMPLETE or MouseEvent.CLICK, that in the most part are dispatched by any child elements/instances within your component. To avoid your internal events from being picked up and used externally, make sure that whatever dispatches an inward-facing event is private or, at the very least, internal.

External events, on the other hand, are usually custom events related to the component that are passed out by the component itself and contain relevant internal data as part of their payload. If you look at the following code, I have an internal MouseEvent.CLICK event from a button called Submit within this component. When a user clicks it, the createPayload() method is called and we create an simple object containing three values: id, typed, and name. We then pass this into the event dispatcher who's ready to dispatch it.

```
package com.developingcomponents.components
{
  import com.developingcomponents.events.ExampleEvent;

  import flash.events.MouseEvent;

  import mx.core.UIComponent;

  import spark.components.Button;

  [Event(name="defaultEvent",
  ➥type="com.developingcomponents.components.events.ExampleEvent")]
  public class EventDispatchingComponent extends UIComponent
  {
    private var _submitBtn    :Button;
    private var _data         :Object;

    override protected function createChildren():void
    {
      super.createChildren();
      _submitBtn = new Button();
      _submitBtn.label = "Submit";
      _submitBtn.setActualSize(100, 50);
      _submitBtn.addEventListener(MouseEvent.CLICK, createPayload);
      addChild(_submitBtn);
    }
```

```
  protected function createPayload(e:MouseEvent):void
  {
    _data = {name:"Event Component", typed:false, id:1};
    dispatchEvent(new ExampleEvent(ExampleEvent.DEFAULT_EVENT, _data));
  }
 }
}
```

I removed much of the superfluous code from this example so that it is easier to read. Also, I added an [Event] metadata tag so that I can immediately take advantage of the handler generation within Flash Builder. Don't worry about the ExampleEvent used in the code—we look at creating custom events shortly.

In the following code, you can see where defaultEvent is referenced within the MXML. This is possible because we exposed this event name within our component code (by using the [Event] metadata tag) and the reciprocal handler (eventExample_defaultEventHandler) that was automatically generated.

```
<?xml version="1.0" encoding="utf-8"?>
<s:Application xmlns:fx="http://ns.adobe.com/mxml/2009"
               xmlns:s="library://ns.adobe.com/flex/spark"
               xmlns:mx="library://ns.adobe.com/flex/mx"
               xmlns:components="com.developingcomponents.components.*"
               minWidth="955" minHeight="600">
  <s:layout>
    <s:HorizontalLayout/>
  </s:layout>

  <fx:Script>
    <![CDATA[
      import com.developingcomponents.components.events.ExampleEvent;

      protected function eventExampleHandler(event:ExampleEvent):void
      {
        output.text = event.data.name;
      }

    ]]>
  </fx:Script>
  <components:EventDispatchingComponent id="eventExample"
            defaultEvent="eventExampleHandler(event)" />
  <s:TextArea id="output" />
</s:Application>
```

Just in case you forgot, be careful with metadata. I had a typo in the metadata tag, and it took me a few minutes to spot it. Fingers crossed, Adobe will include code complete for metadata tags in a future version. This is where the typo I mentioned tripped me up. I love the automation features in Flash Builder 4—if only it was human-proof, too.

Adding Event Listeners

Dispatching an event is only one part of the event process; you need to add a listener to your event if you want to interact with it. (This is obvious, I know, but I guarantee you'll forget at least once when using internal event handling in your components.)

When adding a listener, you have a set of parameters that you can define to determine when the listener is called and whether it can be canceled. You are probably used to creating event listeners, but I want to discuss the remaining parameters because we will explore them later in this chapter and, if you aren't aware of them, it may cause some confusion. The format of an `addEventListener()` method is as follows:

```
addEventListener(eventType, listener, useCapture, priority, useWeakReference);
```

Of the parameters just listed, only the `eventType` and `listener` are required. By default, `useCapture` is set to false. If this is set to true, the listener responds only when the event is in the capture phase of the event flow and ignores the Target and Bubbling phases.

If you want your listener to respond to all three phases—Capture, Target and Bubbling—you need to add two listeners: one with `useCapture` set to true and one set to false.

The `priority` parameter enables you to set the event priority, which we look at later in this chapter; by default, this parameter is set to 0.

The last parameter, `useWeakReference`, is a `Boolean` flag that indicates how the component dispatching the event should be treated when marked for garbage collection. I'm not going to discuss garbage management too much, because it's out of the scope of this book; what I will say is that if you have a normal listener associated with a component and you nullify the component (destroy, set null, incinerate, bury in quick drying cement, and such), because of the strongly bound listener (`useWeakReference=false`, which is the default value), the component won't be garbage collected and it is retained in memory—not ideal.

Generally speaking, when it comes to component development, you have a finite amount of internal listeners, and they are generally required throughout the component's life cycle. The use of `useWeakReference` is more of a consideration when assigning the stage or application as a listener and forgetting to remove the listener from the component's event stack prior to nullification. If you need to dispose of an internal item that has listeners on it, the best approach is the good old-fashioned process of doing it manually.

Custom Events

Although there are a plethora of events to choose from within the Flex framework, it is best to create your own custom events for use with your components. The reason for this is twofold: because it provides a clean separation between framework events and your component and, probably more important, you will be safe in the knowledge that something else within the framework isn't listening (or worse, still broadcasting an event type that your component uses).

Creating your own events isn't that tricky—you just need to decide which event you want to inherit from and create the relevant event. Personally, I always subclass my events from flash.events.Event.

Extending the Event Class

Creating an event is a fairly subjective affair, from the properties within it to the package in which it resides. When it comes to component development, I keep the event's package inside the components package. Not only because it keeps everything associated with my components all in one location (within the aforementioned components package), but it also means that when I finally create a Flex Library project ready to package up my components, I have to select only the components entry and everything below it is included. If you've never packaged your components before, don't worry; you get the complete lowdown in Chapter 12, "The Flex Library Project."

I created this custom event for a media player controller. As you can see, it contains various constants representing the event types it dispatches. The constructor has an additional parameter to the default type, bubbles, and cancelable, which is data. This is the payload for this particular event.

```
package com.developingcomponents.components.events
{
  import flash.events.Event;

  public class MediaControlEvent extends Event
  {
    public static const PAUSE      :String = "pause"
    public static const PLAY       :String = "play";

    public static const STOP       :String = "stop";

    public static const FORWARD    :String = "forward";
    public static const REWIND     :String = "rewind";

    public static const MUTE       :String = "mute";
    public static const SCRUB      :String = "scrub";

    public var data                :Object;

    public function MediaControlEvent(type:String, data:Object,
                            bubbles:Boolean=false,
                            cancelable:Boolean=false)
    {
      super(type, bubbles, cancelable);
      this.data = data;
    }
```

```
    override public function clone():Event
    {
      return new MediaControlEvent(type, data, bubbles, cancelable);
    }
  }
}
```

You don't need to have a property called data; I do it out of habit. Sometimes, you need to pass only a single piece of information or nothing at all. In other cases, you may want to pass a lot of information out in the event—take the Mouse events that pass a vast amount of information regarding x and y position, what object is directly beneath the hit point, and so on.

Cloning Events

One aspect of creating custom events that a lot of people ask the most questions about is the clone() method. What is it, and do you need to override it? Well, the clone() method is, as it sounds, a method for cloning your event. You don't need to override it if you don't want to, but you may get a coercion error if you don't.

```
TypeError: Error #1034: Type Coercion failed: cannot convert
flash.events::Event@21e44b3 to
com.developingcomponents.components.events.ExampleEvent.
```

This can happen when you try and re-dispatch a custom event; without the overriding the clone() method, it can be returned as a generic Event instance and as such will lose any custom data that it may normally associate with your custom event. The documentation for custom events is quite clear—if you create your own events, override the clone() method.

The process of implementing an override on clone() is straightforward: define the method override and return a new instance of your custom component passing in the relevant properties. Here is the clone() method from the custom event you saw earlier:

```
override public function clone():Event
{
  return new MediaControlEvent(type, data, bubbles, cancelable);
}
```

Given the flexibility it offers, should you or another developer want to bubble / re-dispatch your events, it doesn't make too much sense to omit the clone() override. I always implement it and rarely, if ever, need it. That said, if you do need to re-dispatch one of your custom events, it can be a real time-waster trying to work out what is going wrong—it's worth the few seconds it takes to override the clone() method, and it's a good habit to get into.

Dealing with Event Priority

You can add any number of listeners to a single event. When a corresponding event occurs, Flex calls each listener in the order that they were registered. Most of the time, this is fit for purpose; but there may be an occasion when you want to make sure that listener A is notified before listener B. To achieve this, you can use event priorities.

Event priorities enable you to assign a integer (positive or negative) to a listener, and when the associated event is dispatched, Flex first calls the listener with the highest value and proceeds to call each listener in order until all listeners are notified. If you have one or more listeners with the same priority, Flex calls them in the order they were registered. So, take the Submit button from the earlier example of dispatching an event:

```
protected function addComponentListeners():void
{
  _submitBtn.addEventListener(MouseEvent.CLICK, cleanUpDisplay,
                              false, -1);
  _submitBtn.addEventListener(MouseEvent.CLICK, resetButton,
                              false, 2);
  _submitBtn.addEventListener(MouseEvent.CLICK, createPayload,
                              false, 10);
  _submitBtn.addEventListener(MouseEvent.CLICK, verifyCall,
                              false, 5);
}
```

In this example, the Submit button (_submitBtn) has four listeners, each with an event priority value. When a user clicks the Submit button, all four listeners are notified that an event has occurred. However, the first to be called is createPayload, because this has a priority of 10; next is verifyCall, with a priority of 5; then, resetButton, with a priority of 2; and finally, cleanUpDisplay, which has a priority of -1.

Just because you have assigned even priorities to the listeners doesn't mean that Flex waits until the first listener has finished executing before calling the next one in the priority list. So, don't rely on event priorities as a basis for using one listener to produce data for a lower priority one. If you want to do that sort of thing, you are better off dispatching an event from the initial listener after it finishes executing and using that for your subsequent listeners that need the data it produces.

One final point: If you need to change the priority of a listener and it is already registered, you have to remove the original and add it back again with the new priority value.

Event Priority Constants

Within the mx.core package is a class called EventPriority. This utility class contains a selection of constants that represent different event priorities based on function. This can be useful if you need to assign a standard event priority to some of your listeners, as these will be consistent across the Flex framework. Table 8.1 lists the constants.

Table 8.1   **Event Priority Constants**

Constant Name	Event Priority Value	Description
BINDING	100	Auto-generated data bindings need to execute before any other event so require a high event priority.
CURSOR_MANAGEMENT	200	`CursorManager` hooks into mouse events and needs to execute before other mouse-related events.
DEFAULT	0	All component instances have an event priority of DEFAULT unless otherwise indicated.
DEFAULT_HANDLER	-50	Some components dispatch and listen to their own events but rely on other listeners to call `preventDefault()`.
EFFECT	-100	Auto-generated effects need to execute after all other events on the specified component. Therefore, they have a low event priority.

The interesting thing about these constants is that, although they can be useful, the documentation does come with a warning:

> Do not write code that depends on the numeric values of these constants. They are subject to change in future versions of Flex.

Now, it's up to you to decide if you want to heed this warning. If you choose to ignore it and use them within your component, you have to make sure that you check the documentation regularly to make sure they are still valid for your requirements.

Countering Events

There are certain circumstances when you want to stop an event dead in its tracks or kill it off after the associated listener receives the event. There are a few ways to achieve this, from halting the propagation of the event within the event flow to preventing its default behavior.

Event Propagation

During any of the event phases, you can stop the events traversal of the display list by call-ing stopPropagation() or stopImmediatePropagation(). The key differences between these two methods is that stopImmediatePropagation() halts the event and prevents any other listeners from executing, even those on the same node. stopPropagation(), on the other hand, halts the event but still enables any remaining listeners that are at the same node to execute based on the event. Look at the following example; both the panel and the button within it are listening for a mouse down event.

```xml
<?xml version="1.0" encoding="utf-8"?>
<s:Application xmlns:fx="http://ns.adobe.com/mxml/2009"
               xmlns:s="library://ns.adobe.com/flex/spark"
               xmlns:mx="library://ns.adobe.com/flex/mx"
               minWidth="955" minHeight="600"
               initialize="init(event)">
  <fx:Script>
    <![CDATA[
      import flash.events.Event;
      import flash.events.MouseEvent;

      import mx.controls.Alert;

      public function init(e:Event):void
      {
        panel.addEventListener(MouseEvent.MOUSE_DOWN, displayInfoAlert);
        button.addEventListener(MouseEvent.MOUSE_DOWN, displayInfoAlert);
      }

      public function displayInfoAlert(e:Event):void
      {
        Alert.show("This an alert from the " + e.currentTarget.id,
                   e.currentTarget.id );
      }
    ]]>
  </fx:Script>

  <s:layout>
    <s:HorizontalLayout horizontalAlign="center" verticalAlign="middle" />
  </s:layout>

  <s:Panel id="panel" title="Propagation Example" width="250">
    <s:layout>
      <s:HorizontalLayout horizontalAlign="center"
                          verticalAlign="middle" />
    </s:layout>
    <s:Button id="button" label="Click Me!" />
  </s:Panel>
</s:Application>
```

Without using `stopPropagation()`, the mouse-click event is picked up by both and, therefore, two alert dialogs display (see Figure 8.1).

Figure 8.1   Displaying an Alert dialog for each
listener (not using stopPropagation())

By placing a `stopPropagation()` call on the event passed to the listener's handler, you get only one dialog. Because the button is uppermost in the display hierarchy, it invokes the `displayInfoAlert()` method and stops the propagation before the panel calls the same method and creates an additional Alert, as this revised code demonstrates:

```
public function displayInfoAlert(e:Event):void
{
  Alert.show("This an alert from the " + e.currentTarget.id,
             e.currentTarget.id );
  e.stopPropagation();
}
```

Prevent Defaults

Many standard Flex 4.0 components have default behaviors that are associated with the events they dispatch. This is a good thing; if it weren't, you would dispatch the associated event to access that behavior. Sometimes, however, there are situations where you want to add a listener to a particular event on a component, but you don't want it to perform that associated behavior. This is where the `preventDefaults()` method on the event that is dispatched comes into play. As the name implies, this prevents the component from performing the default behavior for that event type. From a component development perspective, this is a useful feature, not only to use within your own component structure, but also when compositing child components within your own component, because there may be certain forms of feedback from a child component that can be negated by using `preventDefault()`.

To invoke `preventDefault()` on an event, it has to be dispatched with `cancelable` flag set to true. If this isn't set to true (the default being false), `preventDefault()` has no effect. The `cancelable` flag is usually the last entry in an event class's constructor signature but, depending on how you define your custom components, it may be in another location.

```
component.dispatchEvent(new Event(Event.EVENT, false, true));
```

By default, the vast majority of events within the Flex framework are cancelable. However, if you need to make an event cancelable and by default, it isn't, you can achieve this by getting the component to manually dispatch the event directly, as just shown.

Summary

This chapter discussed the benefits of events over polling classes to see if the respective class instances have updated. You now have a better understanding of the various phases of the event life cycle.

You saw how to create your own events for use both dispatching internally and externally. In doing so, you saw that you can assign your event listeners a priority to order how listeners of a particular event are notified.

We discussed how to prevent an event behavior associated with an event after it has been dispatched, and stopping an event from continuing its propagation immediately or after it notifies all listeners within a particular scope.

Next, we look at how to work with data, both defined internally and that which is passed in from an external source. So, let's move on....

Manipulating Data

Most components within the Flex framework rely on data to function. Complex controls tend to rely on more data than simple components, thus employ a dual data handling strategy: display and management.

Defining Component Data

It may sound like an obvious question, but what is data in relation to components? After all, there are the properties and values that the component uses internally and there are the properties that can be set externally that affect how the component displays or reacts to the application it inhabits.

Both are correct answers. However, for the sake of this chapter, I concentrate on the latter: setting properties externally that affect how your component displays or reacts to the application it inhabits. The first thing to understand is how to get data in and out of your components, and monitor values both internally and externally, if need be. To that end, let's start by looking at data providers. Although there is a property on most data-aware components called dataProvider, I'm not specifically referring to that. I'm talking about the process by which you provide and retrieve data to and from your component.

Data Providers

Providing data to your components can be as simple or as complex as you need it to be. The main crux of the process is to provide a clean and transparent set of properties and methods by which developers can plumb your controls into their applications without having to jump through hoops to achieve this. Although it is fairly simple to support basic data types within your components, after you start looking at passing large amounts of data in—regardless of whether it is complex—you're going to want to manage both the manipulation and display of this information.

KISS

Remember: If you have a multistep approach to configuring and initializing your components that others need to follow just to get them to work, you'll find that they are replaced quickly. Likewise, if your component requires a specific type of object passed into it so it can operate, be that functionally or from a visual standpoint, again, it will likely be replaced.

This is because it has no direct relationship to your components—it's the simple rule of Keep It Simple, Stupid (KISS), and I don't mean that in a disrespectful way. It just so happens to be a term used when situations or processes start to spiral out of control. All the standard components, both in the Halo and Spark sets, require only standard object types, regardless of whether they are simple or complex in nature. If you compare a button to a list, although radically different in design and purpose, they exhibit similar traits when it comes to data. Take the following simple example where I have a Halo button and list. All I am providing them with is a simple string value of Hello, yet both can render this value perfectly easily without external assistance.

```
<?xml version="1.0" encoding="utf-8"?>
<s:Application xmlns:fx="http://ns.adobe.com/mxml/2009"
               xmlns:s="library://ns.adobe.com/flex/spark"
               xmlns:mx="library://ns.adobe.com/flex/mx"
               minWidth="1024" minHeight="768">
  <s:layout>
    <s:VerticalLayout horizontalAlign="center" />
  </s:layout>

  <s:Button label="Hello" />
  <mx:List dataProvider="Hello" height="22" />
</s:Application>
```

As you can see, when compiled and executed, both the button and list display the data as expected for their component type (see Figure 9.1).

The list has the advantage over the button component because you can pass it complex data and it will happily accept it. (Although it needs assistance to render it correctly as part of the visual display.) Don't worry about that now because we discuss rendering the data in a bit.

The takeaway from this example is that although you can provide data to a list component in as simple a format as a solitary string, it is also capable of handling far more complex data. Many people are put off by this level of customization and management because it may seem daunting to define where you should actually start. With that in mind, let's discuss actually managing the data after it is passed into a component.

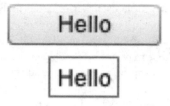

Figure 9.1   Simple data rendered by both a button and list

Managing Data

The simplest form of data management within a component is exactly the same as pretty much any other object—setting values on properties which the object (or component) exposes.

```
myObject.myValue = value;
```

The main rule to try and stick to when focusing on component development is that all public properties should be, at the very least, mutators (setters); with those that can be, they should be bound to externally supporting accessors (getters).

This is because, as we have seen in previous chapters, invalidation routines may need to be fired off when a value is set or updated. Fortunately, Flash Builder 4 makes this easy for us by automatically creating the getter/setter methods for our private/internal variables as we create them. Automation aside, it is easier to extend a mutator or accessor (getter/setter) at a later date while refactoring than to have to go through your code base and update all entries that were initially pointing to a public variable because other processes have to happen that initially weren't required.

```
// Not very flexible as only allows setting of single value.
public var isPlaying    :Boolean = false;

// More flexible as you can now process this value and update the component if
// needed - note the ability to execute another method.
public function set isPlaying(value:Boolean):void
{
  _playing = value;

  if(value != _playing)
    updateSomeOtherFunctionality();
}

public function get isPlaying():Boolean
{
  return _playing;
}
```

That's all well and good for simple data that is passed in, but what about collections of objects. How do we go about setting up our components to handle different groups of objects? Well, the first stage is to use only the standard objects; this alleviates any reliance on additional custom classes that may not be flexible enough to be useful in the multitude of applications that your components may be used within. That being said, no written-in-stone rule says that all components should only accept standard data types. If you have a valid reason to use a custom class or object as the data for a component, feel free to use it—just be aware that, further down the line, it may not be as customizable as initially thought. There is nothing stopping you from passing in an array of custom objects into your component; your component just has to be able to deal with them, happy in the knowledge it is tied tightly to that data type.

There are ways around this, which you see later on in this chapter, but for now, work with the notion that passing in custom object instances creates a tight coupling between those object instances and your component. If you keep the data that is passed in as generic as possible, you reap the benefits when you start looking at how to handle and render it. This is not to say that tight coupling is bad, but you have to weigh the pros and cons of tight, or loose, coupling.

With that in mind, let's look at how you can provide your data-centric components with a simple `dataProvider` property that accepts various standard object types.

```
private var _dataProvider     :ICollectionView

public function get dataProvider():Object
{
  return _dataProvider;
}

public function set dataProvider(value:Object):void
{
  if (value is Array)
  {
    _dataProvider = new ArrayCollection(value as Array);
  }
  else if (value is ICollectionView)
  {
    _dataProvider = ICollectionView(value);
  }
  else
  {
    var _tmp     :Array = [];
    if (value != null)
      _tmp.push(value);

    _dataProvider = new ArrayCollection(_tmp);
  }
}
```

What does this enable you to do? Well, if you think back to the list component, this starts to make a bit more sense.

Let's start with the lowest common denominator: A string, if it were passed into our component via the `dataProvider` property, would be evaluated to check to see if it were initially an array. If it were, it would create a new instance of an `ArrayCollection` and pass the value to the `ArrayCollection` constructor, casting it as an array and assigning it to the internal `_dataProvider` property. If, on the other hand, it were an object that implemented the `ICollectionView` interface, it would just cast it as an `ICollectionView` object and, like the previous process, it would assign it to the internal `_dataProvider` property. However, we passed in a simple string; therefore, it steps over these two options and defaults to creating a temporary array, checks to see if the actual object is null and, if it isn't it, pushes it into the temporary array and finally creates a new `ArrayCollection`, again passing this temporary array as part of the constructor, and assigns it to the internal `_dataProvider` variable. Simple, right?

What does this actually give you? For starters, you can pretty much handle any data type passed into your component (even custom ones). It wouldn't be too hard to extend this to support `IList`, `XMLList`, or `XMLListCollection` if need be. But, why cast everything to a collection? Well, that's a good question, so let's look at collections.

Collections

If you've never used the various collections that Flex provides, opting to use arrays instead, you could be missing out on some useful and time-saving additions that collections offer. Not only can you access the content of a collection as if it was an object (no more numeric access modifiers, like arrays), but you also gain the ability to receive notifications when the data changes. Obviously, collections generally wrap a group of objects in either an array as required by an `ArrayCollection` or an `XMLList` as used by an `XMLListCollection`. At this point, you may not be convinced that collections provide any massive benefit beyond the established approach, even with the event notification they support. I appreciate that, so let me introduce you to my personal favorite aspects of collections (and why I use them whenever applicable): cursors, filters, and sorting.

Cursors

Cursors enable you to move around your collection without having to manually set up some form of storage variable to represent the current index. For example, iterating over an array is easy through a loop, but storing the current item in an array generally requires some form of position variable that represents the item within the array that you wanted to locate.

With collections, you can just store a reference to the cursor and simply move it forward or backward through the collection, because it always provides you with access to the current position it occupies within the collection.

To work with a cursor, you need to define a variable that is of type IViewCursor and assign it the cursor of the target collection through the collections createCursor() method. I highlighted these lines so you can see where it happens in this example:

```
<?xml version="1.0" encoding="utf-8"?>
<s:Application xmlns:fx="http://ns.adobe.com/mxml/2009"
               xmlns:s="library://ns.adobe.com/flex/spark"
               xmlns:mx="library://ns.adobe.com/flex/mx"
                 minWidth="640" minHeight="480"
                 creationComplete="creationCompleteHandler(event)">

  <fx:Script>
    <![CDATA[
      import mx.collections.CursorBookmark;
      import mx.collections.IViewCursor;
      import mx.controls.dataGridClasses.DataGridColumn;

      [Bindable]
      public var dpCursor      :IViewCursor;

      protected function creationCompleteHandler(e:Event):void
      {
        dpCursor = productColl.createCursor();
        dpCursor.seek(CursorBookmark.FIRST);
      }

      protected function movePrevious(e:MouseEvent):void
      {
        dpCursor.movePrevious();

        if(dpCursor.beforeFirst)
          dpCursor.seek(CursorBookmark.LAST);
      }

      protected function moveNext(e:MouseEvent):void
      {
        dpCursor.moveNext();

        if(dpCursor.afterLast)
          dpCursor.seek(CursorBookmark.FIRST);
      }
    ]]>
  </fx:Script>
```

```
    <fx:Declarations>
      <s:ArrayCollection id="productColl">
        <s:source>
          <fx:Array id="productArr">
            <fx:Object name="AIR" bu="Platform"
                       icon="assets/images/icons/AIR.png" />
            <fx:Object name="Dreamweaver" bu="Creative Suite"
                       icon="assets/images/icons/Dreamweaver.png" />
            <fx:Object name="Fireworks" bu="Creative Suite"
                       icon="assets/images/icons/Fireworks.png" />
            <fx:Object name="Flash Professional" bu="Platform"
                       icon="assets/images/icons/Flash.png" />
            <fx:Object name="Flash Player" bu="Platform"
                       icon="assets/images/icons/Flashplayer.png" />
            <fx:Object name="Flex Builder" bu="Platform"
                       icon="assets/images/icons/Flex.png" />
            <fx:Object name="Illustrator" bu="Creative Suite"
                       icon="assets/images/icons/Illustrator.png" />
            <fx:Object name="Photoshop" bu="Creative Suite"
                       icon="assets/images/icons/Photoshop.png" />
          </fx:Array>
        </s:source>
      </s:ArrayCollection>
    </fx:Declarations>

    <s:layout>
      <s:BasicLayout/>
    </s:layout>

    <mx:Panel title="Cursor Example"
              status="{productColl.getItemIndex(dpCursor.current) + 1} of
                      {productColl.length} item(s)"
              width="200" height="200"
              horizontalCenter="0" verticalCenter="0"
              horizontalAlign="center" verticalAlign="middle">
      <mx:Image source="{dpCursor.current.icon}"
                width="100%" height="100%"
                scaleContent="false"
                horizontalAlign="center" verticalAlign="middle"/>
      <mx:ControlBar>
        <mx:Button label="Previous" id="prevBtn"
                   click="movePrevious(event)" width="75"/>
        <mx:Spacer width="100%" height="20"/>
        <mx:Button label="Next" id="nextBtn"
                   click="moveNext(event)" width="75"/>
      </mx:ControlBar>
    </mx:Panel>
  </s:Application>
```

The previous example displays the relevant image based on where the cursor is within the collection. Clicking either the Move Next or Move Previous buttons moves the cursor forward or backward through the collection, as Figure 9.2 shows.

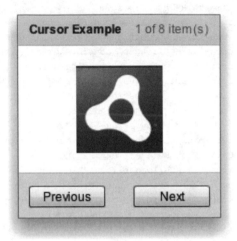

Figure 9.2   Simple image navigator using
collections and cursors

Although cursors are good to navigate within the collection of data, you may want to have it loop around when it reaches the end or beginning. This is easy to implement because the cursor provides some constants to enable you to check against, which enables you to determine if you are at the beginning or end of it. If you look at the following code block, you see that, when the button is clicked, the relevant click handler moves the cursor and then checks to see if it has go out of bounds (for example, because it's before the first item or after the last item in the collection). If it is, it moves the cursor to the first or last item (depending on which button was clicked).

```
protected function movePrevious(e:MouseEvent):void
{
  dpCursor.movePrevious();

  if(dpCursor.beforeFirst)
    dpCursor.seek(CursorBookmark.LAST);
}

protected function moveNext(e:MouseEvent):void
{
  dpCursor.moveNext();
```

```
    if(dpCursor.afterLast)
      dpCursor.seek(CursorBookmark.FIRST);
}
```

Note that the cursor represents the item located at that location in the collection, so if you change the item order or elements within it, the cursor updates to reflect this; it is only a pointer and doesn't retain the actual object located within the collection. So, be careful not to move the cursor or manipulate the underlying data until you are confident that it is no longer required.

Filtering

One thing that always takes time is slicing and dicing data after you have it within your component. If it's stored in an array, for example, you need to iterate over it, create a new array based on the current data display requirements, and use that as the basis for the current view. This is, all in all, time consuming and awkward.

Collections provide the same functionality; however, they do it all under the hood for you, so all you need to do is define a filter, apply it to the collection, and the data displays as desired without you having to manage switching out one data set for another. After you finish, you can just as easily revert it back safe in the knowledge that the entire process is nondestructive.

In the following example, I created a simple data model and passed it into an `ArrayCollection`; which in turn is passed in to a `DataGrid`. Below it is a `ComboBox` that just sets what the filter value is based on the selected entry from the drop down. As you can see, to set a simple filter like this doesn't take much code, and although this is externalized for clarity, it is just as easy to place this level of functionality inside a component that provides this type of functionality—think `Calendar` component filter my event.

```
<?xml version="1.0" encoding="utf-8"?>
<s:Application xmlns:fx="http://ns.adobe.com/mxml/2009"
               xmlns:s="library://ns.adobe.com/flex/spark"
               xmlns:mx="library://ns.adobe.com/flex/mx"
               minWidth="640" minHeight="480">

  <fx:Script>
    <![CDATA[
      [Bindable]
      private var _filterOptions    :ArrayCollection = new ArrayCollection(
                                                ['No Filter',
                                                'Platform',
                                                'Creative Suite']);

      protected function filterProducts(e:Event):void
      {
        if(filterCombo.selectedItem == "No Filter")
          productColl.filterFunction = null;
        else
```

```
            productColl.filterFunction = processFilter;

        productColl.refresh();
    }

    protected function processFilter(item:Object):Boolean
    {
        return item.bu == filterCombo.selectedItem;
    }
  ]]>
</fx:Script>

<fx:Declarations>
  <s:ArrayCollection id="productColl">
    <s:source>
      <fx:Array id="productArr">
        <fx:Object name="Photoshop" bu="Creative Suite" />
        <fx:Object name="Fireworks" bu="Creative Suite" />
        <fx:Object name="AIR" bu="Platform" />
        <fx:Object name="Flash Professional" bu="Creative Suite" />
        <fx:Object name="Flash Player" bu="Platform" />
        <fx:Object name="Dreamweaver" bu="Creative Suite" />
        <fx:Object name="Illustrator" bu="Creative Suite" />
        <fx:Object name="Flex Builder" bu="Platform" />
      </fx:Array>
    </s:source>
  </s:ArrayCollection>
</fx:Declarations>

<s:layout>
  <s:BasicLayout/>
</s:layout>

<mx:Panel title="Filtering Example"
        status="Displaying {productColl.length}/{productColl.source.length}
                item(s)"
        width="300" height="250"
        horizontalCenter="0" verticalCenter="0">
  <mx:DataGrid id="dataGrid"
            dataProvider="{productColl}"
            verticalScrollPolicy="off"
            width="100%" height="100%">
    <mx:columns>
      <mx:DataGridColumn headerText="Product"
                        dataField="name" width="130"/>
      <mx:DataGridColumn headerText="Business Unit"
                        dataField="bu" width="120"/>
```

```
        </mx:columns>
      </mx:DataGrid>
      <mx:ControlBar>
        <s:ComboBox id="filterCombo"
                    change="filterProducts(event)"
                    dataProvider="{_filterOptions}"
                    selectedIndex="0"/>
      </mx:ControlBar>
    </mx:Panel>
  </s:Application>
```

In case it isn't clear, the actual filtering happens in the following two methods. When the user selects an entry from the ComboBox, it calls the filterProducts() method.

```
protected function filterProducts(e:Event):void
{
  if(filterCombo.selectedItem == "No Filter")
    productColl.filterFunction = null;
  else
    productColl.filterFunction = processFilter;

  productColl.refresh();
}


protected function processFilter(item:Object):Boolean
{
  return item.bu == filterCombo.selectedItem;
}
```

Here, we check to see if the filtering option selected from the ComboBox is No Filter; if it is, we set the filter to null; otherwise, we set it to the method processFilter(). When executed, this method sets the return Boolean value based on the ComboBox selection (as shown in Figure 9.3), so it will be either Platform or Creative Suite, and evaluates it with the bu property of the item object; if it resolves to true, it is displayed, and if it resolves to false, it isn't. After this finishes executing, we need to refresh the actual collection so that the filter can be applied. We achieve this by calling the obviously named refresh() method.

Although this example only determines the contents of the filter by comparing a single value, you can provide as complex a set of requirements as necessary within your filter function to determine what is actually displayed.

Given that filtering is exceedingly useful, sometimes all you may need to do is actually order the data based on certain criteria (regardless of whether it has been filtered). Again, collections provide a simple time-saving approach to this without sacrificing functionality.

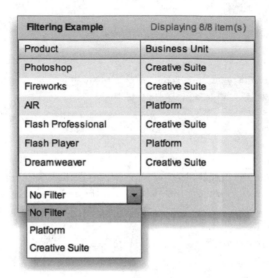

Figure 9.3   Filter example as defined
by the previous code

Sorting

If you've ever used a `DataGrid` within Flex, you have already experienced sorting. By default, the `DataGrid` component enables the user to sort the data it displays by clicking the column header, which provides a simple single-column sort. Collections also support this; however, they can perform far more complex sorts on the data they contain based on the provided criteria.

For example, the previous code is sorting on two properties within the collection. First, it sorts by product type (for example, is it a design-orientated product [Creative Suite] or a Flash Platform product [Platform]); and second, it sorts based on the ordering of the product names after the first sort, so in this case, it should place all the Creative Suite products at the top and all the Platform products at the bottom. Then, when the second sort is applied, it alphabetically orders each grouping, as shown in Figure 9.4.

```
<?xml version="1.0" encoding="utf-8"?>
<s:Application xmlns:fx="http://ns.adobe.com/mxml/2009"
               xmlns:s="library://ns.adobe.com/flex/spark"
               xmlns:mx="library://ns.adobe.com/flex/mx">

   <s:layout>
     <s:HorizontalLayout horizontalAlign="center" verticalAlign="middle" />
   </s:layout>
```

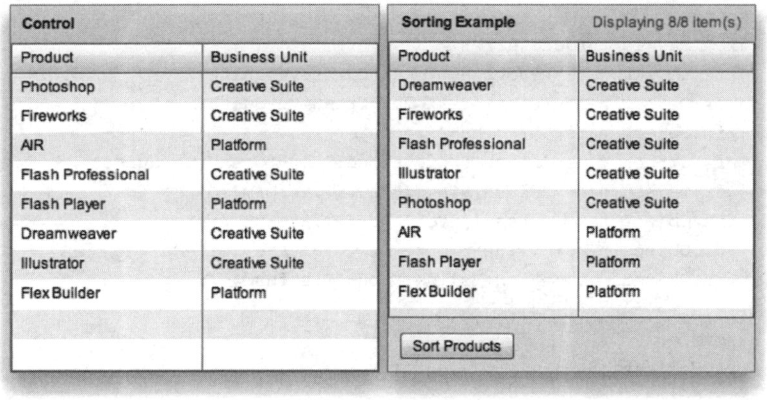

Control			Sorting Example	Displaying 8/8 item(s)
Product	Business Unit		Product	Business Unit
Photoshop	Creative Suite		Dreamweaver	Creative Suite
Fireworks	Creative Suite		Fireworks	Creative Suite
AIR	Platform		Flash Professional	Creative Suite
Flash Professional	Creative Suite		Illustrator	Creative Suite
Flash Player	Platform		Photoshop	Creative Suite
Dreamweaver	Creative Suite		AIR	Platform
Illustrator	Creative Suite		Flash Player	Platform
Flex Builder	Platform		Flex Builder	Platform
			Sort Products	

Figure 9.4   Multisort applied to a collection, with the
original data displayed on the left

```
<fx:Script>
  <![CDATA[
    import com.developingcomponents.components.renderer.CenteredImage;

    import mx.collections.Sort;
    import mx.collections.SortField;
    import mx.controls.dataGridClasses.DataGridColumn;

    protected function sortProducts(e:MouseEvent):void
    {
      var _productSortField    :SortField = new SortField();
      _productSortField.name = "name";
      _productSortField.caseInsensitive = true;

      var _platformSortField    :SortField = new SortField();
      _platformSortField.name - "bu";
      _platformSortField.caseInsensitive = true;

      var _productNameSort    :Sort = new Sort();
      _productNameSort.fields = [_platformSortField, _productSortField];

      productColl.sort = _productNameSort;
      productColl.refresh();
    }
  ]]>
</fx:Script>

<fx:Declarations>
  <s:ArrayCollection id="productColl">
```

```
        <s:source>
          <fx:Array id="productArr">
            <fx:Object name="Photoshop" bu="Creative Suite" />
            <fx:Object name="Fireworks" bu="Creative Suite" />
            <fx:Object name="AIR" bu="Platform" />
            <fx:Object name="Flash Professional" bu="Creative Suite" />
            <fx:Object name="Flash Player" bu="Platform" />
            <fx:Object name="Dreamweaver" bu="Platform" />
            <fx:Object name="Illustrator" bu="Creative Suite" />
            <fx:Object name="Flex Builder" bu="Platform" />
          </fx:Array>
        </s:source>
      </s:ArrayCollection>
    </fx:Declarations>

    <s:Panel title="Control" width="300" height="300">
      <mx:DataGrid id="control"
                   dataProvider="{productArr}"
                   verticalScrollPolicy="off"
                   width="100%" height="100%">
        <mx:columns>
          <mx:DataGridColumn headerText="Product"
                             dataField="name" width="130"/>
          <mx:DataGridColumn headerText="Business Unit"
                             dataField="bu" width="120"/>
        </mx:columns>
      </mx:DataGrid>
    </s:Panel>

    <mx:Panel title="Sorting Example"
              status="Displaying {productColl.length}/{productColl.source.length}
    item(s)"
              width="300" height="300">
      <mx:DataGrid id="dataGrid"
                   dataProvider="{productColl}"
                   verticalScrollPolicy="off"
                   width="100%" height="100%">
        <mx:columns>
          <mx:DataGridColumn headerText="Product"
                             dataField="name" width="130"/>
          <mx:DataGridColumn headerText="Business Unit"
                             dataField="bu" width="120"/>
        </mx:columns>
      </mx:DataGrid>

      <mx:ControlBar>
        <s:Button id="sortBtn" label="Sort Products"
```

```
                    click="sortProducts(event)" />
        </mx:ControlBar>
    </mx:Panel>
</s:Application>
```

Note that sorting large data sets can take time (as does anything that has to process a lot of information), but in my experience, even with very large amounts of data, the sorting doesn't break the user experience or become unresponsive. If it does appear to be taking longer to process than is acceptable, think about what you're sorting on and how you're sorting it—could first filtering the data improve the execution?

Although I've been using the DataGrid as an obvious example of how filtering and sorting operates, don't assume that you can use only complex data in tabular-based components. The use of collections can be as useful in managing the display of more visual content (as you'll see when we get to renderers) as it is for displaying complex spreadsheet-style information.

Note that you can combine filtering and sorting to condense the data displayed and order it based on your requirements. The following example does the same filtering as the earlier example, but the example code also then sorts the data in alphabetical order before displaying the updated results:

```
<?xml version="1.0" encoding="utf-8"?>
<s:Application xmlns:fx="http://ns.adobe.com/mxml/2009"
               xmlns:s="library://ns.adobe.com/flex/spark"
               xmlns:mx="library://ns.adobe.com/flex/mx"
               minWidth="640" minHeight="480">

  <fx:Script>
    <![CDATA[
      import mx.collections.Sort;
      import mx.collections.SortField;

      [Bindable]
      private var _filterOptions    :ArrayCollection = new ArrayCollection(
                                              ['No Filter',
                                               'Platform',
                                               'Creative Suite']);

      protected function sortAndFilterProducts(e:Event):void
      {
        if(filterCombo.selectedItem == "No Filter")
        {
          productColl.sort = null;
          productColl.filterFunction = null;
        }
        else
        {
          var _productSortField   :SortField = new SortField();
```

```
              _productSortField.name = "name";
              _productSortField.caseInsensitive = true;

              var _productNameSort     :Sort = new Sort();
              _productNameSort.fields = [_productSortField];

              productColl.filterFunction = processFilter;
              productColl.sort = _productNameSort;
            }

            productColl.refresh();
          }

        protected function processFilter(item:Object):Boolean
        {
          return item.bu == filterCombo.selectedItem;
        }
     ]]>
  </fx:Script>

  <fx:Declarations>
    <s:ArrayCollection id="productColl">
      <s:source>
        <fx:Array id="productArr">
          <fx:Object name="Photoshop" bu="Creative Suite" />
          <fx:Object name="Fireworks" bu="Creative Suite" />
          <fx:Object name="AIR" bu="Platform" />
          <fx:Object name="Flash Professional" bu="Creative Suite" />
          <fx:Object name="Flash Player" bu="Platform" />
          <fx:Object name="Dreamweaver" bu="Creative Suite" />
          <fx:Object name="Illustrator" bu="Creative Suite" />
          <fx:Object name="Flex Builder" bu="Platform" />
        </fx:Array>
      </s:source>
    </s:ArrayCollection>
  </fx:Declarations>

  <s:layout>
    <s:BasicLayout/>
  </s:layout>

  <mx:Panel title="Sort & Filtering Example"
            status="Displaying {productColl.length}/{productColl.source.length}
  item(s)"
            width="300" height="250"
            horizontalCenter="0" verticalCenter="0">
    <mx:DataGrid id="dataGrid"
```

```
                  dataProvider="{productColl}"
                  verticalScrollPolicy="off"
                  width="100%" height="100%">
      <mx:columns>
        <mx:DataGridColumn headerText="Product"
                           dataField="name" width="130"/>
        <mx:DataGridColumn headerText="Business Unit"
                           dataField="bu" width="120"/>
      </mx:columns>
    </mx:DataGrid>

    <mx:ControlBar>
      <s:ComboBox id="filterCombo"
                  change="sortAndFilterProducts(event)"
                  dataProvider="{_filterOptions}"
                  selectedIndex="0"/>
    </mx:ControlBar>
  </mx:Panel>
</s:Application>
```

Displaying Data

When you create your first few components, thoughts of complex data and how to display it won't be at the forefront of your mind, mainly because you'll be marrying the visual elements to the properties that you'll expose publically. Therefore, it will likely be a one-to-one relationship: one value for one visual element. Think of the label field of the Button component. As your component library grows and you start to introduce components that can consume more complex data sets, you will likely start to consider how to manage this data—this is especially true if you are using the data to inform the actual visual representation of the component and not just displaying it via DataGrid.

Data Renderers

This is where renderers come in. They enable you to define a default view, if you will, for your component based on its most basic set of parameters, but still enable other developers to assign alternative views that can renderer extended data beyond that which you have already defined.

Take a simple image slideshow, for example. You create a slideshow component that allows the user to pass in a collection of URLs that represent the locations of the images. In turn, your component creates an Image component and loads each image in and provides a mechanism (manual or automatic) for the end user to navigate the slides. What if the developer wants to display a title, or additional information, perhaps a link, or even have some mouse-related effects on the slide? All of a sudden, your simple image slideshow now has loads of additional functionality based on the data passed in that you didn't comprehend would be required, and you are starting to change the overall simple functionality of an collection of URLs that you initially intended.

Fortunately, this is where item rendering and data management step in. You've already seen how you can provide a flexible implementation for the data that is passed into this type of component through the `dataProvider` example earlier in this chapter. Now, let's look at how to create an `itemRenderer` to provide the flexibility needed without breaking the simple collection of URLs with which we first started.

Rendering the UI

An `itemRenderer`, as the name suggests, renders an item within a component. However, they are not the sole bastions of the list/grid-based components. You can use this same process to imbue your components with the ability to be both flexible and functional. The basic process is that your component is provided with data from an external source, and it is provided with a view that it can use to render the data that is passed in. For Spark components, you have the `ItemRenderer` class (or any class that implement the `IItemRenderer` interface), but for the likes of `AdvancedDataGrid`, `DataGrid`, and `Tree`, you have specific item renderer classes, which is partly because they are still Halo implementations, but they also provide component-specific hooks within your item renderer that makes sense to have specific ones for each.

One of the key differences between creating item renderers for Halo components (beyond those just detailed) is that Spark item renderers are almost always declared in MXML. You can create them in ActionScript if you choose, but you are more likely to use MXML form both a workflow and time-saving perspective. In contrast, Halo item renderers can be declared in three different ways: directly within the MXML component block, as a fully qualified class reference, or as a `ClassFactory` that is assigned to the component by ActionScript. Because these are Halo/Flex 3 specific, I do not cover them in this book because, for the most part, you will be using Spark-based components and their companion item renderer classes. If you want to know more about working with Halo `itemRenderers`, check out the resource links in Appendix A, "Flex Resources."

Linking itemRenders to External Data

The next question is how do you get the data into your renderer? Well, if your component provides support for `ItemRenderers`, you can provide a consistent workflow for assigning custom renderers to your components. (You can achieve this by extending your component from any class that provides support for `itemRenderers`: `DataGroup` and `SkinnableDataContainer` are probably the most useful.)

Enough theory, let's look at an example: an image viewer to see how you could implement support for `itemRenderers`, allowing you to retain the flexibility of supporting different layouts and additional data through renderers without having to make your component so flexible that it runs the risk of becoming bloated with code.

The basic structure of the `ImageSlideShow` component is a main display area that holds the image and two buttons, one at either end (which, by default, are hidden until you roll over them). When clicked, the buttons show the next or previous image, depending on which one is selected; this enables you to navigate through each image, as Figure 9.5 shows.

Figure 9.5   The ImageSlideShow component with its default
itemRenderer displaying an image

What follows is the `ImageSlideShow` component code. Notice that we set the default skin in the components constructor; Chapter 10, "Skinning and Styling" discusses this, but, for now, all you need to know is that it sets the overall visual look and feel of the component, including making the buttons semi-opaque gray rectangles.

```
package com.developingcomponents.components
{
  import
com.developingcomponents.components.renderer.ImageSlideShowDefaultRenderer;
  import com.developingcomponents.components.skins.ImageSlideShowSkin;

  import flash.events.MouseEvent;

  import mx.core.ClassFactory;
  import mx.graphics.SolidColor;

  import spark.components.Button;
  import spark.components.Group;
  import spark.components.SkinnableDataContainer;
  import spark.primitives.Rect;
```

```
[SkinState("normal")]
[SkinState("disabled")]
public class ImageSlideShow extends SkinnableDataContainer
{

  private var _prevBtnVisible    :Boolean = false;
  private var _nextBtnVisible    :Boolean = true;

  [SkinPart(required="false")]
  public var nextButton      :Button;
  [SkinPart(required="false")]
  public var previousButton :Button;

  public function ImageSlideShow()
  {
    super();
    setStyle("skinClass", ImageSlideShowSkin);
  }

  override protected function createChildren():void
  {
    super.createChildren();
  }

  override protected function commitProperties():void
  {
    super.commitProperties();

    if(itemRenderer == null)
      itemRenderer = new ClassFactory(ImageSlideShowDefaultRenderer);

    autoLayout = true;
  }

  override protected function measure():void
  {
    super.measure();
  }

  override protected function updateDisplayList(unscaledWidth:Number,
                                        unscaledHeight:Number):void
  {
    super.updateDisplayList(unscaledWidth, unscaledHeight);
    this.setActualSize(unscaledWidth, unscaledHeight);

  }
```

```
override protected function partAdded(partName:String,
                                       instance:Object):void
{
  super.partAdded(partName, instance);

  if(partName == "nextButton")
  {
    instance.enabled = true;
    instance.addEventListener(MouseEvent.CLICK, nextBtnHandler);
  }

  if(partName == "previousButton")
  {
    instance.enabled = true;
    instance.visible = false;
    instance.addEventListener(MouseEvent.CLICK, previousBtnHandler);
  }
}

override protected function partRemoved(partName:String,
                                         instance:Object):void
{
  super.partAdded(partName, instance);

  if(instance == nextButton)
    nextButton.removeEventListener(MouseEvent.CLICK,
                                   nextBtnHandler);

  if(instance == previousButton)
    previousButton.removeEventListener(MouseEvent.CLICK,
                                       previousBtnHandler);
}

/*
The calculation in these button handlers are relatively simple - if
you wanted to use content with arbitrary widths this will require a more
granular calculation to take that in to consideration.

Also they don't take in to consideration the actual layout of the items.
*/
protected function nextBtnHandler(e:MouseEvent):void
{
  dataGroup.x -= (dataGroup.width / dataProvider.length);

  if(dataGroup.x == -(dataGroup.width - (dataGroup.width /
                      dataProvider.length)) && _nextBtnVisible)
    nextButton.visible = _nextBtnVisible = false;
```

```
      if(!_prevBtnVisible)
        previousButton.visible = _prevBtnVisible = true;
    }

    protected function previousBtnHandler(e:MouseEvent):void
    {
      dataGroup.x += (dataGroup.width / dataProvider.length);

      if(dataGroup.x == 0 && _prevBtnVisible)
        previousButton.visible = _prevBtnVisible = false;

      if(!_nextBtnVisible)
        nextButton.visible = _nextBtnVisible = true;
    }
  }
}
```

To keep this compact and functional, the ImageSlideShow component inherits from SkinnableDataContainer. This way, your component immediately inherits the capability to be skinned and already has access to a DataGroup instance to deal with the rendering of each of our items—in this case, an image.

As you can see, within the commitProperties() method, there is a check to see if an external itemRenderer has been assigned. If it hasn't, we can assign the default renderer.

```
override protected function commitProperties():void
{
  super.commitProperties();

  if(itemRenderer == null)
    itemRenderer = new ClassFactory(ImageSlideShowDefaultRenderer);

  autoLayout = true;
}
```

Note that the variable itemRenderer only accepts IFactory instances, so you need to pass the custom item renderer to it as an ClassFactory instance to instantiate it. This is because, before rendering it all to the display list, we'll create the renderer and pass the data into it after it is initialized.

What does the default renderer consist of? Well, by default, when you create an ItemRenderer in MXML, it automatically provides you with a label bound to data.label. In the case of the ImageSlideShow default renderer, I extended it a bit more and added in support for an Image component that maps to data.image, as the following code shows:

```
<?xml version="1.0" encoding="utf-8"?>
<s:ItemRenderer xmlns:fx="http://ns.adobe.com/mxml/2009"
                xmlns:s="library://ns.adobe.com/flex/spark"
```

```
             xmlns:mx="library://ns.adobe.com/flex/mx"
             autoDrawBackground="false"
             showsCaret="false">

  <s:layout>
    <s:VerticalLayout horizontalAlign="center" verticalAlign="top" />
  </s:layout>

  <mx:Image source="{data.image}" autoLoad="true" />
</s:ItemRenderer>
```

If you want to provide a custom renderer and map a complex object to it, you now only need to assign the relevant `itemRenderer` class to the `ImageSlideShow` and it will then support any additional properties defined in the `data` object and, as the following code shows, even support greater functionality—in this case, transitions and view states.

```
<?xml version="1.0" encoding="utf-8"?>
<s:ItemRenderer xmlns:fx="http://ns.adobe.com/mxml/2009"
                xmlns:s="library://ns.adobe.com/flex/spark"
                xmlns:mx="library://ns.adobe.com/flex/mx"
                rollOver=" rollOverHandler(event)"
                rollOut=" rollOutHandler(event)"
                showsCaret="false">

  <fx:Script>
    <![CDATA[
      protected function rollOverHandler(event:MouseEvent):void
      {
        currentState = "panelView"
      }

      protected function rollOutHandler(event:MouseEvent):void
      {
        currentState = "normal";
      }

    ]]>
  </fx:Script>

  <fx:Declarations>
    <!-- Place non-visual elements (e.g., services, value objects) here -->
  </fx:Declarations>

  <s:states>
    <s:State name="normal" />
    <s:State name="panelView" />
  </s:states>
```

```
<s:transitions>
  <s:Transition fromState="*" toState="panelView">
    <s:Move target="{panel}" yFrom="-30" yTo="0"/>
  </s:Transition>
  <s:Transition toState="*" fromState="panelView">
    <s:Move target="{panel}" yFrom="0" yTo="-30" />
  </s:Transition>
</s:transitions>

<mx:Image source="{data.image}" autoLoad="true" scaleContent="true"
          left="0" right="0" top="0" bottom="0"/>

<s:BorderContainer id="panel" backgroundColor="0x333333"
                   alpha="0.7" width="100%" height="30"
                   y="-30"
                   y.panelView="0">
  <s:layout>
    <s:VerticalLayout horizontalAlign="center" verticalAlign="middle" />
  </s:layout>

  <s:Label text="{data.label}" color="0xffffff"/>
</s:BorderContainer>
</s:ItemRenderer>
```

In this enhanced `itemRenderer`, when a user rolls over the image, a semitransparent panel drops down from the top, displaying the label data, as Figure 9.6 shows. The great thing is that there has been no requirement to alter any of the `ImageSlideShow` component's code to achieve this.

To assign the enhanced item renderer to the `ImageSlideShow` component, you just need to declare within the component's MXML, as this code snippets shows:

```
// Additional code has been removed for brevity


<components:ImageSlideShow
itemRenderer="com.developingcomponents.components.renderer.EnhancedImageRenderer"
 dataProvider="{myData}" width="320"/>
```

One thing to consider about the `ImageSlideShow` component is that, although it provides support for custom item renderers, it does have limitations; for example, it has no way to react if the layout changes from horizontal to vertical. However, I didn't include this functionality to keep the code as compact as possible—it's something you might want to do to extend this example and implement yourself....

Figure 9.6   ImageSlideShow using an enhanced item renderer
that provides a drop-down panel

Summary

This chapter gave you insight into how you can design your components so that they can (if needed) render the data passed to them based on a visual renderer that isn't baked into the actual component; this gives you a greater level of flexibility within your component architecture.

You also saw how you can easily harness collections to navigate, filter, and sort data sets, and make working with data within your component a nondestructive process. Finally, you saw a flexible approach to implementing a data provider within your component, allowing you to work with multiple standard data types without having to create separate public methods or properties.

Skinning and Styling

Now that you better understand the more developer-orientated side of component development, we now look at how to actually style our components. This is generally an area where most budding component developers shy away, because it can initially appear to be a black art.

After this chapter, you will understand how the styling and skinning process operates and how you can add various styling properties to your components with ease.

Spark Versus Halo

Probably the first thing to clarify about skinning and styling support is the difference between Halo and Spark components. Halo components still use the legacy architecture, and although you can provide them with MXML-based skins just like Spark components, you can manipulate them visually only so far.

Halo components tend to lean heavily on what are commonly referred to as programmatic skins. These skins directly associate with the component and are created through the combination of ActionScript and Cascading Style Sheets (CSS). The main issue with this approach is that the limitations of layout are built into the component itself. Therefore, you are limited in what you can achieve based on the constraints laid down by the component developer (the Halo button only being able to display a single icon, for example).

The Spark components were architected to remove that tight coupling of skin and component and provide developers with the ability to hook into the exposed functions and properties of the component from within the skin that was assigned to it. This provided a clean separation between the functionality and the visuals and allowed a level of flexibility that wasn't available through the Halo components.

Spark Skin Life Cycle

When it comes to the new Spark skinning model, you must first understand how it relates to the traditional component methods of `createChildren()`, `commitProperties()`, `measure()`, and `updateDisplayList()`. By looking at

Figure 10.1, you see that, when the constructor of the component is instantiated, it sets a flag to indicate that the skin is dirty and needs to be re-created. This is done to make sure that the skin is initialized correctly when the component initializes itself. When the component enters the `createChildren()` phase, it checks to make sure that the skin hasn't changed. If it has, the skin is flagged to be rerendered.

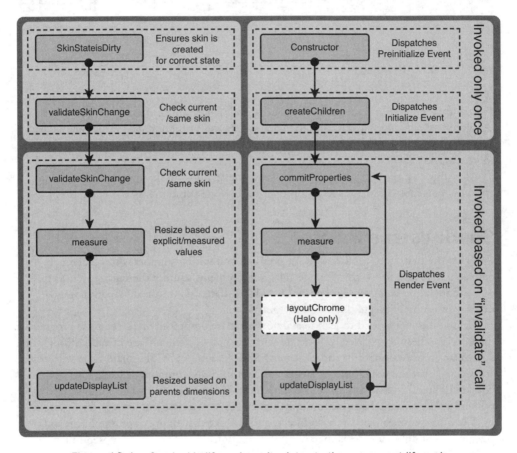

Figure 10.1   Spark skin life cycle as it relates to the component life cycle

After the initialization methods are out of the way (constructor and `createChildren()`), your component enters the main component life cycle. As you may recall, this deals with applying properties and sizing and finally displaying the component.

You can see that the skin's life cycle runs in parallel to that of the host component, which, when you think about it, makes sense. The skin must respond to changes in size or updates to properties that may affect how it is displayed. After the component is fully initialized and rendered to the display for the first time, the skin updates only when it is instructed to do so by the component because of changes in associated properties, styles, or dimension of the host.

Where Do I Start?

Throughout this book, the vast majority, if not all, the examples have generally inherited from UIComponent. All Flex components, be they Halo or Spark, inherit from UIComponent. However, as you may recall from Chapter 3, "Anatomy of a Component," the Spark component framework first extends UIComponent with a new subclass called SkinnableComponent. This is because there are a few changes within the Spark architecture to support the creating, displaying, and managing of visual assets. These deal with attaching and removing skins, reacting to a specific part of a skin after it is added or removed, and determining the current state of the component.

Now, as with most methods within the Flex framework, you need to override only those methods that you are going to add new or additional functionality. In the case of component methods, generally, you are adding additional functionality and, therefore, need to make sure that you invoke the superclasses' reciprocal method. Otherwise, you may get unexpected results.

Working with SkinnableComponent

As mentioned, the SkinnableComponent class (and any Spark component that subclasses from it), provides the hooks needed to enable you to imbue your components with the new Spark skinning model. To achieve this, you need to override a few and add in your component-specific requirements, but it's not that tricky once you know how.

Those methods are attachSkin(), detachSkin(), partAdded(), partRemoved(), and getCurrentSkinState(). Typically you won't need to override attachSkin() or removeskin() because these are low-level methods invoked automatically by the Flex framework—in the case of attachSkin(), whenever the component's createChildren() or UIComponent.commitProperties() methods are called. Likewise when a skin is changed on a component, that component's detachSkin() method is called automatically to remove and destroy the current skin and its associated skin parts. With that in mind, you can safely ignore them.

partAdded(), partRemoved()

The partAdded() method deals with the actual setup of the individual skin parts, adding event listeners, initial values, and so on. The partRemoved() method is primarily used to remove the event listeners on those skin parts, but it can also update your component (if needed) based on the removal of a skin part.

Implementing the part methods requires the addition of the [SkinPart] metadata that relates to the actual part instances within your component. In the following code example, you see two buttons, both of which have a [SkinPart(required="true")] tag marking them as required skin parts for this component. These parts are required because, when it comes to the actual skin, they must be included. I know that sounds obvious, but it can be accidentally overlooked when you work with more complex composite components that have numerous skin parts—both mandatory and optional.

As well as declaring whether a [SkinPart] is required, you can also declare whether the part is dynamic or static in nature. In the majority of cases you will be using static skin parts, whereby you declare the associated variable of the [SkinPart] as a concrete class like a Spark Button for instance. When working with dynamic skin parts, you declare the [SkinPart] tag and include the implementation type within the tag as this code illustrates:

```
/*Declaring a dynamic skin part */
[SkinPart (require="true", type="spark.components.Button")]
private var slideBreadcrumbPip     :IFactory
```

The advantage of using dynamic skin parts over static ones is twofold. First, you may have a skin element within your component that uses the same skin part for multiple instances within your component or is based on a dataset passed in to your component. In this case you can then create an instance of your dynamic skin part for each element in that data as this code example illustrates:

```
protected function createslideBreadcrumbBarItems():void
{
  // Check to see if there is more than one image to display.
  // If so create the breadcrumb items
  if(data.length > 1)
  {
    for(var i:uint = 0; I < _data.length; ++i)
    {
      var _breadcrumbPip :Button = createDynamicPartInstance("slideBreadcrumbPip")
                          as Button;
      breadcrumbBar.addElement(breadcrumbPip);
    }
  }
}
```

The advantage of using dynamic skin parts is that static parts can store only a single instance. Whereas dynamic skin parts are IFactory instances, so they enable the creation of multiple skin parts based on them as the previous example shows. Notice that you need to call createDynamicPartInstance(), passing in the associated skin part's variable name to create a concrete instance of your skin part.

The second benefit is that not all your skin parts may need instantiating when the component is initialized. So it makes sense to mark these as dynamic; then you don't assign memory for skin parts that may not be required.

When a static or dynamic skin part is assigned by the skin to a component, the partAdded() method is invoked, and you can then check to see which part it is. In this case, it's either the next or previous buttons.

```
package com.developingcomponents.components
{
  import com.developingcomponents.components.skins.ExampleSkinnedComponentSkin;

  import flash.events.MouseEvent;

  import spark.components.Button;
  import spark.components.supportClasses.SkinnableComponent;

  public class ExampleSkinnedComponent extends SkinnableComponent
  {
    private var _prevBtnVisible     :Boolean = false;

    [SkinPart(required="true")]
    public var nextButton       :Button;
    [SkinPart(required="true")]
    public var previousButton :Button;

    public function ExampleSkinnedComponent()
    {
      super();
      setStyle("skinClass", ExampleSkinnedComponentSkin);
    }

    override protected function partAdded(partName:String,
                                       instance:Object):void
    {
      if(partName == "nextButton")
      {
        instance.addEventListener(MouseEvent.CLICK, nextBtnHandler);
      }

      if(partName == "previousButton")
      {
        instance.addEventListener(MouseEvent.CLICK, previousBtnHandler);
      }
    }

    override protected function partRemoved(partName:String,
                                         instance:Object):void
    {
      if(partName == "nextButton")
        instance.addEventListener(MouseEvent.CLICK, nextBtnHandler);
```

```
      if(partName == "previousButton")
        instance.addEventListener(MouseEvent.CLICK, previousBtnHandler);
    }

    protected function nextBtnHandler(e:MouseEvent):void
    {
      // handle 'nextButton' click here
    }

    protected function previousBtnHandler(e:MouseEvent):void
    {
      // handle 'previousButton' click here
    }
  }
}
```

You see that, if it's the previous button, the component checks to see if it should be visible based on another property value and sets the visibility of the part as required. Both buttons have listeners added to them to respond to the click event of each button's event. In the partRemoved() method, all that happens is that the listeners that were associated in the partAdded() method are removed so that garbage collection can clean up after the skin is no longer associated with the component.

getCurrentSkinState()

The getCurrentSkinState() method provides a mechanism for determining and setting the current skin state of your component—if your component supports multiple states. (If your component doesn't, you don't need to implement this method.) Like the skin parts, this method works with the [SkinState] metadata tag. Declaring the skin states that the component supports so that any associated skin knows what states it must implement with that skin file.

Skin states aren't the same as view states because they are exposed only to the skin class and not the component. Therefore, if you want to set the state of your skin, you need to do it via an intermediary property, as the following code demonstrates:

```
package com.developingcomponents.components
{
  import flash.events.MouseEvent;

  import spark.components.Button;
  import spark.components.supportClasses.SkinnableComponent;

  [SkinState("normal")]
  [SkinState("enhanced")]
  [SkinState("compact")]
  public class ExampleSkinnedComponent extends SkinnableComponent
```

```
{
  private var _viewMode    :String = "normal";

  public function get viewMode():String
  {
    return _viewMode;
  }

  [Inspectable(defaultValue="normal",
              enumeration="normal,compact,enhanced")]
  public function set viewMode(value:String):void
  {
    _viewMode = value;
  }

  override public function getCurrentSkinState():String
  {
    var _state    :String = "normal";

    if(_viewMode == "compact")
      _state = "compact";
    else if(_viewMode == "enhanced")
      _state = "enhanced";

    return _state;
  }
}
}
```

Here, you have the three skin states. (If you have more than one state, you need to include `normal` by default). When the component invalidates itself, it calls `getCurrentSkinState()` to check if the skin state has changed since it was last checked. If it has, it returns the skin state's value to the skin and updates accordingly. So, in the previous code, we have a variable called `_viewMode` that is linked to an accessor/mutator with some enumerated values. When `getCurrentSkinState()` is invoked, it checks the current value of `_viewMode` and returns the value to the skin class. If the value isn't one of the defined states, we return the `normal` state value. That way, you can be safe in the knowledge that, regardless of what might be assigned to this variable; if it's not one you were expecting, the component defaults to the normal layout as defined by the skin.

Creating Component Skins

You've seen the insides of a Spark component...well, at least from the perspective of adding skin support. So, what do you do to create the actual skin? In previous version of Flex, you created an ActionScript class that was, as mentioned, tightly associated with your component and then passed values from the host component to it to set various visual values (`color`, `backgroundColor`, `radius`, and so on).

Luckily, in Flex 4, we can dispense with that unpleasant process and use MXML to declare skins. The advantages here are that you can easily implement and define the various facets of the skin, use design view to actually see a basic representation of your skin prior to adding it to your component, and finally, get applications like Flash Catalyst to do the vast majority of the work for you.

How can all this happen? Well, it's because of two graphical additions to the Flex framework: FXG and MXML Graphics (MXMLG).

FXG and MXMLG

FXG is an XML-based interoperability format. It enables design software, such as Illustrator or Photoshop, to export their assets so that they can be easily shared between those aforementioned products and Flash Catalyst and/or Flash Builder, and as such, can be used to create interactive visual assets for use within Flex.

MXMLG differs from FXG because it can be rendered at runtime, which enables you to change any of its values on-the-fly through associated component hooks or CSS. FXG is better for static graphics (for example, those that don't need to be altered by user input or rerendered at runtime). Both support an almost identical set of properties, which include the following:

- Graphic primitives
- Text primitives
- Fills, strokes, gradients, and bitmaps
- Effects such as alphas, filter, masks, transforms, and blend modes

Creating a Component Skin

When it comes to creating a skin for your component, you need to consider some additional aspects.

First, the `[HostComponent]` metadata tag provides a mapping between the component class and the skin. That doesn't mean that particular component instance—just what type of component it is. You can omit the `[HostComponent]` tag; some developers do this so that they can reuse a skin on multiple components that have similar visual representations, but honestly, those use cases are generally few and far between compared with the integration benefit that using it offers. This becomes more apparent later, when we look at component properties and styling.

Second, there may be temptation to add functionality to the skin—but, don't! Skins get rerendered only when the component tells it to. Therefore, they are dumb. Don't view them as an extension of a component where you can add additional functionality. If it doesn't have anything to do with defining the component's skin, it shouldn't be in there.

With those pointers out of the way, let's look at the component we've used as a basis for our discussion so far and the associated skin file:

```
package com.developingcomponents.components
{
  import com.developingcomponents.components.skins.ExampleSkinnedComponentSkin;

  import flash.events.MouseEvent;

  import spark.components.Button;
  import spark.components.supportClasses.SkinnableComponent;

  public class ExampleSkinnedComponent extends SkinnableComponent
  {
    private var _prevBtnVisible    :Boolean = false;

    [SkinPart(required="true")]
    public var nextButton      :Button;
    [SkinPart(required="true")]
    public var previousButton :Button;

    public function ExampleSkinnedComponent()
    {
      super();
      setStyle("skinClass", ExampleSkinnedComponentSkin);
    }

    override protected function partAdded(partName:String,
                                          instance:Object):void
    {
      if(partName == "nextButton")
        instance.addEventListener(MouseEvent.CLICK, nextBtnHandler);

      if(partName == "previousButton")
        instance.addEventListener(MouseEvent.CLICK, previousBtnHandler);
    }

    override protected function partRemoved(partName:String,
                                            instance:Object):void
    {
      if(partName == "nextButton")
        instance.addEventListener(MouseEvent.CLICK, nextBtnHandler);

      if(partName == "previousButton")
        instance.addEventListener(MouseEvent.CLICK, previousBtnHandler);
    }
```

```
  protected function nextBtnHandler(e:MouseEvent):void
  {
    // handle 'nextButton' click here
  }

  protected function previousBtnHandler(e:MouseEvent):void
  {
    // handle 'previousButton' click here
  }
 }
}
```

You see in the component class that I set the component skin in the constructor via the setStyle() property. That way, the component always uses this skin if no other is supplied.

Here is the actual skin class. I highlighted the [HostComponent] tag so that you can see how the component class is mapped to the skin. At the bottom of the skin, you can see the two buttons. Omitting one or both buttons causes an error; these are both required.

```xml
<?xml version="1.0" encoding="utf-8"?>
<!--ExampleSkinnedComponentSkin.mxml -->
<s:Skin xmlns:fx="http://ns.adobe.com/mxml/2009"
        xmlns:s="library://ns.adobe.com/flex/spark"
        xmlns:mx="library://ns.adobe.com/flex/mx">

  <!-- host component -->
  <fx:Metadata>
    [HostComponent("com.developingcomponents.components.ExampleSkinnedComponent")]
  </fx:Metadata>

  <s:Rect top="0" right="0" left="0" bottom="0">
    <s:fill>
      <s:SolidColor color="0x999999" />
    </s:fill>
    <s:stroke>
      <s:SolidColorStroke color="0x000000" />
    </s:stroke>
  </s:Rect>

  <s:HGroup width="100%" height="100%"
            horizontalAlign="center"
            paddingTop="10">
    <s:Button id="nextButton" label="Next"
              width="80" height="30" />
    <s:Button id="previousButton" label="Previous"
              width="80" height="30" />
  </s:HGroup>
</s:Skin>
```

The beauty of this separation is that you can literally create the layout of your dreams (within reason). You're still constrained to the dimensions of the component itself and to the skin parts that are required, but as you can see for this simple skin (and Figure 10.2), I also added a grey background and a black border by using the new graphical primitives in Flex 4.

Figure 10.2   Skin as rendered on our ExampleSkinnedComponent component

Declaring dynamic skin parts differs slightly from the static skin parts shown in the previous code example. The main difference is how you declare the dynamic skin part in your skin class. First, you need to wrap it in a `<fx:Component />` tag and place it in the `<fx:Declarations />` block. If you don't supply both of these, you get a runtime error. So instead of declaring the elements inline within the skin, they are kept separate. The downside of placing the dynamic skin part within the `<fx:Declarations />` tag block is that the skin has no idea where a new instance of this part should go. This means you need to add it to the display list as the code example from our component shows:

```
protected function createslideBreadcrumbBarItems():void
{
  // Check to see if there is more than one image to display.
  // If so create the breadcrumb items
  if(data.length > 1)
  {
    for(var i:uint = 0; i < data.length; ++i)
    {
      var _breadcrumbPip :Button = createDynamicPartInstance("slideBreadcrumbPip")
                              as Button;
      // Add our new skin part to the breadcrumbBar
      breadcrumbBar.addElement(breadcrumbPip);
    }
  }
}
```

As you can see I'm adding each new instance of my deferred skin part instance to a variable called `breadcrumbBar`, which is an `HGroup` in the skin class. The revised skin class example shows the `breadcrumbBar` and the dynamic skin part in the `<fx:Declarations/>` block:

```xml
<?xml version="1.0" encoding="utf-8"?>
<!--ExampleSkinnedComponentSkin.mxml -->
<s:Skin xmlns:fx="http://ns.adobe.com/mxml/2009"
        xmlns:s="library://ns.adobe.com/flex/spark"
        xmlns:mx="library://ns.adobe.com/flex/mx">

  <!-- host component -->
  <fx:Metadata>
    [HostComponent("com.developingcomponents.components.ExampleSkinnedComponent")]
  </fx:Metadata>

  <fx:Declarations>
    <fx:Component>
      <s:Button id="slideBreadcrumbPip"
                skinClass="com.developingcomponents.components.skins.
                breadcrumbPipSkin" />
    </fx:Component>
  </fx:Declarations>

  <s:Rect top="0" right="0" left="0" bottom="0">
    <s:fill>
      <s:SolidColor color="0x999999" />
    </s:fill>
    <s:stroke>
      <s:SolidColorStroke color="0x000000" />
    </s:stroke>
  </s:Rect>

  <s:HGroup width="100%" height="100%"
            horizontalAlign="center"
            paddingTop="10">
    <s:Button id="nextButton" label="Next"
              width="80" height="30" />
    <s:Button id="previousButton" label="Previous"
              width="80" height="30" />
  </s:HGroup>
  <s:HGroup id="breadcrumbBar" width=""100% bottom="10" />
</s:Skin>
```

Drawing Nonlinear Content

It's all well and good if you want to create components that are rectilinear in nature, but what if you want to create a skin for your component that is more fluid in its visual representation? If you need more control over a shape beyond a rectangle or ellipse, use the

`<s:Path />` tag, which enables you to draw nonlinear graphics that can be stroked, filled, and rendered. However, unlike most of the other FXG/MXMLG tags, drawing with paths isn't particularly user friendly so it is unlikely (but not beyond the bounds of reason) that you would write them by hand because of the syntactic complexity of the values needed to define nonlinear shapes. Take this example:

```
<?xml version="1.0" encoding="utf-8"?>
<s:Group xmlns:s="library://ns.adobe.com/flex/spark"
         xmlns:fx="http://ns.adobe.com/mxml/2009"
         width="300" height="300">

  <!-- draw the circle -->
  <s:Ellipse height="300" width="300" x="1.5" y="1.5">
    <s:fill>
      <s:SolidColor color="0xfcee21"/>
    </s:fill>
    <s:stroke>
      <s:SolidColorStroke caps="none" joints="miter"
                          miterLimit="4" weight="3"/>
          </s:stroke>
  </s:Ellipse>

  <!-- Draw the left eye -->
  <s:Path data="M 10.78 39.429 L 30.422 33.358 C 29.109 14.373 22.853
              -0.015 15.329 -0.015 C 6.851 -0.015 -0.022 18.246 -0.022 40.774
              C -0.022 63.301 6.851 81.563 15.329 81.563 C 23.51 81.563 30.194
              64.556 30.652 43.123 L 10.78 39.429 Z" winding="nonZero"
              x="166" y="75">

    <s:fill>
      <s:SolidColor/>
    </s:fill>
  </s:Path>
      <!-- Draw the right eye -->
      <s:Path data="M 10.821 39.429 L 30.463 33.358 C 29.15 14.373 22.894
              -0.015 15.37 -0.015 C 6.892 -0.015 0.019 18.246 0.019 40.774
              C 0.019 63.301 6.892 81.563 15.37 81.563 C 23.551 81.563 30.235
              64.556 30.693 43.123 L 10.821 39.429 Z" winding="nonZero"
              x="99" y="75">
  <s:fill>
    <s:SolidColor/>
  </s:fill>
  </s:Path>

  <!-- Draw the smile -->
  <s:Path data="M 62.784 44.639 C 29.845 39.313 4.874 20.192 2.534 -0.019
              C 1.507 2.184 0.764 4.496 0.372 6.921 C -3.302 29.636 23.613
```

```
                    52.884 60.486 58.847 C 97.359 64.811 130.23 51.232 133.904 28.517
                    C 134.296 26.093 134.32 23.663 134.039 21.249 C 125.448 39.693
                    95.722 49.967 62.784 44.639 Z" winding="nonZero" x="72" y="181">
        <s:fill>
          <s:SolidColor/>
        </s:fill>
      </s:Path>
  </s:Group>
```

This is a simple illustration of a smiley face brought into Flash Builder (see Figure 10.3). I highlighted a path tag so you can see how `<s:Path />` tags are not very user friendly if you look at the main attribute `data`. This holds all the information to draw, of all things, the left eye of the smiley face. The basic syntax for the `<s:Path />` tag is M (move), L (line), C (curve), and Z, which is the terminator character. In between any combination of these characters are the points on the stage based on the initial x and y position of the object. Think of this as using the drawing API in MXML (for example, `lineTo()` and `curveTo()`).

Figure 10.3   Smiley face drawn in FXG
using the <s:Path/> tag

Spark Skins and Halo Components

Although you are limited in what you can redefine, and more important, rearrange within a Halo component, it doesn't preclude you from using MXMLG to create your skins. You need to use one of the Halo-specific skin classes `SparkSkin` or `SparkSkinForHalo`. `SparkSkin` is the base skin class for Halo (mx) components, although you should use the `SparkSkinForHalo` as your root skin tag if your component defines a `border` because this class implements the ability to alter the `border` with the `errorColor` style when validation failure occurs. Here is a simple `SparkSkin` class for a Halo button component:

```
<?xml version="1.0" encoding="utf-8"?>
<s:SparkSkin xmlns:fx="http://ns.adobe.com/mxml/2009"
             xmlns:s="library://ns.adobe.com/flex/spark"
             xmlns:mx="library://ns.adobe.com/flex/mx">
```

```
<fx:Declarations>
  <s:AnimateColor id="transitionEffect"
                  targets="{[fillBG, strokeBG]}" duration="250" />
</fx:Declarations>

<s:states>
  <s:State name="up"/>
  <s:State name="over"/>
  <s:State name="down"/>
  <s:State name="disabled"/>
</s:states>

<s:transitions>
  <s:Transition fromState="up" toState="over"
                effect="{transitionEffect}"/>
  <s:Transition fromState="down" toState="over"
                effect="{transitionEffect}"/>
  <s:Transition fromState="over" toState="up"
                effect="{transitionEffect}"/>
  <s:Transition fromState="down" toState="up"
                effect="{transitionEffect}"/>
</s:transitions>

<s:Rect id="background" radiusX="4" radiusY="4"
        width="100%" height="100%">
  <s:fill>
    <s:SolidColor id="fillBG" color="0x666666"
                  color.over="0x999999"
                  color.down="0x888888" />
  </s:fill>
  <s:stroke>
    <s:SolidColorStroke id="strokeBG"
                        color="0x333333"
                        color.over="0x666666"
                        pixelHinting="true"/>
  </s:stroke>
</s:Rect>
</s:SparkSkin>
```

I also included some transitions and associated effects within the skin so that you can
see how to chain effects to state changes. In this example, the `AnimateColor` effect animates the color values of both the fill and the stroke on the Button component when the
button changes from state to state:

```
<fx:Declarations>
  <s:AnimateColor id="transitionEffect"
                  targets="{[fillBG, strokeBG]}" duration="250" />
</fx:Declarations>
```

```
<s:transitions>
  <s:Transition fromState="up" toState="over"
                effect="{transitionEffect}"/>
  <s:Transition fromState="down" toState="over"
                effect="{transitionEffect}"/>
  <s:Transition fromState="over" toState="up"
                effect="{transitionEffect}"/>
  <s:Transition fromState="down" toState="up"
                effect="{transitionEffect}"/>
</s:transitions>
```

Working with Properties and Styles

The previous section mentioned the usefulness of the [HostComponent] tag and its relationship between the skin and the host component. This is so important because it deals with how you access and apply properties and values from within the host component to your skin; generally, this will be through the styles assigned to your component via CSS.

If you inherit from SkinnableComponent, you don't need to do anything because the style properties are passed to your component at runtime. You do need to create a set of default values for your component styles, however; otherwise, any color styles will default to black. This is simple to do: Just add the relevant style properties to the constructor of the component, just like you saw when the skin itself was associated with the component.

```
public function ExampleSkinnedComponent()
{
  super();
  setStyle("skinClass", ExampleSkinnedComponentSkin);
}
```

Using CSS

So far, you've seen how to define skins for your components and set values for the relevant skin parts. You've also seen how easy it is to pass styles assigned to your components to the associated skin class.

Next, we discuss how to link this all together with external Cascading Style Sheets. This is especially useful if you are developing composite components and want to use descendant selectors on your components.

Custom Namespaces

First, let's talk about namepsaces. Because the Flex framework supports more than one component framework, CSS in Flex 4 requires the use of namespaces. The reason for this is to easily separate out components that potentially have the same class name or are in a different package. By default, when you create a new CSS file, Flash Builder automatically adds the namespaces for Spark and Halo, but you need to add a `namespace` for each package that you want to declare CSS entries for. So, if you have two packages that contain components that can be styled, you need to do something similar to this:

```
/* Added by Flash Builder automatically */
@namespace s "library://ns.adobe.com/flex/spark";
@namespace mx "library://ns.adobe.com/flex/mx";

/* Defining namespaces for custom components */
@namespace comp "com.developingcomponents.components.spark.*";
@namespace mxcomp "com.developingcomponents.components.halo.*";
```

Although the two namespaces don't necessarily contain components with the same class names because they are in different packages, they need to be added to the CSS file so that they can be declared.

When declaring a new namespace, make sure it only contains letters and numbers and doesn't contain any special characters (beyond hyphens and underscores) or spaces. You can mix case if you want; I follow the common naming conventions of all lowercase unless I'm concatenating two words together, where I prefer to capitalize the additional word. Some prefer to use an underscore or hyphen as the word separator, but you can decide which you prefer.

Descendant Selectors

Looking back at the `ExampleSkinnedComponent`, recall that it had two buttons as part of its design. At the moment, these don't have any styling beyond the default style sheet. To assign styling to these two buttons, we can leverage the new CSS descendant selectors. This allows you to define a style for your component's children. So, for the example we skinned earlier, I added some styling information for the buttons as a descendant selector in the CSS.

```
comp|ExampleSkinnedComponent
{
  backgroundColor: #ff0000;
  borderColor: #000000;
}

comp|ExampleSkinnedComponent s|Button
{
  skinClass:
  ClassReference("com.developingcomponents.components.skins.ExampleButtonSkin");
}
```

As you can see, it is simple to define the skin class (and any other style properties) on subcomponents within your components without having to resort to convoluted routines to set the internal styles of your components.

ID Selectors

If you want to change the style of one of these buttons, you need to approach it in a slightly different manner and use ID selectors:

```
comp|ExampleSkinnedComponent #nextButton
{
  skinClass:
  ClassReference("com.developingcomponents.components.skins.NextButtonSkin");
}
```

Here, I added another skin class but, this time, it is only for the `nextButton` within the `ExampleSkinnedComponent`. To do this, set the style property on the child component, so in this case, when the `partAdded()` method is called, I add the following so that I can apply the relevant style if needed:

```
nextButton.styleName = "nextButton";
```

Implementing the style ID selector this way means that, if you don't declare it, the next button falls back on any descendant selectors that have been declared for the more generic Button skin class.

The final aspect of CSS selectors that I want to cover are the aptly name pseudo selectors.

Pseudo Selectors

Pseudo selectors enable you to define styling based on a component's skin states. This makes it easy to add styling to the component based on the state it is currently in. These CSS declarations apply only when the component is in the associated state and are transient in nature because they do not persist and are removed over time.

```
s|Button:up
{
  chromeColor: #ffcc00;
}

s|Button:over
{
  chromeColor: #ff3300;
}

s|Button:down
{
  chromeColor: #ff6600;
}
```

Summary

This chapter showed you how to add skin support to your Spark-based components by extending them from `SkinnableComponent` or a subclass. You also saw how to implement the `partAdded()`, `partRemoved()`, and `getCurrentSkinState()` methods.

You also saw that, although Halo components don't provide the same level of configuration, you can use FXG/MXMLG to create an associated skin for most Halo components by extending their skin classes from `SparkSkin` or `SparkSkinForHalo` classes.

Finally, we saw how to externalize your skin association and additional styling values through the use of CSS, specifically through the use of descendant, ID, and pseudo selectors.

Creating Flex Components with Flash Professional CS5

There comes a time where you might want to get more visually creative with your component development and decide that creating programmatic skins, styles, or graphical elements for your Flex-based components isn't quite enough.

For those of you who are familiar with using Flash Professional, you can easily create your components in the Flash IDE and convert them so that they can be integrated into your Flex applications.

Picking a Starting Point

Interestingly, you can use a couple of routes to begin developing components in Flash Professional. (I use CS5, and I just refer to it as Flash Professional. You can achieve the same results in Flash CS4 and CS3, but you need to download and install the Flex Component Kit from Adobe's website; see Appendix A, "Flex Resources," for the link.)

Although the overall process isn't that different, you can choose from two distinct starting points. The first starting point is directly from Flash Professional, which, although more labor intensive, gives you a better understanding of how to create a Flex component from scratch. Also, it doesn't require you to have Flash Builder installed. The second starting point is driven from Flash Builder 4, through to Flash Professional, and back again. So, it provides a cleaner workflow, but it requires that you have both Flash Builder 4 and Flash Professional installed. As they say, no pain, no gain, so let's start with the more detailed Flash Professional approach.

Starting with Flash Professional

Fire up Flash Professional, open a new ActionScript 3.0 FLA file, and save it with the name `SimpleFlashComponent.fla`. I am saving this in the `assets` directory that I created in the root of my Flex project. After the file is saved, you can create your Flash component. Create a new `MovieClip` symbol and call it `SimpleFlashComponent`.

(The filename and symbol name are mutually exclusive, so there is no technical reason that requires you to give them the same name. I just did for consistency.)

At this point, you have nothing but a common or garden Flash symbol, so we need to convert this to one that includes the relevant hooks that enable you to integrate it within the Flex framework. Fortunately, this is as simple as clicking a button—no honestly, it is. To do this, just open the Commands drop down in Flash's main menu, and choose Convert Symbol to Flex Component, as Figure 11.1 shows.

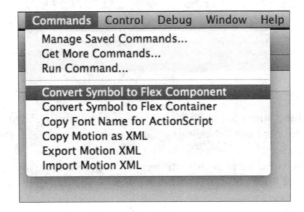

Figure 11.1   Choose Convert Symbol to Flex Component
to update your symbol.

As soon as you click this entry, a few things happen. First, a component called FlexComponentBase is copied into the root of the symbol library; you may remember it from Chapter 10, "Skinning and Styling," and the Output window opens and lists a few behind-the-scenes changes that have been performed on the file. Figure 11.2 shows you the output.

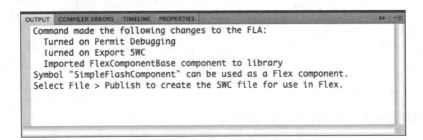

Figure 11.2   Behind-the-scenes updates to your file

Starting with Flash Builder 4

Flash Builder 4 takes some of the more manual processes out of the process covered in the section, "Starting with Flash Professional," and, for the most part, you are likely to use this workflow more often than just firing up Flash Professional and starting from scratch. The first thing to do is open any MXML file in Flash Builder and switch to design view. From design view, the components panel opens and you see a folder called Custom, which contains two entries that are prefixed with the words Flash Professional (as shown in Figure 11.3). These two basic component types are used within the Flex framework: those that are a self-contained component and those that can contain other components as defined by the developer at author time: container. These are currently just placeholders ready to add functionality and visuals via Flash Professional.

Figure 11.3   Flash Professional component
markers in the component's panel

Select and drag an instance of the Flash Professional component to the design view and drop it in place. As soon as you drop the component, the Property panel updates to display the common attributes of your Flash component placeholder, and you see a button that reads Create in Flash Professional, as shown in Figure 11.4.

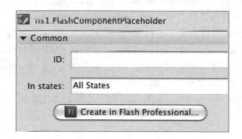

Figure 11.4   Create in Flash Professional button lets you
create/edit your component in Flash Professional.

After you click the button, a dialog titled New Adobe Flash Component opens in the middle of the design view. Here, you can set the class name and the name of the SWC

that will be created. Place `SimpleFlashComponent` in the class name and
`SimpleFlashComponent.swc` in the SWC file name,[1] as shown in Figure 11.5.

Figure 11.5   Set the Class Name and the SWC File
Name for your new Flash component.

At this point, Flash Professional opens and you now see a new FLA file with a gray
rectangle in the middle of the stage. Feel free to delete this gray rectangle, because it is
purely there as a marker and serves no purpose. If you open the symbol library, you can
see that our `FlexComponentBase` component has been copied into it and a symbol with
the same name as the class you supplied has been created. The FLA file has also been
named based on the value you supplied for the SWC. One thing you may not have
noticed yet, however, is that there is a button in the top left of the stage area that reads
Done. This is how we go back to Flash Builder. Clicking this saves the FLA file, compiles
the SWC, and places it back in the `libs` folder in Flash Builder for us. Pretty neat, huh?

Where Has Flash Builder Put the Source Files?

As you may recall, I suggested that you create a folder called assets in the root of your
Flex project. That's fine and dandy for components you have created from beginning to
end in Flash Professional, but what about the ones that are created as part of the Flash
Builder/Flash Professional CS5 workflow? Well, it should come as no surprise that these
are put in a folder called assets in the root of the Flex project you started the process in.
Hence, the insistence on the folder name earlier. Believe me, this may seem like

---

[1] If you already created the SimpleFlashComponent.fla in the section, "Starting with Flash
Professional," you need to provide a different class and SWC name; otherwise, Flash Professional
opens that FLA file instead of the newly created one. There is no real difference between the files
they each create, but to see the Flash Builder/Flash Professional workflow in operation, it is worth
giving it an alternative name. The rest of the information in this chapter works with an FLA created by
either process.

superfluous information now, but it took me several minutes to work out where Flash Builder had placed the FLAs within my Flex project.

Is That All There Is to Create a Component with Flash?

Yes, that is pretty much the entire Flash Builder / Flash Professional component work-flow. Obviously, you now need to add the functionality that you require for your component to operate as envisioned; but to actually create a component in Flash Professional that works with the Flex framework, you just need to follow those steps.

Regardless of which process you choose to employ, a few things have happened that you need to be aware of. First, your component symbol now has a base class of `mx.flash.UIMovieClip` and has had its frame rate set to 24fps. For any component created in Flash Professional to function correctly in the Flex framework, its base class must be `UIMovieClip` or a subclass thereof.

`UIMovieClip` extends `MovieClip` and implements the following interfaces from the Flex framework: `IToolTipMangerClient`, `IDeferredInstanceUIComponent`, `IStateClient`, `IConstraintClient`, and `IFocusManagerComponent`. These are implemented because they provide the majority of the hooks required for a Flash Professional component to function within the Flex framework, be that as a skin or as a component. These hooks enable you to set Tooltips, both internally and externally, and enable your component to be instantiated immediately or as part of a deferred instantiation, as we saw with `Template` components in Chapter 3, "Anatomy of a Component." It also enables Flex to set the layout of the component based on the traditional width, height settings and through layout constraints. In addition, it provides the inputs within your component so that it can respond and react to focus events. Last but no least, it provides access to the setting and managing of view states, which we look at next. Before we do, however, let's cover a few quirks when creating components in Flash Professional.

Limitations

Be aware of a few limitations when creating components in Flash Professional for use in Flex. These aren't showstoppers, but if you aren't aware of them, they can eat your time as you try and "fix" them when they aren't actually broken.

First, you can't apply zoom effects to Flash-authored components; you need to wrap them in a Flex `<s:Group/>` or another such container.

I already mentioned this, but just to make sure it isn't missed again: Flex uses x/y coordinates based on the top-left point of a component. Therefore, make sure your registration point is set to top left when you create your components in Flash.

If you created a container component in Flash (which we looking at shortly), and you need to modify any visual characteristics (like the alpha value, for example), you need to embed the fonts used by the child Flex components that are held within it; otherwise, they will be inconsistent when rendered.

Finally, if you enable tabbing in your Flash component and want to override the Flash Player's default yellow bounding box when a focused element is selected, you have to handle the `focusIn` and `focusOut` events of each Flash symbol. However, in a container component, only the Flex components contained within the content area can receive focus, because they use the standard Flex highlighting to indicate when an item is selected.

Implementing States

Although the concept of view states should be fairly familiar, the idea of implementing them in Flash may seem difficult to visualize. Funny enough, they are probably far easier to create in Flash than they are in Flex. To define a state in a Flash component, you only need to add a label to a specific frame. So, if you want to have a state for a Flash component called "open" and another called "close," you simply create two frames and give them the relevant label of either "open" or "close." Then, all you need to do is add the relevant symbols to your component to reflect those states. Take the example shown in Figure 11.6.

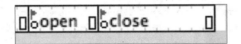

Figure 11.6   Setting frame labels corresponds
to states when referenced in Flex.

Bear in mind that you don't actually want to place any state frame labels on the first frame of your component because this will be likely be your default state. Also, don't forget to place a `stop()` action in the first frame so that you don't accidentally play any transitions or states. One thing I want to point out about states in components created in Flash Professional is that they do not support implied state names. By this, I mean that you cannot call the following to return to the default state, like you would in Flex:

```
myComponent.currentState = "";
```

This seems to have to do with how `UIMovieClip` determines state frame labels to frame numbers within the compiled component. You can't set an empty frame label; by default, all frames contain empty frame labels if you follow my twisted logic. The easiest way to get around this is to call your default frame `normal` or `default`, like the Flex 4 state model docs.

Now that you've seen the theory, let's get into the practical. If you switch back to the `SimpleFlashComponent.fla` file, enter edit mode for the symbol of the same name you created earlier and add the following:

- Rename the current layer to `States`.
- Add additional key frames so you have a total of 15 key frames.
- Give frame 1 a frame label of `default`.

- On frame 5, add a new blank key and give it the frame label open.
- On frame 10, add a new blank key frame and set the frame label to close.

Your layer should now look similar to Figure 11.6. If it does, save the file, because next, we look at how to implement transitions.

Implementing Transitions

Implementing transitions is similar to implementing view states. All you need to do is provide the animation that you want to be played when the state changes. To do this, add a special set of frame labels that conform to the startState-endState and suffix it with either start or end.

For example, if you want to have an animation play from the open state to the close state, you need to add a frame label, like the one shown here, at the start of the animation:

open-close:start

Likewise, to let Flex know where this animation ends, you need to add the complementary end label at the end of the animation:

open-close:end

This way, when you change the currentState value of your component in Flex from open to close, Flex looks for the frame label open-close:start and plays the animation until it hits the open-close:end label and then switches the state to close. When you set the currentState from close to open, Flex does one of two things: It first examines the component to see if there are frame labels close-open:start and close-open:end and, if there are, it plays the corresponding animation within them. If, however, it doesn't find those specific labels, it just plays the open-close animation in reverse. That way, if you want to use the same animation for both state changes, you need to define only one set, and Flex just plays it in reverse for the other.

You can also define a wildcard (*) within your label names, just like you can use the wildcard symbol in Flex to switch between states. However, Flex has a specific order in which it checks the component label names for these.

First, it checks to see if there is a set of labels marking an animation between the current state and the target state (startState-endState:start startState-endState:end); if not, it checks to see if there is a reversed set of frame labels. If neither of these is present, it then looks for a single wildcard for the startState part of the frame label. Likewise, if this isn't found, it looks for the reverse. Again, if neither of these are found, it checks to see if there are frame labels where the endState part of the frame label is a wildcard, both normal and reversed. Finally, if it doesn't find any of those permutations, it looks for a frame label where both the startState and endState are wildcards. For ease of reference, the order is shown here:

- `startState-endState` (normal)
- `endState-startState` (reversed)
- `*-endState` (normal)
- `endState-*` (reversed)
- `startState-*` (normal)
- `*-startState` (reversed)
- `*-*`

When you use timeline animations, for transitions, as obvious as this may sound, make sure that you keep your transitions separate from your states. Otherwise, you can get unpredictable results when playing the transition for one particular state to another. I suggest grouping your animations at the end of your timeline, and don't feel that you have to use a single frame to hold your state—add a few blank frames to each one, because they won't be affected by the play head as these additional frames are never played. This way, you can see the frame labels should you need to come back to your components at a later date (see Figure 11.7). Obviously, the number of transition frames dictates the speed at which the transition animation is played, based on the fact that Flex components have a default frame rate of 24fps. Keep this in mind when you create your transitions.

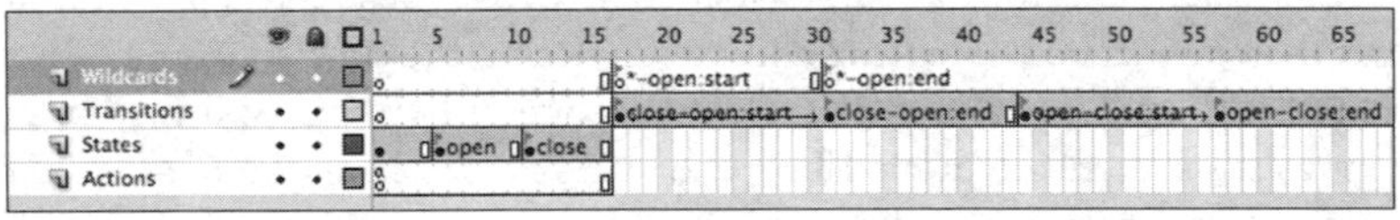

Figure 11.7   Keeping the timeline organized and legible

To access those state labels in Flex, all you need to do is set the `currentState` variable for the component to the new state name. The following MXML sets the state on the component states previously shown:

```
<?xml version="1.0" encoding="utf-8"?>
<s:Application xmlns:fx="http://ns.adobe.com/mxml/2009"
               xmlns:s="library://ns.adobe.com/flex/spark"
               xmlns:mx="library://ns.adobe.com/flex/mx"
               xmlns:components="com.developingcomponents.components.*">

    <components:TransitionStateExampleComponent id="tse" x="200" y="200" />
    <s:Button id="Open" label="Set State 'open'"
            click="tse.currentState='open'"   x="10" y="40"/>

    <s:Button id="Close" label="Set State 'closed'"
            click="tse.currentState='close'"   x="10" y="10"/>
</s:Application>
```

It's time for you to switch back to your `SimpleFlashComponent` symbol. This time, you add a set of transitions to the component:

1. Add a new layer and call it **Transitions**.

2. Make the new layer 70 frames long.

3. Add a blank key frame to this layer at frame 16 and give it the frame label `close-open:start`.

4. Add another blank key frame at frame 30 and give it the frame label `close-open:end`.

5. On frame 45, create a new blank key frame and give it the frame label `open-close:start`.

6. Add a blank key frame at frame 60 and set the frame label to `open-close:end`.

7. Now add another new layer. Position this one above the Transitions layer and call it **Wildcards**.

8. On frame 16, add a blank key frame and set its frame label to `*-open:start`.

9. On frame 30, add a blank key frame and give it the value of `*-open:end` as the frame label.

If you're not sure if it's correct, look at Figure 11.7. Yours should look almost identical except for the animated transitions, which are present in the image. Let's sort those out next.

Now we have the transitions and states in place, all that is left to do is add the transition animations and the default graphics for each state (including the default state). Before we get into that, however, let's talk about managing the resizing of your Flash component.

Controlling Component Resizing

One thing that you may want to consider when you create components in Flash is what happens if your component size changes because of an effect or animation you have defined within your component. Normally, Flex uses the default size of your component as the size of it at runtime; if its size changes, Flex resizes it to make sure that it doesn't accidentally overlap other components in the UI.

This may not be what you want to happen and, if it occurs regularly, it could prove detrimental to the application's performance that the component is used in. To avoid this, you can define a bounding box in Flash and use that to indicate to Flex when it should take over the resizing responsibilities. As long as any effects, animations, or tweens remain within the boundaries of the bounding box clip, Flex ignores the changes to the component. As soon as it extends beyond those boundaries, Flex steps in to retain a cohesive layout with any other components.

Bounding Boxes

To define a bounding box for your Flash component, you need to create a `MovieClip` assign it a layer within your component symbol, and give it the instance name of `boundingBox`. Alternatively, you can access the `boundingBoxName` property of the `UIMovieClip` class and assign a symbol to that. In most cases, the former is the easiest and quickest way to implement a bounding box for your component. Don't worry if it is visible in your symbol while you create your component in Flash, because Flex automatically sets its visibility to false so it cannot be seen when compiled.

When using bounding boxes, something to consider is to avoid using one that is larger than the overall initial visual size of your component. Otherwise, you will have a lot of white space around it when Flex lays it out for the first time. Take the example in Figure 11.8: The first component (a simple blue lozenge) has been laid out as expected, as its default size is the same as its bounding box. However, if you look at the second component, you see a large amount of white space below it (tinted gray to show the dimensions of the bounding box), as the default visual size is smaller than the actual bounding box that has been associated with it.

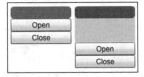

Figure 11.8   Bounding boxes sometimes have a
negative effect on layout (boundingBox tinted
to show impact on layout)

External Manipulation

Now, if you resize your component internally, you can dispatch an event (custom or a relevant one from the built-in event packages) to notify Flex that your component is resizing, and Flex takes care of the rest of the layout that may be impacted by the change in dimensions. However, what do you do if you change the size of your component from Flex from, say, a button component? Well, the answer is that you don't need to do anything. The following code illustrates this point. Here, we have a Flash Professional authored component called `grayBox`, and our Flex button just resizes the component and updated the layout as expected. In fact, the `greyBox` component contains no custom code whatsoever. I merely created the placeholder, altered the placeholder rectangle in Flash Professional, and saved it back to Flash Builder.

```
<fx:Script>
  <![CDATA[
    protected function btn_clickHandler(event:MouseEvent):void
    {
```

```
      grayBox.height = 500;
    }
  ]]>
</fx:Script>

<dfc:GrayBox id="grayBox"/>
<s:Button id="btn" label="Resize Box" click="btn_clickHandler(event)"/>
```

If you want more control over how your component handles resizing, you can override the `setActualSize()` method within your component and tailor what your component does when it is resized by Flex. The advantages of overriding this method is that you can deal with any layout issues that may arise should the component be resized disproportionally or to a size that is out of operational bounds (too small, for example). The following code snippet shows a `setActualSize()` method that has been overridden because this particular component can only function if its size is greater than width 200 and height 200. If it falls below that, it displays a simple error view state within the component to notify the developer that its operational bounds have been reached.

```
package com.developingcomponents.components
{
  import mx.flash.UIMovieClip;

  public class ErrorComponent extends UIMovieClip
  {
    private static const MINIMUM_WIDTH     :Number = 200;
    private static const MINIMUM_HEIGHT    :Number = 200;

    private static const ERROR_VIEW        :String = "error";
    private static const DEFAULT_VIEW      :String = "default";

    public function ErrorComponent()
    {
    }

    override public function setActualSize(newWidth:Number,
                                           newHeight:Number):void
    {
      var _error    :Boolean = false;

      if (newWidth != _width || newHeight != _height)
      {
        _width = newWidth;
        _height = newHeight;

        if(newWidth < MINIMUM_WIDTH)
        {
          _width = MINIMUM_WIDTH;
```

```
       _error = true;
    }

    if(newHeight < MINIMUM_HEIGHT)
    {
      _height = MINIMUM_HEIGHT;
      _error = true;
    }
  }
  currentState = (_error)? ERROR_VIEW : DEFAULT_VIEW;
  }
 }
}
```

Obviously, this is a literal implementation, but you can see that, by overriding this method, you have more granular control over how your component reacts when Flex manipulates its dimensions, as shown in Figure 11.9. Here, the component has reset its dimensions to 200x200 pixels and is showing its error message.

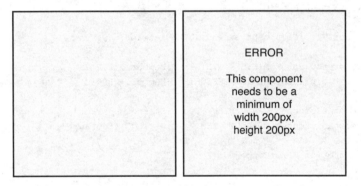

Figure 11.9   Same component, the second showing an error
message because its dimensions were below 200px

Creating Component Visual Assets

Although you can happily use ActionScript to create your graphical assets, it defeats the point of using Flash to create your components if you don't capitalize on the ability to actually draw your graphical elements. If you are going to create any assets that can be resized but you don't want them to get distorted, make sure that you enable 9 scale slicing on the symbol. This process is identical to the steps detailed in Chapter 10; in fact, we use the same steps to create a background to use in this component.

Putting It All Together

Now that you've had all the theory, let's make the component; it is nothing more than a hollow shell at the moment. The first thing is to draw a rectangle in Flash: Make it about 200x200 pixels and give it rounded corners—a radius of 8 is fine. You can fill it with any color you like; like the previous example, I colored this square light grey and added a border. After you are happy with its size, convert it into a symbol and give it the name `Background`. Remember to pay attention to the registration point when you do. Make sure it is set to top left, as Figure 11.10 shows.

Figure 11.10   Making sure the registration point
is set to the correct option

If you accidentally forget to set the registration point, you can still align the rectangle to 0,0 within its symbol. If you do need to do this, open the Properties panel and set the x and y values to 0. You also need to check the Enable Guides for 9-Slice Scaling (refer to Figure 11.10). This turns on the guide markers within the symbol.[2] With the guides active, move each of them so that they are on a straight edge, but as close to the beginning of a corner curve as possible, as Figure 11.11 shows.

I placed the guides 5 pixels from each edge. Zoom into the graphic to make it easier to place the guides, because this can be fiddly, even with the rulers on. After you're happy with the placement of your guides, exit the edit screen of your component and save the file.

Now that the symbol is finished, you can use this as the basis for the three states of the component, the default state, and the open and close states. For the default and the close states, I resized the panel symbol to 40 pixels. So, drag an instance of the Background symbol out and place it in each of the state key frames on the Timeline (which we added to the States layer). Resize the panel to 40 pixels for both the default (the first frame state) and the close state. Make sure that each one is positioned so that its x and y are set to 0,0 within the component symbol.

---

[2] If you didn't enable 9-slice scaling, you can turn it on by opening the properties of the symbol by right-clicking it in the Symbol library and selecting Properties.

Figure 11.11   Panel symbol with the scale 9
guides in place

Adding the Transition Animations

Next, add the transition animations that will play when your component switches from one state to another. I leave you to do the hard work of making the actual tweens, but what I did was create the following animations between these frame labels:

- **close-open:start/close-open:end:** The panel starts at 40 pixels and ends at 200 pixels.

- **open-close:start/open-close:end:** The panel starts at 200 pixels and ends at 40 pixels.

Simple, really. There's not much more to transition animations. Feel free to be more creative if you want—these examples only give you insight into how the process works.

Properties and Methods

Something you want to do is provide properties that can be written to or read from. The same goes for methods. Bear in mind that anything that you place on the stage within the symbol, if it has an instance name, can be accessed. This isn't always ideal, because you may not want something to be publically accessible. One solution is to wrap that element within another symbol. This moves it one level deeper within the symbol so it won't be automatically picked up when it is converted into a SWC. Or you can use ActionScript to create the assets in the first frame of your main component symbol. The only downside to this is that you cannot declare the access modifiers.

A cleaner solution is to use ActionScript to declare and even manage those variables and assets that you want to keep private. So, you can either opt to bury your assets inside other MovieClips—to shield them—so that they aren't easily accessible, or you can use an external class and define the properties that you want to make public. I opt for the latter of the two, because I like to keep the class files separate. The added advantage is that they use the package name as the identifier in Flex Builder, so if they are in a folder called components, that's the name of the namespace that Flex Builder uses to reference them; it doesn't use local, like you get if you let Flash create the class for your component on the fly.

Adding methods to your component is the same as adding methods to any other Flash symbol or class. Just declare them and provide the relevant access modifier and parameters and wire it in to your component as required. A word to the wise: Like standard Flex components, you can't access methods from the attribute list in MXML. So, if you want to use them as the default set of parameters that are accessible in MXML, either change them to public variables or accessors and mutators (getter/setters) so that they can be easily exposed in MXML as attributes.

Metadata

Like Flex, you can use the `[Bindable]` tag within your Flash components to allow the binding of values to and from your component, including triggering the binding via custom events. This is useful if you want to provide a visual feedback mechanism to a user when the data changes within your application's model or within the component itself. In the `SimpleFlashComponent` example, I use it to bind the `title` getter/setter in the component so that it can be changed, and the result is immediately reflected. Here is code taken directly from the first frame of the `SimpleFlashComponent` symbol:

```
// Start frame based code
stop();

[Bindable]
function get title():String
{
  return _title.text;
}

function set title (value:String):void
{
  _title.text = value;
}

[Inspectable(defaultValue="false", enumeration="true,false")]
var startOpen    :Boolean = true;
```

Remember that, although [Bindable] will function as expected, [Inspectable] doesn't respond at all when used within code on the actual timeline. To enable the [Inspectable] tag, you need to use an external ActionScript class linked to your component symbol. Honestly, as soon as you go beyond the basic layout of your component, you should realistically replace the class reference in the symbol's properties panel with that of an externalized class, because it makes adding programmatic functionality far easier.

Events

If you want to provide custom events for your component, you can easily create them in the same way you would for a Flex-based component and include metadata tags within the component's class file to indicate to Flash Builder that your component supports a specific event. For example, here is a simple SimpleFlashComponentEvent:

```
package com.developingcomponents.events
{
  import flash.events.Event;

  public class SimpleFlashComponentEvent extends Event
  {
    public static const OPEN        :String = "open";
    public static const CLOSE       :String = "close";
    public static const OPENING     :String = "opening";
    public static const CLOSING     :String = "closing";

    public function SimpleFlashComponentEvent (type:String,
                                          bubbles:Boolean=false,
                                          cancelable:Boolean=false)
    {
      super(type, bubbles, cancelable);
    }

    override public function clone():Event
    {
      return new SimpleFlashComponentEvent(type, bubbles, cancelable);
    }
  }
}
```

You can then add a metadata tag to the top of your component's class to indicate that it dispatches this event, as the following code illustrates. I highlighted the method that dispatches the event, just so you can see how it relates to the metadata tag at the top of the class. If you're still fuzzy about how the metadata relates to the actual event, go back to Chapter 7, "Working with Metadata," and Chapter 8, "Events and Event Handling," to refresh your memory.

```
package com.developingcomponents.components
{
  import com.developingcomponents.events.SimpleFlashComponentEvent;

  import mx.flash.UIMovieClip;

  [Event(name="open",
         type="com.developingcomponents.events. SimpleFlashComponentEvent")]
  [Event(name="close",
         type="com.developingcomponents.events. SimpleFlashComponentEvent ")]
  [Event(name="opening",
         type="com.developingcomponents.events. SimpleFlashComponentEvent ")]
  [Event(name="closing",
         type="com.developingcomponents.events. SimpleFlashComponentEvent ")]

  public class SimpleFlashComponent extends UIMovieClip
  {
    public function SimpleFlashComponent()
    {
    }

    protected function dispatchSimpleFlashComponentEvent ():void
    {
      dispatchEvent(new SimpleFlashComponentEvent(
                    SimpleFlashComponentEvent.OPEN));
    }
  }
}
```

If you have more than one event type that your event can dispatch, you just need to add in the additional event metadata tags for each event type, as you can see in the code. If you omit the metadata, it doesn't affect the event dispatching—it just means that Flash Builder won't offer code hinting when implementing your component in MXML. Therefore, you can't take advantage of the natty handler generation it offers.

Externalizing Component Classes

As mentioned in the last section, certain aspects of component development in Flash Professional don't function as expected when placed within the actual timeline—the [Inspectable] metadata tag for one. To fix this, you need to externalize your ActionScript into a separate class file. To do this, place the fully qualified path of the class you are linking to the symbol in the class field.[3] (Remember that the class must have

---

[3] To access a symbol's linkage information, select the symbol in the Symbol Library, right-click to open the context menu, and click the Properties entry.

the same name as the symbol to which you are attaching it.) Next, you can delete the `Base class` reference below it; as soon as you link your symbol to an external class, it no longer uses the `Base class` reference within the properties panel, so to avoid confusion, I delete it entirely. The revised linkage information within the Properties panel should look similar to Figure 11.12.

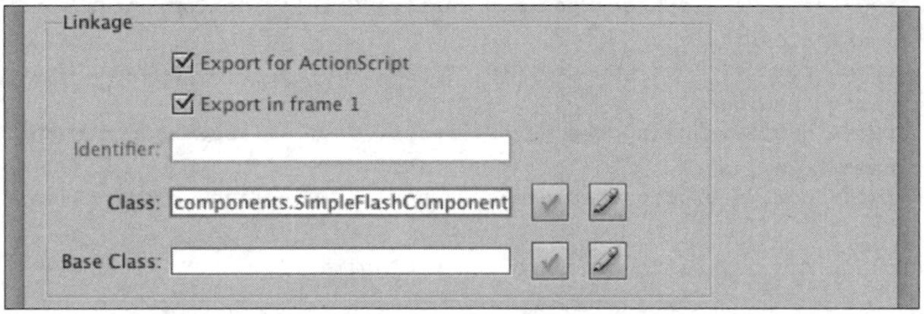

Figure 11.12   Linkage information of a symbol that uses an external class

When externalizing classes, if you place your classes in packages, you should use the same folder that contains your FLAs as the root of your package structure. If you copied my suggestion from earlier, this will be in a folder called `assets` that is located within the root of your Flex project. You can then just reference them by full package name, and you don't have to worry about updating the class paths within Flash Professional. Remember that you still need to create the folder structure to reflect the package path within your `assets` directory, just as you would for a class in the `src` directory of your Flex project.

After you link your external ActionScript class, you just need to make sure it extends from `UIMovieClip` and add the relevant properties and methods as required. Here is the source for the `SimpleFlashComponent`, detailing all the aspects we have discussed.

```
package com.developingcomponents.components
{
  import com.developingcomponents.events.SimpleFlashComponentEvent;

  import mx.flash.UIMovieClip;

  [Event(name="open",
         type="com.developingcomponents.events. SimpleFlashComponentEvent")]
  [Event(name="close",
         type="com.developingcomponents.events. SimpleFlashComponentEvent ")]
  public class SimpleFlashComponent extends UIMovieClip
  {
    public function SimpleFlashComponent()
    {
      super();
    }
```

```
protected function dispatchOpenEvent():void
{
  dispatchEvent(new SimpleFlashComponentEvent(
                SimpleFlashComponentEvent.OPEN));
}

protected function dispatchCloseEvent():void
{
  dispatchEvent(new SimpleFlashComponentEvent(
                SimpleFlashComponentEvent.CLOSE));
}

public function get title():String
{
  return componentTitle.text;
}

public function set title(value:String):void
{
  componentTitle.text = value;
}

[Inspectable(defaultValue="true", enumeration="true,false")]
public function get closed():Boolean
{
  return _closed;
}

public function set closed(value:Boolean):void
{
  _closed = value;
}
  }
}
```

Now that you have externalized your class for the component, the `[Inspectable]` metadata tag functions as expected when placed on a property or accessor. So, when your component is compiled into a SWC and imported into Flex Builder, the tag parameters appear as expected, as shown in Figure 11.13.

Note

This source code functions, but the events are not linked in. Why not link the dispatching of the open and close events to their respective view states?

If you're not sure where to start, think about using `currentState` and the events that are fired by state changes.

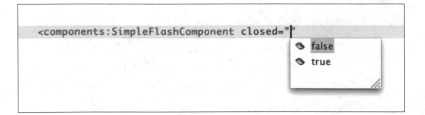

Figure 11.13   Inspectable tag operating correctly in Flash Builder

Container Components

The process for creating container components in Flash Professional is almost identical to that of the standard components we have been looking at. To create them, just follow one of the two processes that are detailed at the beginning of this chapter, either working completely in Flash Professional or as part of the Flash Builder/Flash Professional work-flow. Either way, start by selecting a Container component—in Flash Professional, this is from the same drop-down you used earlier to create a standard component and, in Flash Builder, you just drag a Flash Professional Container placeholder onto the design view and precede as before. Either way, set the component's name to `SimpleFlashContainer`.

The reason there is a different option for creating container components is because Flash needs to add additional components to your symbol library to provide the container functionality.

Besides `FlexComponentBase`, a Container component also includes an additional symbol called `FlexContentHolder` (see Figure 11.14), which is an instance of `mx.flash.FlexContentHolder`, which in turn inherits from `ContainerMovieClip`.

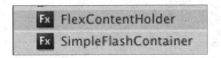

Figure 11.14   FlexContentHolder symbol, used
to define the content area of your component

If you use the Flash Builder/Flash Professional workflow, it creates the component symbol and placea the `FlexContentHolder` symbol within it. If you create it directly in Flash Professional, you need to do this yourself by dragging it from the symbol library and adding it to your main component symbol.

Your component also needs to have the base class property set to
`mx.flash.ContainerMovieClip`, not `UIMovieClip`. `ContentMovieClip` inherits
from `UIMovieClip` and provides additional support for displaying visual elements by
implementing `IVisualElementContainer`. This provides the support necessary for displaying Spark components within your container component.

As `ContainerMovieClip` inherits from `UIMovieClip`, it also supports all the same
functionality that a standard component does. It can include view states, effects, and
respond to events, and hold and display child components. However, there is a caveat with
that last point. The way that this class is structured, it can contain only one `IUIComponent`
child. If you do try manipulating the contents of your container component by invoking
`addElement()`, `addElementAt()`, `removeElement()`, `removeElementAt()`,
`removeAllElements()`, `swapElement()`, `swapElementAt()`, or `setElementIndex()`, you
get an argument error because these are not supported.

This may seem limiting, but that child can be a Flex container or group, so in reality, it
can hold numerous children, but only through a layer of separation, and you can freely
make those calls on that container. The following code shows how you would include a
group of buttons inside a container component created in Flash Professional:

```xml
<?xml version="1.0" encoding="utf-8"?>
<s:Application xmlns:fx="http://ns.adobe.com/mxml/2009"
               xmlns:s="library://ns.adobe.com/flex/spark"
               xmlns:mx="library://ns.adobe.com/flex/mx"
               xmlns:components="com.developingcomponents.components.*">

  <components:SimpleFlashContainer>
    <s:HGroup>
      <s:ComboBox id="myCombo" />
      <s:Button id="myButton" label="Submit"/>
    </s:HGroup>
  </components:SimpleFlashContainer>
</s:Application>
```

Like `UIMovieClip`, you are free to define your own external class that extends
`ContentHolder` and add additional functionality to it. Likewise, if you want to create your
own content area in ActionScript instead of using the symbol `FlexContentHolder`, you
need to create an instance of `mx.flash.FlexContentHolder` or a subclass of it and add it
to your component on creation. That's pretty much it when it comes to creating Flex
components in Flash Professional

Summary

This chapter showed you how you can leverage the visual nature of Flash Professional to
create components for use within the Flex framework. By creating your visual assets in
Flash and converting your symbols to Flex components through the Flex Component

Kit for Flash, you saw how easily and quickly you can create and deploy your components to Flex.

You now have a better idea of what you can implement and how within your Flash-based components, and the two types of components that you can create in Flash for use in Flex. With that in mind, let's move on to the last few chapters, which deal with integration and distribution—starting with the Flex Library project.

III

Distribution

The Flex Library Project

You are almost at the end of this journey into developing components for use in Flex and AIR applications. The final three chapters are more about workflow and distribution. However, this doesn't make them any less important; it actually makes them the most important chapters in this entire book.

With that in mind, this chapter looks at how to package and distribute your components and looks at the Flex Library project and its underlying command-line compiler, compc.

Packaging Your Component

There comes a time in the component development cycle when you need to distribute your components to members of your development team or to the developer community at large. When this time comes, the most obvious way to distribute them may not be the most useful.

The most obvious method is to just zip the classes and mail them to the team. Or place them on a website for others to download. However, before you race to zip all your shiny new components, there is a more distribution-friendly approach you can take: the SWC (generally pronounced "swick").

Before discussing how you create a SWC, let's look at what an SWC actually is because you may be in for a surprise.

SWC Format

As surprising as this may sound, an SWC is basically a zip archive. There—how ground-breaking was that! However, note that SWCs contain a specific set of files and beware if you mess with them (cue chain-rattling and spooky moaning). If you do want to look inside an SWC, make sure that you do it on a copy of the actual SWC to avoid any mishaps.

To avoid any of those mishaps, I took the liberty of opening up an SWC to provide some information about what is included within one.

An SWC is usually made up of the following elements (optional items are only added when a content type that requires it exists):

- library.swf
- catalog.xml
- Locale (folder)
- Assets (folder/)

library.swf

The `library.swf` contains your component classes compiled down into a SWF. This is also how Live Previews are generated. When you drag an instance of your class onto the design view in Flash Builder, all it does is grab the `library.swf` and reference the relevant component.

catalog.xml

The `catalog.xml` contains various pieces of information about the contents of the SWC, including the version of the SWC and the version of the Flex SDK. Here is an example of the catalog file:

```xml
<?xml version="1.0" encoding ="utf-8"?>
<swc xmlns="http://www.adobe.com/flash/swccatalog/9">
  <versions>
    <swc version="1.2" />
    <flex version="3.2.0" build="3958" />
  </versions>
  <features>
    <feature-script-deps />
    <feature-files />
  </features>
  <libraries>
    <library path="library.swf">
      <digests>
        <digest type="SHA-256" signed="false"
➥value="03fd31623f767aa5669d00c8b156e39dae930e6f5c0dd1502bce2efd04338dcc"
  />
      </digests>
    </library>
  </libraries>
  <files>
    <file path="assets/css/SimpleComponentGraphicalSkin.css" mod="1230206400000" />
</files>
</swc>
```

You can happily ignore the vast majority of the content, but it is worth looking at a couple of key elements. The `catalog.xml` file holds only a simple reference to the library.swf within its libraries node, as shown in the following code. Besides a reference to the library.swf, it also contains a reference to the library.swf's digest information.

```
<libraries>
  <library path="library.swf">
    <digests>
      <digest type="SHA-256" signed="false"
▶value="03fd31623f767aa5669d00c8b156e39dae930e6f5c0dd1502bce2efd04338dcc"
  />
    </digests>
  </library>
</libraries>
```

Digest

The digest entry is mainly used when you use signed Runtime Shared Libraries within you Flex/AIR applications. The process is to extract the library.swf from the SWC, run the optimizer (a command-line tool included in the SDK) to remove debug information, and use the digest signing tool (another command-line application) to actually sign the SWF. This is beyond the scope of this book, but if you want to find out more, see Appendix A, "Flex Resources."

Files

Finally, the file entries just detail files that are to be included within the SWC, but cannot be compiled within the library.swf for one reason or another. Usually, this consists of nonembedded files and/or CSS files. Notice the mod entry on the file path:

```
<file path="assets/css/SimpleComponentGraphicalSkin.css" mod="1230206400000" />
```

This is just the date/time it was added to the SWC in UNIX time (or Epoch time, as it is sometimes referred to). If you were to convert the one just listed, it would actually be Thursday, 25 December 2008 12:00:00 GMT. The last three digits are not required to do this conversion and, in all honesty, I'm not sure what or if they are actually used for anything at this point. The reason the time is stored is so that, when the SWC is rebuilt, it can check to see if the timestamp on the file has changed and, if so, include the newer version in the SWC.

Locale

The locale folder contains the default messaging strings that Flex displays when there are errors or responses. We tend to take this aspect for granted, because it is English by default, so it is one of those things that tend to pass us English speakers by. However, this folder is created if you produce multilingual applications because the locale hooks directly into the resource bundles in Flex 4. By default the locale contains a set of .properties files contained within a folder named after your current locale—in my case en_US.

Assets

The assets folder listed as an item within the SWC. This is where any nonclasses files are located. So if you have any images or CSS used by your components, you can find it here.

It is worth mentioning that you may see two additional folders named mx and spark. These folders just contain the images used as the icons for the Halo and Spark components.

Now that you have a better idea of what a SWC can consist of, let's see how you actually create one.

Working with the Flex Library Project

After you finalize your component, start thinking about how you are going to distribute them. You have a couple of options—the most obvious one, as mentioned at the beginning of this chapter, is to zip the contents and place it on your website. This allows anyone to download and unzip it, place the classes and related assets within the application, and use your components as he chooses.

However, if you don't want to distribute your source code, this proves troublesome because you have no way to separate the source code and still provide your components in a usable form. Fortunately, there is a far better and more streamlined solution, known as the Flex Library Project in Flash Builder (or compc, if you want to use the command line). The Flex Library Project provide a more responsive and feature-rich interface that wires itself directly into compc to produce a SWC, allowing you to distribute this to any other Flex developers so they can include this in their current application and directly access your component.

Setting up a Flex Library Project can initially be daunting as it doesn't actually offer anything to you as an end user; it works best when it's coupled with a project that already has classes or components ready to be compiled into a SWC. Therefore, let's look at how you actually create a Library project.

Creating a Flex Library Project

The first thing to do is to open Flash Builder workspace and switch to the workspace that we have been using to create our components. From within the Flex navigator panel, right-click and select New > Flex Library (see Figure 12.1). Alternatively, you can just choose File > New > Flex Library Project from the Flash Builder menu. As soon as you select this, the New Flex Library Project dialog opens, which you can see in Figure 12.2.

In the Project Name field, I use the name the DFC_ExportComponents, just so there is some consistency with the other project that you have created—feel free to call this what you want. The next option is the location of the project on your file system. I generally leave this as the default setting used by the currently active workspace. Actually, as you'll see in a bit, this is the best approach, so leave the check box selected on Use Default Location. The final option is which version of the Flex SDK you want to use. This is set to Use Default SDK (Currently "Flex 4.x") where x is the current version of the SDK (in my case, 4.0). You don't have to use this specific version; this just happens to be the most recent version of the SDK as I was writing this book.

Figure 12.1   Select New Flex Library

Figure 12.2   Main project configuration dialog

Click the Next button because you need to supply some configuration setting before you can finalize the creation of this library project. The next stage of the process is divided into four sections, separated into tabs at the top of the screen (see Figure 12.3).

Figure 12.3   Library project configuration
options screen

As you can see, like a normal Flex project, there are also two fields at the bottom for you to configure the main source folder and the folder for the project output (which in this case, is a SWC). By default, the main source folder maps to the Flex Library Project's own src folder, which is created when you click Finish. However, this isn't the source folder that you will use. We will add an external source folder.

This is useful for two reasons: It saves you from having to copy source files from your main Flex project into the library project and risk them going out of sync if you update the original Flex project files; and it can cause a headache if you use classes from multiple sources. To get around this and, in my opinion, the only way you should set up a library project, is to use the external source folders that are mapped into the library project. To do this, you need to select the third tab: Source Path. Within this tab, you can add additional external source folders to your library project (see Figure 12.4).

Figure 12.4   External sources tab

If you click the Add Folder button, a small pop-up dialog appears with an input field and a Browse button. Clicking the Browse button takes you to a file system window that enables you to navigate to any folder on your computer. This is slightly annoying because you are more likely to use the source of a project that is in the same workspace as the library project that is being configured. Say that you have a DFC_DevelopingComponents project, which is located in the same workspace—and therefore folder—where this new library project will be created. Having a file system dialog means that navigating to this folder could be a few button clicks, depending on where the content folder of your file system window was last located.

A simpler solution is to use one of Flash Builder's environment variables. You may have seen these in passing—especially if you have had a good nose through the Flash Builder Preferences panel. They are usually uppercase and, when used, are surrounded by curly braces, a bit like a data binding in Flex, and prefixed with a dollar sign. The one that we will use is the reference to the current workspace, which is represented by the keyword DOCUMENTS (see Figure 12.5).

As you can see in Figure 12.5, with the DOCUMENTS variable in place, you just need to insert the name of the project and add its src folder so it can be linked correctly. With this in place, click OK and close the dialog. You should now see the reference to this folder within the Source Path window. Now that you have the external source present, you can update the main source folder reference to this use this new source folder.

Figure 12.5   Using Flash Builder's environment variables to set the
location of external source files

To do this, click the Browse button next to the Main source folder input field, and you are presented with a dialog like the one shown in Figure 12.6. If the project root isn't expanded by default, open it and you see the three entries shown in the figure. Notice the cryptic [source path] src entry. This is the external source folder that you just mapped into the project.

Figure 12.6   Selecting the default source folder
for the project

Be aware of one quirk with the external source libraries in Flash Builder. It has to do with the default mapping of external source path: As you've seen, the naming of an external source path isn't clear where that external source is located (refer to Figure 12.6), unless you are actually in the Source Path tab. Fortunately, Flash Builder takes care of this should you have more than one external source folder mapped. If you do, it suffixes the [source path] entry with the name of the folder hyphen source:

[source path] DFC_DevelopingComponents-src

Select the relevant [source path] entry to make it the default src folder and click OK to apply it. The main source folder entry should have updated to reflect this after the dialog closes. With the external source folder selected as the default, you can now finish configuring the library project.

Next, add the required classes (or, in our case, components) to the source selection so that when the project performs a build, it knows what to place within the SWC. You can be as granular as you want. In this case, I want you to add all the components that you have been working on. You have two options on this screen, indicated by a pair of radio buttons just below the Classes tab. The first reads Include All Classes from All Source Paths and is selected by default. You don't actually want to use this one, because it includes everything in the src folder. Instead, select the second radio button: Select Classes to Include in Library. After this is selected, the main central area of the panel becomes active. Click the disclosure arrow next to the [source path] src entry and expand it out one level.

You should now see something similar to Figure 12.7, although the exact content may vary. Keep in mind that you don't actually want to include any of the application MXML files (those that are in the root of your src folder based off of the application class). You don't need to include those; all you should be concerned with including are the actual component classes (and any that your components use are needed for distribution).

To save yourself time, select the base class folder, which—if you have followed the recommended reversed domain name format—will likely be something along the lines of com, co.uk, net, and so on. (In my case, it is com.) Look at Figure 12.7 and notice that I have an assets folder listed in the tree structure. This is where I store all the elements that are not classes, such as my CSS, SWF/SWC skin files, and any graphical elements that my components need to function correctly. However, if you try and expand this to add any of those items while in the Classes panel, the disclosure arrow just disappears because the Classes panel is set to filter out anything that doesn't have a .as or .mxml file extension. Don't worry—you can add these items in the next tab, Assets.

The Assets tab is almost identical to the Classes tab, except that it has a traditional folder tree (as you can see in Figure 12.8) like you see in Windows Explorer or Finder (if you're in list view).

Figure 12.7   Selecting the classes
to include within the SWC

Figure 12.8   Selecting the Assets
to include within the SWC

Within this panel, you can add all the nonclass files, which need to be included within the SWC for distribution. A point worth remembering is that the project cannot see beyond the root of the src folder, so make sure that your assets are stored within a structure within the src directory. This is especially important for assets that are not embedded within the component and isn't just isolated to the library project. It also affects how Flex interprets content when you perform a build of your application, while it can reference assets that are in the root of your actual project while testing. After you package those files and deploy them, it loses all reference to them. Think of the src folder as the root of your website; anything outside of it cannot be seen or accessed. This is doubly important when developing for AIR, because it can be a costly mistake to suddenly realize that assets that worked on your development machine are not present in the application you just distributed to the public. With that in mind, I make sure that all my assets are stored within the src folder, so nothing ever gets left out.

After you are happy that all the assets you want to export with your components are selected, click Finish to create the library project and get it to create your initial SWC. If all goes well, after a brief pause, a little disclosure arrow should appear next to the bin directory, indicating that the SWC has been created. If you expand this folder, you should have something similar to Figure 12.9.

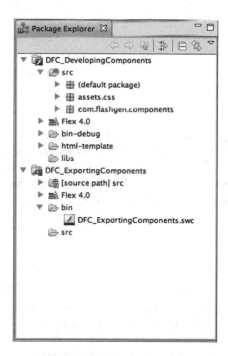

Figure 12.9   Compiled SWC

What If It All Goes Wrong

Hopefully, you'll only have issues creating a SWC on the rarest of occasions. However, it is worth knowing what can cause the SWC to fail to compile. Before we cover those, let me show you an error that you may get through no fault of your own. This is the automatic build error. If, when creating the library project, instead of mapping in those external classes, you just named the project and clicked Finish, you might see this (see Figure 12.10). This error is caused because the default setting of Flash Builder is set to build a project automatically. However, if your library project has no source classes selected, it cannot build anything; hence, the error.

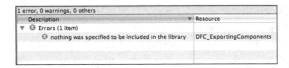

Figure 12.10   Nothing to Include error

This shouldn't actually be an error because it is actually a warning; after all, if nothing is selected, it's obvious it wouldn't be able to include anything. The common errors that you will receive when using external source files relate to unterminated variables and package-naming inconsistencies. Unfortunately, many of them won't actually cause an error message to be pushed to the Problems panel in Flash Builder, unless the actual project that they are mapped from is open in the workspace. A common one that regularly trips me up is errors in embedded assets in classes. These seem to fail silently and never refresh the SWC—something that is hard to determine if it has happened unless you run clean on your project and/or delete the SWC from the `bin` directory.

My general rule is, if the SWC fails to compile correctly, check that the classes you are trying to compile into it are error free. (This may mean that you have to actually try and compile them in their original Flex project to spot the error.) This is generally the issue. Remember that the Flex Library tends to fail silently, so don't panic if nothing seems to have changed within the SWC; just recheck your code, clean the project, and attempt to build the SWC again.

compc

What if you don't want to use the Flex Library Project in Flash Builder? After all, you may want to link the creation of your SWCs to an Ant script or do it externally on a separate machine that isn't running Flash Builder, or you may just want to "keep it real." Regardless of why you want to, if you do, you need to use `compc`, which is a command-line compiler that enables you to bundle your components in to a SWC by passing parameters into it from the command line. We're not going to cover this in any detail, so if you want to know more about how to use the command-line compilers, read the supporting documentation that comes with the Flex SDK.

However, so you can get a basic idea of the syntax, here is a simple example:

```
compc -source-path c:/flexapp/src -output c:/mycomponents/components.swc
-include-classes myClasses.MyComponent myClasses.MyDataComponent
-include-file icon.png c:/flexapps/assets/icon.png
```

What you have is the call to command compc, supplying three distinct parameters. First, we have the directory where we have our classes that will be included in our SWC. In the case of this example, we are using the -source-path parameter, and we are pointing it at a directory called src, which is located in the folder flexapps on the c:\ drive. (Note that we use UNIX-style forward slashes in our path, not the traditional backslash that Windows uses.)

Next, we have the output directory. This is where you want to output your SWC, and it provides you with the ability to set the name for the SWC you are going to create. If you omitted this, it would create the SWC in the -source-path directory. For this example, we call it components.swc and output it to the folder c:/mycomponents.

The next parameter allows us to define the classes we want to actually include within this SWC. There are a few different ways to achieve this, but for this simple example, we can just list them as values within the -include-classes. The final parameter, -include-file, allows you to add nonsource files to the SWC. Unfortunately, this can get long winded because you need to use the -include file flag for each asset you include that isn't able to be compiled. The first parameter of this flag is the name of the asset once it is embedded; this way, you can reference it if you want. As the name is used to create a global variable, it goes without saying that you need to make sure they are all unique.

The compc compiler has a detailed list of parameters that you can use to tweak and tailor the inclusion of classes and the output of the resultant SWC, but this is a pretty dry read at the best of times; therefore, as mentioned at the beginning of this section, if you want to know more, check out Appendix A for links to further information.

Summary

Whew! I know it's a lot to take in. Don't worry—you're almost at the end of this interesting journey. This chapter covered how to create and configure a Flex Library Project and export a SWC.

We looked at the structure of a SWC and some of the core items that are included within it. You also got a feel for what is actually under the hood in the form of the compc compiler and how to invoke it from the command line.

The next chapter looks at how to integrate components into the Flash Builder IDE to make life easier.

Component Integration
in Flash Builder 4

You are now in the final stages of developing component. Up to this point, you have seen how to create the structure of a component, add events, data binding, and styles to your components and package it up for distribution. This chapter explains how you can provide hooks so that your components integrate with Flash Builder directly.

This makes life a lot easier for other developers who may be integrating your components within their applications, and it adds the final level of polish to make a great component and make it into a solid publically distributable one.

Why Integrate with Flash Builder?

As with most things in life, familiarity breeds contempt. Although you and I can probably write ActionScript and MXML with our eyes closed on a napkin with a bit of ketchup, we are a minority. The vast majority of developers aren't interested in showing off their 1337 5|<1llz. They just want to get the job done as quickly and efficiently as possible. After all, there wouldn't be much of a demand for development tools like Flash Builder if everyone was as proficient with wood pulp and fermented pressed tomatoes.

With that in mind, if adding this support for Flash Builder makes your job longer and harder, you're not going to be that enthusiastic about providing these hooks because there is nothing in it for you beyond taking away your Xbox time. However, integration is quite painless and takes no real time to add the support within your component.

In the end, you may have a cool component, but if it's hard to configure or has loads of parameters that may or may not need configuring, people will lose interest in using it. By providing hooks and integration points with Flash Builder, you provide easy access to the core properties and leave the more advanced ones for those who want to read all the documentation (more on that later on). The flip side is that you may want to hide certain classes or properties from the IDE so that they don't appear as an option. Although this may sound a bit backward, there are cases—one of which I cover later in this chapter.

What Can I Integrate With?

For the most part, your main integration points within Flash Builder will be with the code-hinting engine and the MXML editor. You can also integrate with the Properties and Components panels, which makes the life of a component developer easier—especially if you are distributing your components as SWCs, because the guy who is using your components in his application is unlikely to have access to the actual source code.

Panel Integration

Chapter 12, "The Flex Library Project," showed you how to package up your components into a SWC so that you can easily distribute them without having to provide the actual source code. One thing you probably noticed is that, when you create your own components, they get grouped in the to the Custom Components folder in design view's Components panel. This is OK, but wouldn't it be nicer if you could have more control over how your components were organized in Flash Builder? Well, if you compile them into SWCs, you can do just that and more.

To achieve this, however, you have to create some additional files in your component project's `src` folder that will contain the information necessary to manipulate Flash Builder and organize your components. These files are called `manifest.xml` and `design.xml`. Actually, they just need to be suffixed as that—the common approach is to prefix the files with the name of the Flex project file to avoid confusion when viewed alongside other projects that use them. So, for my component development, they are named `FGComponents-manifest.xml` and `FGComponents-design.xml`, but for the ease of explanation, let's stick with `manifest.xml` and `design.xml` for the rest of this chapter.

Manifest

The `manifest.xml` file contains a list of all the components that you want to include in a SWC; this is similar to how you add components via the Class tab of a Flex Library Project, as discussed in Chapter 12. However, it has the added capability of enabling you to define a URL-based namespace for your components; like core namespaces, take the namespace for the core Flex 4 classes (`fx`), which uses a URI-style namespace: `xmlns:fx=http://ns.adobe.com/mxml/2009`.

To use this form of namespacing over the more common uncompiled namespace convention of using the local package structure (`xmlns:views="com.developingcomponents.views.*"`), you need to tell the manifest file what components will be included in the SWC and their fully qualified package path, like the following example:

```
<componentPackage>
  <component id="SimpleComponent"
 class="com.developingcomponents.components.SimpleComponent"/>
  <component id="SimpleContainerComponent"
 class="com.developingcomponents.components.SimpleContainerComponent"/>
</componentPackage>
```

As you can see, you have a root node called `componentPackage` and, within this, you place only the components you want to include in the SWC, each represented by a child node called `component`. The `component` node `id` attribute represents the actual component name and the `class` is the fully qualified path to that class, be it an MXML or ActionScript file—the manifest isn't choosy.

After you create the manifest file, update the compiler settings in your Flex Library Project and point it to the `manifest.xml` file. You can do this in two ways: the easy way and the more complex way.

Let's start with the easy way. If you look at Figure 13.1, you see that the namespace URL has been set manually, and I included the `manifest.xml` file that it should be associated with. The namespace URL is an arbitrary string, but it is recommended that you use a URL, because it is unique to the individual or organization; feel free to append any identifying path information to it. One thing to bear in mind is that if you were to go to this URL in your browser, you wouldn't find anything because it doesn't represent a page containing any special information. It's just a string identifier—nothing more.

Figure 13.1   Setting your component's namespace with
a manifest file within the Flex Library compiler settings

The advantages of using a namespace URL is that when you include those components that have been compiled in to a SWC with one, instead of the using a local package path, when your components are declared in MXML, they will be referenced by the namespace. By default, it takes the last part of the URL and prefixes it with ns. So, if you

used my namespace http://www.flashgen.com/fgc/2010, Flash Builder interprets this as
`xmlns:ns2010="http://www.flashgen.com/fgc/2010"`. This isn't ideal, because I want
to use `fgc` as my namespace prefix. Admittedly, I could just put that at the end of the
namespace and suffer the `ns` prefix, but that's not how I roll, and I'm sure it's not how you
roll, either. Fortunately, you can "have you namespace and prefix it," and it has to do with
the `design.xml` file I mentioned at the beginning of this section.

Before we look at `design.xml`, recall that I mentioned an easy and complex way of
working with a `manifest.xml` file. Well, the more complex way is to create a `config.xml`
file in your project root and manually set all the relevant attributes. This is useful if you
want to apply a selection of compiler directives to the project without having to type
them all into the single input field in the compiler preferences for that project. The easier
way is to just set the parameters in the aforementioned Flex project compiler preferences.
Because we're only looking at integrating our components, let's just stick with this way,
but feel free to try the `config.xml` way if you want to experiment/have greater control
over the entire compilation process.

Design.xml

So, what does the `design.xml` file actually do? Well, it's responsible for telling Flash
Builder what the namespace prefix is for each component and enables you to configure
the folder that these components will be displayed in when the Component panel is displayed. Instead of placing all your components in the Custom folder, you can define separate folders for your components. Figure 13.2 shows the same components in design
view's Component panel: the first one without a design file and the second one with the
file included. Notice how the second one has placed my components in a folder called
FlashGen.Com, whereas the first one has just added them to the default Custom folder.

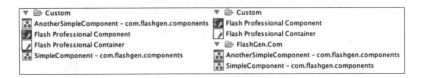

Figure 13.2   Same components, the first without the design.xml file
and the other with it applied

You have to agree that the ability to customize the folder your components appear in
within the Component panel is more desirable that opting for the generic Custom folder.
Let's look at the `design.xml` file to see how we tap into all this coolness. Here is the
actual `design.xml` file I used to place my components within their own folder, as shown
in Figure 13.2. The design file is broken down in to three parts: namespaces, categories
and components.

```
<?xml version="1.0" ?>
<design>
  <namespaces>
    <namespace prefix="fgc" uri="http://www.flashgen.com/fgc/2010" />
  </namespaces>
  <categories>
    <category id="fgcomps" label="FlashGen.Com" defaultExpand="true" />
  </categories>
  <components>
    <component id="com.developingcomponents.components.SimpleComponent"
               name="SimpleComponent"
               namespace="fgc"
               category="fgcomps" />
    <component id="com.developingcomponents.components.AnotherSimpleComponent"
               name="AnotherSimpleComponent"
               namespace="fgc"
               category="fgcomps" />
  </components>
</design>
```

The namespaces node enables you to declare namespace nodes; as you can see from the namespace, I declared it has a prefix attribute, which I have set to fgc and the URI to which it maps. Notice that this is the same URI I declared within the Flex Library compiler settings in Figure 13.1.

The next section is the categories node. Within this node, you can declare multiple categories, which require an id and an optional label property. The label entry can have spaces, symbols, and so on within it because it is just used as the *friendly* name of the category. Flash Builder uses the id attribute to actually reference the folder and its contents.

The final section within the design file is where you actually declare your components and associate them with the previous namespace and category nodes. If we have a closer look at the component node, you can see it has a selection of attributes including id, which is where you declare your components complete package path. You then have the name property, where you can give your component a user *friendly* name. I just use the component class name to avoid confusion. Next, you have the namespace where you associate the namespace node that you declared earlier with the component and, finally, you have the category attribute. Like namespace, it is mapped back to one of the category nodes within your design.xml file.

```
<components>
  <component id="com.developingcomponents.components.SimpleComponent"
             name="SimpleComponent"
             namespace="fgc"
             category="fgcomps" />
</components>
```

After you're happy with your design.xml file, you need to associate this with your Flex Library Project. To do this, open the preferences of the project and select the Flex Library Build Path entry. From the tabs at the top, you need to select the Assets tab, and if you placed your design.xml file in the src root of your project, you should see it listed here—you may need to expand the src folder (see Figure 13.3). Make sure its check box is selected and click OK to close the preferences.

Figure 13.3   Adding the design.xml file to your
Flex Library Project

Your SWC should be rebuilt at this point (although as I mentioned in Chapter 12), you may want to delete it from the bin directory and force it to build it again so you know that it was definitely rebuilt. Now, all you need to do is drag it from the bin folder and drop it into the libs folder of one of your Flex projects to test it. If you already have the an earlier version of the SWC in your Flex project, make sure you delete it and switch back to Source view, because I noticed that refreshing the design view sometimes doesn't update the Component panel correctly if it's still visible. If nothing went awry, upon switching back to design view, you should see your components in their own folder in the Components panel. If you drag and drop one on to the design area and switch back to view the code, you'll see it now uses your custom namespace.

Setting Some Ground Rules

The `design.xml` file has additional properties that can be declared within it, some of which are simple one-line settings; others, like the Design View Extensions, require additional code to function. For example, you can set defaults for the various properties of your components from within the `design.xml` file. This is a relatively simple process; all you need to do is declare a `defaultAttribute` node within your component node:

```
<component id="com.developingcomponents.components.SimpleComponent"
        name="SimpleComponent"
        namespace="fgc"
        category="fgcomps">
  <defaultAttribute name="width" value="250"/>
  <defaultAttribute name="height" value="200"/>
  <defaultAttribute name="title" value="FlashGen.Com"/>
</component>
```

As you can see, I set the width, height, and title properties of my component so that they use these when placed within a developer's application (if no other values are set). This approach allows you to set your component's properties without needing to set these defaults in the actual component class. Either way is acceptable; so pick the one you are most comfortable with.

Chapter 7, "Working with Metadata," mentioned that the limitation of the `[Inspectable]` tags category attribute is that it can only affect the list or tree view within the Properties panel. Wouldn't it be great if you could manipulate the main Property pane? Well you can, within the design.xml. Remember that these all have to be merged into a SWC for this to be accessible.

```
<?xml version="1.0" ?>
<design>
  <namespaces>
    <namespace prefix="fgc" uri="http://www.flashgen.com/fgc/2009" />
  </namespaces>
  <categories>
    <category id="fgcomps" label="FG Components" defaultExpand="true" />
  </categories>
  <components>
    <component id="com.developingcomponents.components.SimpleComponent"
            name="SimpleComponent"
            namespace="fgc"
            category="fgcomps">
    <defaultAttribute name="width" value="250"/>
    <defaultAttribute name="height" value="200"/>
    <designExtension
➥class="com.developingcomponents.extensions.SimpleComponentExtension" />
    <mxmlProperties>
      <textfield id="selectedIndex"
              name="%propertyLabel.selectedIndex"/>
```

```
        <combo id="enabled" name="%propertyLabel.enabled"/>
      </mxmlProperties>
    </component>
  </components>
</design>
```

If you look at the previous code, you see that, within the `<mxmlProperties/>` tag, numerous attributes are defined in the following format:

```
<attributeType id name/>
```

The `attribute` is the type of edit field you want to display in the Common section of the main property panel. The `id` relates to the actual component property the field relates to, and `name` is the name of the actual edit field as it appears within the panel. So, the following entry adds a `ComboBox` to the panel, gives it the label of enabled, and maps it back to the enabled property within the component it is declared within.

As you can see in Figure 13.4, the Properties panel has been updated to reflect the changes we assigned to the `SimpleComponent`. Pretty cool, eh!

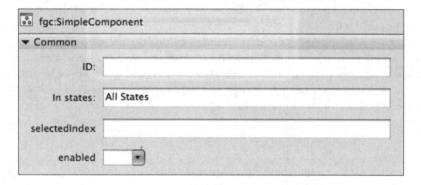

Figure 13.4   Using design.xml and mxmlProperties to define
custom fields in the Properties panel

Valid attribute types are

- `textfield`
- `combo`
- `colorpicker`
- `filepicker`
- `slider`

- `rowcolsize`
- `configColumns`
- `dataTextfield`
- `rendererTextfield`

Now that you've seen what can be done via the `design.xml` file, let's look at the design view extensions and how they can be used to add additional functionality to your components when used within the design view of Flash Builder.

Design View Extensions

One thing you may have noticed when working with in Flash Builder's design view is that some components have additional visual overlays to their visual layout that hook directly into Flash Builder. These are known as design view extensions, and they are based on a set of ActionScript classes that allow you to provide greater integration between your components and Flash Builder without polluting the actual component code itself.

For example, the add/remove tab option in the `TabNavigator` component (see Figure 13.5) is displayed if you override the `isNavigator()` design extension method within the associated design view extension class of your navigator component.

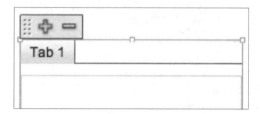

Figure 13.5   The TabNavigator component displaying the add/remove navigator overlay

To take advantage of this feature set, you need a copy of the **Design Extension Kit**. (The URL to download the kit is in Appendix A, "Flex Resources.) Bear in mind that when you download the extension kit, it is saved as an FXP file, so be careful if you have Flash Catalyst installed, because it will try and open it by default and that's not what you want it to do. You need to import it into Flash Builder via the import option in the file menu.

After you have the Design Extension Kit imported, you'll see it contains three Flex Library Projects and a single Flex project (`DesignExtension`, `Picnic`, `PicnicExtensions`, and `DV4ExtensionKit`, respectively), as shown in Figure 13.6.

We talk only about the `DesignExtensions` project in this chapter, but feel free to look through the others if you want. (Hopefully, the picnic metaphor will make more sense to you than it did to me.) If you expand the `DesignExtensions` library project `bin` folder, you see it contains a SWC called `DesignExtensions.swc`. You need to copy this into the `libs` folder of any Flex projects that you want to use component design view extensions within. If you want to know what's in the SWC, feel free to look at the actual source files for the design extensions—you'll find them inside the `com.adobe.flexide.extensions` package in the `DesignExtensions` library project. Once expanded, you see a few base classes and an interface, `DesignUtils`, `IComponentExtension`, and `NullExtension`, as well as two packages containing the individual design extensions for each component: one for the Halo components (`mx`) and one for the Spark components (`spark`).

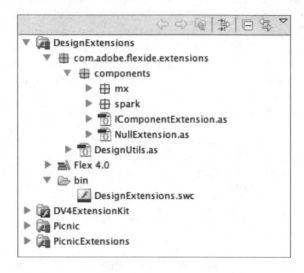

Figure 13.6   Imported contents of the DV4ExtensionKit.fxp

All these component-specific extension classes implement the interface `IComponentExtension`, although most achieve this by inheriting from `UIComponentExtension`, subclassing from this, and overriding the method stubs as needed. When working with the extensions, remember that API subclasses your extension from the same class that your component inherits from. So, for example, if you had a component that extends from `Group` use the `GroupExtension` as the inheriting class for your extension.

Like most class inheritance, this takes the hassle out of implementing all the methods that your component may require, unless you need to override them. This poses an interesting quandary. Suppose you don't use one of the Flex framework components, but use `UIComponent` as your base class. Well, you'd use the `UIComponentExtension`, but be aware that although you get a lot of flexibility when doing this—just like having your component inherit from `UIComponent`—you need to implement all the methods you need to hook into. This is because, as I mentioned, these are just method stubs within `UIComponentExtension`.

So, with this high-level overview out of the way, let's look at how we combine our component extension classes with our components for distribution and how you go about actually integrating your components with a component extension class.

Distributing Your Design View Extensions

Just like in Chapter 12, the easiest way to distribute your extension classes are within a SWC. This mainly shields them from prying eyes, and it makes managing them easier both from a component developer perspective, but also from the implementing developer's point of view.

You don't need to keep your extensions in a separate Flex project from your components (see Figure 13.7), but I recommend creating an extensions directory and storing them inside that—in fact, if you are creating both Halo and Spark components, I'd create subpackages for both of these and place your extensions within the relevant package.

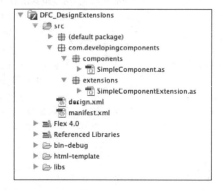

Figure 13.7   Package structure of a Flex project
that contains components and design
view extensions

After you create your extension for your component, it is just a matter of selecting it to be included within the SWC. I'm not going to replicate the process here—it would be pointless because it adds no extra insight or value. Just follow the steps that you were shown in Chapter 12 because the process is identical—except you need to include the extension classes and the components themselves within your SWC.

Linking Your Component to Your Extension

So, we talked about importing the extensions and distributing them with our components, but that's no use if you have no idea what you can do with them. Fortunately, that's what the rest of this section is about. First, let's look at Table 13.1 to see all the methods that IComponentExtension provides.

Table 13.1 **IComponentExtension** Methods

Method	Description
adjustDropContainer	Manages the adjustment of a container in which a drop occurs if the original drop container isn't suitable. It's recommended that you only use this for move actions (drag-move) and not insertions (drag-insert). Returns the container in which the drop occurred as a `DisplayObjectContainer`. If the container isn't suitable, it returns `null`.
canShowBorder	Determines whether the component can have a border drawn around it. Returns a `Boolean`.
childIsSuitable	Determines whether the component can support child items. Returns a `Boolean`. See also `parentIsSuitable`.
createComponent	Creates an instance of the component that is associated with it for management by the extension. Returns the component as a `DisplayObject`.
drawBackgroundInComponentView	Useful if you have a component that, by default, doesn't have a background (the `VideoDisplay` component, for example). In these cases, you can draw the background when displaying the component the design view. Returns a `Boolean` to indicate whether it supports design view background creation.
getEditField	Provides a hook so you can use an inline edit field to set textual data within your component. Returns an `Object` with the following properties: `fieldStringName`: Name of the text to edit `compDisplayObject`: Component that contains the text to edit `xNumber`: x location of the inline edit field `yNumber`: y location of the inline edit field `widthNumber`: Width of the edit field `heightNumber`: Height of the edit field `multilineBoolean`: Determines use of multiline edit field If edit field is valid, it returns `null` instead.

Table 13.1 **IComponentExtension Methods**

Method	Description
getLayoutDirection	Returns the layout applied to the component as a String; values are "" for absolute, "vertical" if vertical, and "horizontal" if the layout is horizontal.
getPropOpenSize	Returns the default size of a component, because Point. Containers are calculated differently than normal components. This is because they may have a default size in x but not necessarily have in y. You can assign the returned values only when the useDefaultSize returns true.
isContainer	Returns a Boolean based on whether the target component is a Container. Extension classes that extend ContainerExtension return true; if you have a requirement for a Container component to return false, you need to override this method.
isDockedItemHit	Determines if a component that is part of a ControlBar has been hit. Returns a Boolean.
isDraggable	Returns a Boolean based on whether the component is draggable.
isNavigator	Determines whether the component is a Navigator. If it is, an overlay is displayed, allowing for the addition and removal of subviews. Returns a Boolean.
mayPropOpen	Determines whether a component should be set to a default size ("propped open"). Useful when dealing with containers that rely on their children to determine their size. Otherwise, adding children to such a component would be difficult because its dimensions would likely be zero by default. Returns a Boolean that indicates whether the component supports sizing. See also getPropOpenSize.
mayUseAlignmentBounds	Determines whether a component supports snapping at its bounds. Generally only valid when a container uses absolute layout.

Table 13.1 **IComponentExtension Methods**

Method	Description
navigatorWidgetStyle	Defines the style of the navigator overlay widget. Returns a `Number` that determines the style. 0 = No navigator widget 1 = No arrows 2 = Show arrows
parentIsSuitable	Determines if the target parent is suitable and allows the component to be placed within it. Returns a `Boolean`.
postAddItemToContainer	Invoked after the component instance has been added to its parent and all of its initial properties have been set. Provides a hook so you can add event listeners or set the current view state.
preDeleteItem	As the name implies, this is called prior to a component being deleted. Returns a `Boolean` of `true` if `preDeleteItem` actually deleted the item and, therefore, shouldn't attempt to delete it again. Or in normal operation, `false`.
preDeleteChildItem	Like `preDeleteItem`, this allows `Container`-based components to update based on the removal of a child item.
processChildAtPoint	Returns the child of a component that is located under the current Point as a `DisplayObject`. Override this method if you want to alter the normal hit test behavior.
processMouseDown	Enables your component extension to handle `mouseDown` events. This is performed on a from-root-inwards approach, invoking the method on each component until it receives a true response. If no component returns true, the `mouseDown` event is handled by the design view.
revealChildItem	Enables stacked view containers, like `Accordion` and `ViewStack`, to display their contents within the design view, showing the currently selected one and hiding the others. Overlays a control within the design view so you can navigate through these containers.

Table 13.1   `IComponentExtension` Methods

Method	Description
`setIPAtView`	Draws an insertion point icon on a drag operation when inserting a component into a `Container`. The extension draws an insertion icon based on the mouse location. Returns a number for relative layouts (`VGroup`, `VBox`, and so on) and a `Point` for absolute layouts (`Canvas`, `Group`).
`setProperty`	As the name implies, allows the extension to set a property on the component instance. Returns a `Boolean`.
`setPropertyWithDataBinding`	Like `setProperty`, allows the extension to set a property that is linked by data binding. Returns a `Boolean`.
`setStyle`	Assigns a style to the component instance. Returns a `Boolean`.
`snapToBaseline`	Returns a `Boolean` that indicates whether baseline snapping is supported.
`useItemBoundsForSelection`	Returns a `Boolean` that indicates whether a component can be selected by clicking within its bounds (for example, `DataGroup`). `Containers`, as a rule, implement their own form of hit testing, so don't use this.
`usesAbsolutePositioning`	Determines whether the component's layout is absolute. Override this if your component implements a custom layout that supports `absoluteLayout` in some instances. Returns a `Boolean`.

As you can see, you can hook into an awful lot of methods to provide a richer integration with design view. So, let's look at a few examples so you can see it in action.

Something that will likely frustrate you is that all the extension classes are marked with the `[ExcludeClass]` metadata tag—the upshot being that you cannot easily import the class nor use the class creation wizard to add it as a superclass to your extension. So, be prepared to spend a few minutes manually adding the right path only to have to switch back to the source directory of the `DesignExtensions` library project to dig into the packages to find the location of the class you need. This needs to be changed, because it stumps productivity and turns off many people from using the design view extension, because it takes time to do such a simple thing, like import a class.

I don't cover all the methods that are exposed by IComponentExtension, because there isn't enough space in this book. However, I highlight some methods that you'll likely use on a regular basis when you develop your own component extensions: createComponent(), postAddItemToContainer(), setProperty(), setStyle() and preDeleteItem().

I emphasize that the ones that are most useful are createComponent(), postAddItemToContainer(), and preItemDelete()/preChildItemDelete() because these provide the basic startup and tear down for the component controlled by its associated extension implementation.

createComponent()

createComponent() is the starting method when working with extensions. Within this method, you create the instance of the associated component. By overriding this method, you can manipulate how the component is instantiated before being rendered within design view. This is if you need to add any event listeners to the component so you can perform additional actions. If you don't override this method, design view just calls the default constructor of the component.

```
override public function createComponent(inItemType:String):DisplayObject
{
    var _comp    :SimpleComponent = new SimpleComponent();

    _comp.addEventListener(FlexEvent.CREATION_COMPLETE,
                           creastionCompleteHandler);

    return _comp;
}
```

postAddItemToContainer()

After you place your component on the design surface—be that directly onto the application of an alternative Container component—the postAddItemToContainer() method is executed. This method is, in some respects, similar to adding a creationComplete() listener. However, as mentioned, it only gets fired when the component is added to a container (be that the root application or another Container component. At this point, you may want to execute additional methods that update or manipulate the component in design view.

setProperty(), setStyle()

Overriding this method allows you to manipulate property values as they are set on your component. It is advisable to override this method if you are setting any properties within the postAddItemToContainer() method. This is because, under certain circumstances, when values are updated directly in MXML, those initial properties can be reset.

So, it's worth reapplying them in the `setProperty()` method, as the following example illustrates:

```
override public function setProperty(item:DisplayObject,
                                    inProperty:String, inValue:*):Boolean
{
  // apply the updated property and store whether it is successful
  var _propApplied:Boolean = super.setProperty(item, inProperty,
                                               inValue);

  // Reapply any properties that were initially set.
  setVideoControlBar(VideoController(item));

  return _propApplied;
}
```

`setStyle()`, like `setProperty()`, allows for the applying of style values to the relevant style attribute within your component. Again, like all the extension methods, if you want to perform additional processing, you need to override the `setStyle()` method and add that functionality.

preDeleteItem(), preDeleteChildItem()

One golden rule is this: Always remove any event listeners that have served their purpose and that applies doubly to any that are still present when the component is removed from design view while in Flash Builder. If you don't you run the risk of tying up your machine, or that of the developer using your components as orphaned event listeners, keep the extensions in memory even after the actual component has been removed. Luckily, Adobe included some event handlers within the extension framework that get invoked prior to the actual removal event.

The first event handler relates to the removal of the component instance itself and allows you to kick off any processes that need to happen when your component is removed. The basic method signature is

```
preDeleteItem(parent:DisplayObject, child:DisplayObject):void { }
```

The second handler method is the child component equivalent `preDeleteChildItem()`. The signature for this method is exactly the same as `preDeleteItem()`. This particular method is useful when children get removed because it enables you to update your container component in case the removal of the child alters its display.

Live Previews

One of the most obvious pieces of integration that we, as component developers, can provide is the live preview. Live previews have always been hit and miss in the past. When components were first introduced to the Flash Authoring tool many years ago, it was up to the developer to create a visual representation of the component so that other developers could see what the component actually looked like within the Flash Authoring tool.

Fortunately, time has moved forward, and so has the process by which live previews are created. Now, all you need to do is convert your components into a SWC. After you create a SWC of your components, distribute it and the recipients just need to drop it into their `libs` directory in their Flex project to access the components it contains. The full process is detailed in Chapter 12.

Note that, if you fail to provide a default width and or height for your component (generally by defining private static constant values or through `DefaultAttribute` tags within the `design.xml` entry for the component) for both of these properties, once compiled and dragged to design view, it will not be visible (beyond a black-bordered 1x1 pixel square). Although it's not a showstopper, it forces the developer using your components to insert explicit values for both width and height and makes the live preview redundant. If your component doesn't have a background by default, you can also create a design extension that overrides the `drawBackgroundInComponentView()` method and create the background that way, as well as the `prop open` methods to set the width and height of components that rely on their children to define their dimensions.

Setting Default Styles

One aspect of component distribution via a SWC has to do with CSS styling. If your component has a default set of styles, you need to provide a process by which these can be accessed; otherwise, if left up to the implementer of your component, he may forget to do it or not be aware that it requires certain CSS properties to display properly by default. To avoid this, you can include a special type of CSS file within your SWC. This file is special, not because it contains anything sophisticated compared to a normal CSS file used in Flex, but because of its name. You see the compiler is pretty clever in Flex, and it has certain directives it scans through and executes if the required criteria are present (in this case, the default CSS values for your components).

It probably comes as no surprise that the CSS file is called `defaults.css`. By default, the Flex framework has a `defaults.css` that provides all the CSS values for the Flex components, and this is applied to the components at compile time. You can create a local version of this for use with your components and, when your SWC is compiled within a Flex project, the compiler looks to see if there are any default styles for them and applies those values to your components.

When adding a `defaults.css` file to your SWC, make sure it is placed in the root of your component source files (by default, the `src` folder); otherwise, the compiler ignores it. Also, you can only have one of them per SWC.

Check out the section on handling and applying default styles within your component in Chapter 10, "Skinning and Styling," if you're still unsure on how to apply CSS to your own custom components.

Summary

Although this wasn't the largest of chapters, it helps to collate all the various elements that have been detailed in previous chapters to provide a process by which you can easily integrate your components into Flash Builder. This makes other developers lives easier and adds polish to your components when distributed.

The final chapter discusses documentation and why it is even more important to document your code if you are a component developer. With that in mind, let's end this book on a high note.

Documentation

Although this may be the final chapter in this book, it is probably the most import chapter—not only in relation to component development, but also for software development in general. This chapter gives you a feel for the level of documentation that a commercial component requires and advice on how to incorporate code comments in your components as you develop your own component library. It also shows how to hook those in to the auto documentation tool ASDoc.

Finally, this chapter shows you how to use some third-party tools to make the insertion of comments a less painful process and, ultimately, save you time and effort. Without further ado, let's get documenting....

Why Should I Document Code?

Documentation is often treated as "last in, first out" for a project. It is treated with the reverence of an annoying little brother who takes up all your time. It also generally has the stigma of being a time-wasting exercise when viewed by those who neither code nor understand what it is to code but need to deliver the project on time and budget. (I know, a sweeping generalization, but you get the idea.) Few projects ever factor in time or budget to enable developers to document their code because it eats into profit. Oh, and it never gets read anyway because each project is unique, so the vast majority of code is created on a bespoke basis.

Last to the Party, First to Leave

Most documentation gets left until the last moment, the end of the project, or when the project is finally archived. This is a bad approach. Having just written 300+ pages for this book, I assure you that remaining focused on writing stuff down when you'd sooner be coding is hard to do. That said, it is a rewarding experience, but if you can break it up into small chunks, you rapidly forget that you are commenting and documenting your code as you go.

If you leave documenting your code until the end of the project, it is almost always dropped usually on the grounds of no more time/no more budget.

Be warned; this won't pay any dividends in the future. This is because that project will likely come back and haunt you many months down the road and immediately suck up a few days of precious development time as you, your team, and any additional resource pour over the classes and the application to try and understand how it worked the first time around.

This is more likely to happen if you have a retained client because I suspect most of you have experience doing a site refresh for a client every 12 to 24 months.

Documentation Is Boring

I agree, documentation can be dry at times, and without the right level of consideration when crafting your documentation, it can be boring. Let's be realistic: You're not writing the next Pulitzer Prize winner here! You're providing a concise explanation of how the methods and classes you have written operate. (There are a few exceptions when commenting code, and I show you those later.)

However, it would be far worse for all of us if we had no documentation for, say, something like the Flex framework. Imagine how much longer it would take to achieve anything if you have to use trial and error to work out what properties and methods were available and what each did on every class within the Flex framework. Obviously, you could just crack open the code and have a long and slightly winding read through each and every class, but if the framework came only as an SWC, you'd likely come unstuck rather quickly.

My Code Is Easy to Read

Granted, you may have the most elegant code known to humankind, and it may have a logical approach to both naming conventions and structure, but when you have a selection of classes that instantiate instances of other class types within themselves, and execute methods on externalized or pseudo anonymous functions, it won't be long before you need to start adding comments, and ultimately documentation, to aid not only yourself, but also your colleagues and external developers who may want to use your class library.

OK I Get It, Enough Already

Now that I've berated you for doing exactly what I used to do, let's look at how you can make your life easier by documenting as you go. I assure you that it is worth reading the rest of this chapter because it makes developer life much easier.

Commenting Your Code

Obviously, to provide documentation, you need to comment your code at the very least. However, if you've never commented your code before, you may find this slightly confusing given the various types of comment markers you can use. So, before you get into the tags that you can use in a comment block, let's look at the various comment types and what they offer.

Basic Comment Types

First are the most common comment types used just to provide inline commenting or simple block commenting not for public consumption. By this, I mean that these types of comment markers are ignored by ASDoc when automatically generating your class documentation and, therefore, can be read only if you open the actual class itself. This style of comment can also be used as a delimiter on a single or multiple lines of code so that the compiler ignores them. Following are examples of these comment markers demonstrating their use as both information blocks and delimiters to bypass code elements when the application is compiled into a SWF.

This chapter isn't about commenting out code, so these examples are detailed here to only illustrate both uses.

```
// This is an inline comment - The compiler ignores this as does ASDoc


/*
This is the same as the comment above but it allows you to have a comment
 that is longer than a single line. Ideal if you need to put a reminder or
 temporary explanation in about a method or property.
*/


// public var _myVariable :String; // This variable is ignored


/*
  This method is ignored as it is within a comment block

  public function myMethod():void
  {
    ...
  }
*/
```

As you can see, they are self-explanatory (no pun intended), and for the rest of this chapter, that is as much as you need to know about those particular types of comment blocks.

ASDoc Comment Blocks

The next set of comment blocks are the ones that you need to use to wrap your documentation tags so that ASDoc can generate all your HTML documentation for you. ASDoc comments are a derivation of the more widely known JavaDoc notation. This notation consists of tag-style syntax to enable keywords and simple formatting commands to be interpreted by the document compiler and displayed correctly in the resultant documentation that it generates. If you have never used ASDoc, don't worry. I go over it in the next section.

You probably already noticed that these ASDoc comment blocks look similar to the previous block comments except that they start with a /** and each additional line is prefixed with a *, like the following simple example. Don't worry about the leading * and any tab spaces prefixing your comments. ASDoc automatically removes these on document creation.

```
/**
 *     This is a simple document block.
 *     Everything I write here will be converted by ASDoc
 *     and added to the documentation for the class where this
 *     is placed.
 */
```

Flash Builder kindly colors the various comment blocks so that you can easily see which one you are using. The nonpublic variants are colored in green, and the public blocks (such as those that ASDoc can interpret) are colored in blue by default. Obviously, if all you could do in your document comments were write reams of text, it would get laborious. Luckily, Flash Builder provides a few enhancements that create the stub comment block based on the element upon which it was placed. For example, it provides tag markers in the block for method signatures and return types when placed over a function that provides either or both. If placed over the class declaration, it automatically inserts your author name (usually defined by your login name on your machine). To get Flash Builder to do this automatically requires using the insert ASDoc comment command (CMD + SHIFT + D on OS X and SHIFT + CTRL + D on Windows).

```
/**
 * If you need to access the videoControlBar component directly you
 * need to do it via this accessor.
 *
 * @return VideoControlBar
 */
public function get controlBar():VideoControlBar
{
  ...
}
```

This raises a valid point: Where do you place your comment blocks so that they are correctly read and converted by ASDoc? Its actually pretty obvious: anywhere! However, as these are still human-readable when viewed in the actual source file, it makes sense to place ASDoc comments above class, method, property, interface entries, or metadata tags so that there is a logical association with the element on which you are commenting. Plus, you can't take advantage of Flash Builders stub comment creation. From this point, when I use the term "comments," unless explicitly indicated, I refer to ASDoc comments.

ASDoc Tags

You probably saw that the return comment in the previous example was prefixed with an @. This enables ASDoc to format your documentation by type and tag. In this case, it knows that the @return tag is a marker and, therefore, treats it differently when applying the document styling to it.

ASDoc has an extensive array of @*tag* markers—not as many as JavaDoc but enough for you to create a decent level of documentation for archiving, or in the case of public distribution of components, a concise set of documents that enables other developers to understand what your components can and can't do; after all, you may just want to provide the SWC and keep the source code to yourself.

The following tables list the ASDoc common tags. Table 14.1 shows the tags you are likely to see and use on a regular basis. Table 14.2 lists the remaining tags in alphabetical order. Both tables give a brief description of what the tag does and, where relevant, include an example of its usage.

Table 14.1   Common ASDoc Tags

Tag	Description
@param	Enables you to add a comment specific to the relevant parameter in the following format: @param value description For example: @param myVar This var is mine, so leave it alone.
@private	Enables you to exclude the entire comment from being included within the documentation that ASDoc generates. If you want to exclude an entire class, place this in the top of the comment block for the class definition.
@return	Similar to the @param: @return myvalue A value that will be returned.

@see	Enables you to provide a linked reference to any element. You can reference classes and properties within those classes by fully qualified package names or, if they are within the same package, just their name and/or property.
	
	For example:
	
	@see VideoPlayer //Class in the same package
	
	@see VideoPlayer#play() //Method on that class. In this case the play() method
	
	@see com.developingcomponents.view.FlipPanel() //Class is a different package.
	
	@see http://developer.flashgen.com //An external site

Table 14.2   **Additional ASDoc Tags**

Tag	Description
@copy	Similar to the @see tag, except it copies the main comment, @return, and @param comments from one class and places it in the comment block.
@default	Enables you to define an entry for the default value of a property effect or style.
@eventType	Can be declared in two formats:
	@eventType package.event.CONSTANT
	Use this when commenting an [Event] metadata tag. This enables you to specify the constant defined by the value Event.type. ASDoc then copies the description of the event constant to the referencing class.
	The second format:
	@eventType String
	Use this form in the comment for the actual constant definition. You must supply the name of the event associated with the constant. If this tag is omitted, ASDoc cannot copy the constant's comment to the referencing class.
@example	Use with the <listing></listing> HTML tag to provide a formatted code block with the header "Example."
@inheritDoc	Similar to @copy, but use this to copy comments from inherited methods and properties.
@mxml	Generally used within the class comment block. Enables you to provide an MXML example code block that can be expanded or contracted in a similar manner to the show Inherited entries for various class attributes.
@includeExample	An advanced and undocumented tag. Enables you to include an MXML file for use as a code example placed at the bottom of the documentation.
@playerversion	Indicates the version of either the Flash or AIR players. For example, @playerversion Flash 10 or @playerversion AIR 1.5.
@productversion	Indicates what version of the Flex framework is required. For example, @productversion Flex 4.

A few other tags exist, but these are the ones that you are likely to use most of the time.

Accessors and Mutators

One thing to know is how ASDoc treats accessors (getter) and mutators (setter) methods. This is because ASDoc treats accessor/mutator methods, like ActionScript, as a single property definition and not as separate methods. When adding ASDoc comments, Adobe recommends that you place the accessor before the mutator and apply the comments to the accessor. It also recommends that you then mark the mutator as private to avoid ASDoc throwing errors that are difficult to immediately spot within the code, as this example illustrates:

```
/**
 * This is myProperty
 */
public function get myProperty():String
{
  return _myProperty;
}

/**
 * @private
 */
public function set myProperty(val:String):void
{
  _myProperty = val;
}
```

ASDoc has a set of rules that it applies to accessors and mutators when it processes them, so if you have documentation issues with your accessor or mutator, quickly look through the following list to see if you have fallen foul of one of ASDocs rules:

- If you precede an accessor/mutator with a comment block, it is included in the documentation output.
- If you define both parts of an accessor/mutator, you need to place only the comment block on one part.
- As just indicated, if you have both parts of an accessor and mutator, mark the mutator @private and place the comment block before the accessor.
- Providing only an accessor marks it as read-only in the documentation.
- Providing only a mutator marks it as write-only in the documentation.
- The accessor and mutator do not have to be put in any particular order or in the same location within the class. (Although, for clarity and consistency, it's easier to keep them together.)

- If you have both a public accessor and mutator and want to omit both from your documentation, mark both as @private.
- If you have only one part of an accessor/mutator, you need to apply only the @private tag to that part to have it omitted from the documentation.

Finally, a subclass always inherits its parent's visible accessors and mutators.

HTML Formatting

ASDoc comments don't just support plain text and marker tags. ASDoc can also parse XHTML compliant tags, although you are limited to a subset of those tags. That said, there is still enough flexibility in ASDoc to enable you to format text, define paragraphs, create lists, and anchor elements internally and externally to make it worth adding them to your comments.

Table 14.3   **ASDoc HTML Tags**

Tag	Description
` `	Avoid using this tag because it may be deprecated in the future. If you do need to use it, make sure that you close it.
`<p>`	Defines paragraphs within your comment blocks. Don't use it for the initial comment block, however; use it only for additional paragraphs within an individual block. You must close this tag.
`<pre>`	Keeps the formatting of the HTML code it contains. This is commonly used in association with the @mxml tag. You must close this tag.
`<listing>`	Provides you with a mechanism to insert formatted code within a comment block. This is not the same as using the `<pre></pre>` and the @mxml tag. You have to close this tag.
`<ul> <li>`	Provides the ability to insert lists within your comment. Make sure that you close these tags.
`<table> <th>` `<tr> <td>`	You can include tables within your comments. However, you need to alter the CSS file used with the generated documents to style it.
`<img>`	Inserts an image into the document. If you want to make sure that it isn't crowded, wrap it in a `<p></p>`. That way, you have an equal mount of white space around it.
`<code>`	Formats the text it encapsulates in a monospaced font. You must close this tag.
`<strong>`	Provides you with the ability to make enclosed text bold. You must close this tag.
`<em>`	Like `<strong>`, this provides you with the ability to display the enclosed text in italics. You must close this tag.

I want to draw your attention to one additional element: the `class="hide"` attribute. Although this isn't an HTML tag, it provides you with the ability to mark sections of your comment blocks so that they are not included within the exported documentation.

This may sound odd, but if you think about it, it provides a nice level of information separation. Instead of having to just include the core information in your class to avoid your documentation becoming verbose, you can include a detailed description within the comment block, but it marks it as hidden so that it can be viewed only when someone looks at the actual source code. A common approach to using this attribute is to include it within a `<span></span>` or `<p></p>` tag.

```
/**
 * This is the class description. Use this to give an overview of your
 * class and provide any example code if need be.
 *
 * <p class="hide">This comment is omitted from the documentation</p>
 *
 */
```

Special Characters

Because the resulting output that ASDoc generates is HTML and that the comment markers and blocks use special characters to delimit or demarcate themselves, using special characters within your plain-text sections cause problems. If you need to use an asterisk (*) in your comment block, use a pair of tilde (~~) instead. For the @ sign and any other special characters (especially < or >), use the standard encoded HTML conventions for them. Although in most cases, leaving them as they are causes no issues—other than they may not appear in the final document—this cannot be guaranteed. If in doubt, convert to HTML-encoded syntax. If you are unsure, Table 14.4 describes the common ones. (If you want to see a more complete list, go to www.w3schools.com/TAGS/ref_ascii.asp.)

Table 14.4   **Common Special Characters and Their HTML Equivalent**

Character	HTML
@	&#64;
<	&lt;
>	&gt;
&	&amp;
%	&#37;
{	&#123;
}	&#125;
[	&#91;
]	&#93;
(	&#40;
)	&#41;

Metadata Comments

Adding comments to metadata is almost identical to adding comment blocks to any other facet of your class. However, metadata blocks exhibit a few nuances, and they can vary between metadata tags.

Bindable

The Bindable metadata tag falls into the preprocessor tag category and, therefore, imbues the property or method upon which it is placed. As such, you cannot add any comments to this tag; however, it adds comments to your documentation. Any property or method that has a Bindable tag placed on it has This property can be used as the source for data binding added to it in the generated documentation. Note that if you use this metadata tag in an <mx:Script /> block in MXML, you won't get this output. It appears to influence the actual read-write properties of the accessor/mutator upon which it is placed.

DefaultProperty

The [DefaultProperty] tag enables you to indicate what property is the default for your component. If you are unsure what [DefaultProperty] does, refresh your memory by looking at Chapter 7, "Working with Metadata." When ASDoc comes across an entry of [DefaultProperty], it adds an entry to the class section of the documentation so that it is clear to the user that there is a [DefaultProperty] defined and what it actually is.

Events and Effects

Events and effects are treated in a similar manner, so I clumped them into one topic to avoid unnecessary repetition. When you place comments on an [Event] or [Effect] metadata tag, include the @eventType tag to indicate what the event type is for this particular event or effect metadata tag references.

Styles

The Style tag is treated pretty much the same way as any other comment block; you can use the @default tag to indicate a default value for each style entry so that another developer knows what the default setting for the styles on your component are.

Documenting MXML

MXML is the weak link in the ASDoc loop. Unfortunately, you can apply comments only to elements that appear inside of <mx:Script></mx:Script> tags. Although you may see this as a limitation, it isn't. Think about the components you have seen and created throughout this book. Notice that almost all of them are written in ActionScript; it is in the examples that they are usually instantiated in MXML. As mentioned in Chapter 3, "Anatomy of a Component," you are only likely to use MXML for component development as prefabricated containers of data. So, because you can place comments only in script blocks shouldn't cause too many issues. It is also worth reiterating that all MXML tags are public, so the vast majority of the MXL will get documented automatically; it's just that you cannot add any additional commenting to the individual tags.

Bypassing Documentation

By default, anything in your class that has an access modifier of public or protected will automatically be documented, even if you haven't put an ASDoc comment block over it. This includes any properties or methods inherited from that class's superclass. That's great unless it is something that you don't want documented and, for coding reasons, it cannot be made private. Now, I know you are wondering where on Earth there would be a case that you didn't want to include a property or method that wasn't private. Well, here are a few relevant examples: `createChildren()`, `commitProperties()`, `measure()`, and `updateDisplayList()`.

The easiest way to exclude these entities is to precede them with a comment block that has the `@private` tag in it, as illustrated here. This is ignored by ASDoc and, therefore, omitted from the documentation it generates.

```
/**
* @private
* This property will be ignored by ASDoc
*/
public var myProperty :String = "Mike!"
```

However, suppose that you want to mark an inherited property or method as private so that it is ignored, but you haven't overridden it. Well then, you need to use a metadata tag called [Exclude]. This comes in two variants: Chapter 7 showed the other [ExcludeClass]. [Exclude] is the sibling of [ExcludeClass] because it targets only the property you declare within its signature. Here is the basic structure of [Exclude]:

```
[Exclude(name="attribute", kind="attributeType")]
```

So, if you wanted to exclude the aforementioned `createChildren()` method, but you hadn't overridden it, you could just place the following at the top of your class to make sure it wasn't documented when ASDoc examined your class:

```
[Exclude(name="createChildren", kind="method")]
```

As mentioned in Chapter 7, [ExcludeClass] marks your class so it isn't added to the code complete in Flash Builder, effectively hiding it. What it also does is marks it so it is also ignored by ASDoc. This can be annoying because you may want to document a class but not have it available via code hinting. (Trust me, there are a few cases.) My advice, because you can't force ASDoc to parse classes marked in this way, is to comment out the [ExcludeClass] tag and run ASDoc; then, remove the comment after it finishes. This is handy if you distribute your components only as SWCs. I know it isn't that elegant a solution, but it's a good-enough workaround until Adobe alters how ASDoc interprets this tag.

Generating Your Documentation

Now, you've got a good idea of what and how you can mark up your classes in preparation for generating documentation from them, let's look at how you run ASDoc to get it to produce the documentation you are chomping at the bit to create.

ASDoc is a standalone application usually run from the command line. Wait...don't close this book yet! This is the most common way to use it. Fortunately, you can mask this with a more user-friendly process. However, like everything, let's try walking before we break into a jog.

Command-Line Document Generation

If you ever looked into using ASDoc before, you probably found a wealth of examples all based on using it as a command-line execution. At that point, you probably thought of a reasonable excuse for stopping and going back to writing code. I know I did. However, there comes a time when you need to document code, and if you've read this far, you are pretty serious about it. So, I cover of the basics of running ASDoc on the command line, and we can move on to see how it can be used with Flash Builder. The basic syntax of ASDoc is

```
asdoc -source-path . -doc-classes
com.developingcomponents.components.MyFirstComponent[1]
```

This tells ASDoc to create the documentation (-source-path) in the same folder (.) as the class com.developingcomponents.components.MyFirstComponent (-doc-classes). You can easily add more class paths to the –doc-classes option, but you need to make sure you include the fully qualified package path, too. However, you can wildcard the parent package to include all the classes within it. An easier solution is to supply a path to your project folder (in most cases, this is /src) and get ASDoc to recurse through all the folders within it.

---

[1] The period just signifies the same folder as the class.

Generating Documentation in Flash Builder

For some reason best known to Adobe, you cannot run ASDoc directly in Flash Builder. In my mind, this is a real oversight; after all, you'd have thought that just as the Flex Project option uses the `mxmlc` compiler and the Flex Library Project uses `compc` that there would be an option to generate documentation from a Menu option. However, that is sadly not the case.

That said, Flash Builder 4 finally provides built-in support for displaying documentation in a Tooltip-style pop-up window when you hover over an MXML tag or ActionScript class, method, or property, as you can see in Figure 14.1. So, although it doesn't provide the ability to generate standalone documentation, it supports the reading of the ASDoc comment tags.

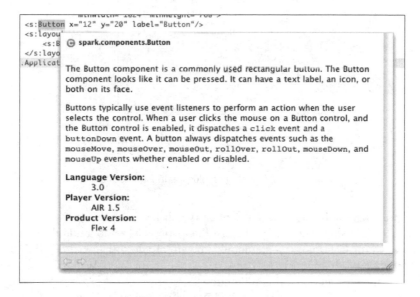

Figure 14.1   Documentation support in Flash Builder 4

This doesn't mean that you can't run ASDoc in Flash Builder. You can, but you need to add a few plug-ins to Flash Builder to achieve this.

Updating Flash Builder for ASDoc

The first thing you need to do is add in the Eclipse Java Development Tool (JDT). This provides support for Ant, which enables you to run build scripts. Build scripts are a set of tasks written in XML that provide access to features within the eclipse IDE and certain features that enable interaction with the operating system. It also gives you access to certain Java processes. Before we get ahead of ourselves, let's get the JDT plug-in installed.

If you have never added an additional plug-in for Flash Builder, the process is fairly simple. The first thing you need to do is open the Install Software dialog. To do this, click the Help entry of the File menu in Flash Builder and select Install New Software, as shown in Figure 14.2.

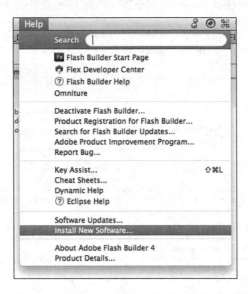

Figure 14.2   Installing plug-ins in Flash Builder

After you click the Install New Software entry, a dialog (as shown in Figure 14.3) opens, which, at this point, is empty. The first thing you need to do is add the update site for Eclipse 3.5 (or Galileo, as it is commonly known)[2]. To do this, insert the URL `http://download.eclipse.org/releases/galileo` to the Work With text field at the top of the dialog box and click the Add button.

This opens a small dialog, which has the URL in the lower of the two text fields. In the upper field, you can place a memorable name for this entry. I suggest calling it Galileo (see Figure 14.4). After you give it a memorable name, the OK button activates, and you can click it to close and apply the entry.

---

[2] Eclipse 3.5 was the current version of Eclipse used by Flash Builder 4.0. Check what version of Eclipse your current Flash Builder version uses before adding JDT to ensure you use the correct update site.

Figure 14.3   Adding an update site to Flash Builder

Figure 14.4   Saving an update site

As soon as the update site is applied, Flash Builder should automatically contact it and start to download information about any packages that you can install based on your version of Eclipse that Flash Builder is using (in this case, Eclipse 3.5). After a few seconds (depending on your connection speed), you see a set of folders grouped by technology, process, or language. Expand the Programming Languages folder, and select the Eclipse Java Development Tool option. Now, you should be looking at something that looks similar, if not identical, to Figure 14.5. Check the box next to the JDT entry and click Next.

You are now presented with a license agreement dialog. If you want to read the license, go for it. However, if you just want to get the JDT installed, accept the license and click Next. The final dialog you are presented with is the installation paths dialog. Some developers like to have separate locations to install their features into. However, that is an advanced topic that's out of the scope of this discussion, so click Finish to start the download and installation process.

Figure 14.5   Select the JDT entry from the
Programming Languages folder.

At this point, Finish Flash Builder downloads all the files it requires to install the JDT. After they are downloaded, you are presented with one final dialog prior to actually installing it. This is the last step where you can cancel the installation of a new feature—just in case you had a funny 5 minutes and decided to install something you didn't actually need. Fortunately, in this case, it is something that you need, so click the Install All button. If you accidentally click the Install button, all that happens is that you have to confirm each set of classes that need to be installed one at a time. Regardless of which you click, after the installation finishes, you reach the final dialog in this process (see Figure 14.6). The restart dialog! To apply the setting and have them initialized, restart Flash Builder.

If you are in the middle of working on something, you can click No and restart after you finish what you were doing. However, in this case, I assume you're not working on anything, so click Yes.

Figure 14.6   Restart dialog: the end of the installation journey

Getting to Grips with Ant

After Flash Builder restarts, open the Ant panel so that you can add your Ant scripts for a specific project to it. To do this, open the Windows entry in Flash Builder's menu, and choose the entry that reads Other Views. This opens a small window with all the various views available to you grouped by perspective[3] (see Figure 14.7).

You should now see an entry called Ant and, if you expand it, there is only one entry inside: Ant. Select this entry and click OK to open it. After the dialog closes, the Ant panel will probably be located next to the Problems panel at the bottom of the workspace. I dock mine next to the Outline panel on the left side, but you can leave it where it is for the moment.

Before you get into making your first Ant script, you need a project to test it out on, so create a new Flex project called `ASDoc_Ant` and in the root of the project, create a folder called `build`. This is where you store your Ant scripts.

Building with Ant

Although I'd love to wax lyrically about how great Ant is and how much you can do with it, it's way out of this book's scope; after all, you didn't buy a book on Ant. Therefore, I show you only how to use Ant with ASDoc. If you want to know more about Ant, you can find more information at http://ant.apache.org.

---

[3] A perspective is Flash Builder terminology for a group of views designed to provide a collective work environment. For example, the Flash Builder debugger is a perspective, as is the default Flash Builder project workspace.

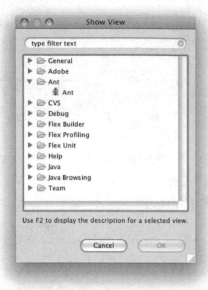

Figure 14.7   Add Views dialog

Ant scripts are just XML files broken down into tasks. By default, Ant associates itself with any script called `build.xml`. In your project root, add a new file inside the `build` folder called `build.xml`. As soon as you save the file, notice that it gets an ant icon in front of it. Open the file (if it isn't already open), add the following to the file, and save it:

```
<project name="ASDoc_Ant" default="Document Export [Full]">
  <property name="ProjectName" value="${ant.project.name}" />
<!--
  The location of your HTML templates directory.
  Copy these files from your Flash Builder installation directory.
  The files are located in the  /sdks/4.x/asdoc/template directory.
  Copy all of the template files to a new location and replace the
  TemplatesPath value below with the new template location.
-->
  <property name="TemplatesPath"
               value="${user.home}/Development/Resources/Flex/Templates"/>
  <property name="ExamplesPath" value="${basedir}/../examples"/>
  <property name="ASDocs.dir"
               location="/Applications/Adobe Flash Builder
               4/sdks/4.0.0/bin/asdoc"/>
  <property name="AppClasses.dir" location="${basedir}/../src"/>
  <property name="Output.dir" location="${basedir}/../docs"/>
```

```
    <target name="Document Export [Full]"
            depends="Document Directory Rebuild, Document Only Export"
            description="Full document export including
            directory recreation"/>

    <target name="Document Directory Rebuild">
      <delete dir="${Output.dir}" failOnError="false" includeEmptyDirs="true"/>
      <mkdir dir="${Output.dir}"/>
    </target>

    <target name="Document Only Export">
      <exec executable="${ASDocs.dir}" failOnError="true">
        <arg line="-doc-sources '${AppClasses.dir}'"/>
        <arg line="-window-title '${ProjectName}'"/>
        <arg line="-output '${Output.dir}'"/>
        <arg line="-templates-path '${TemplatesPath}'"/>
        <arg line="-examples-path '${ExamplesPath}'"/>
      </exec>
    </target>
</project>
```

Before you test it out, let me explain what each part does. At the top, you have the `project` tag: This defines the actual script. However, that doesn't mean that all the content it encapsulates has to relate to a single process or procedure. Far from it—you can have a multitude of tasks within a single build script; it just so happens that this one is specific to generating ASDoc documentation.

Notice that the tag has two parameters: `name` and `default`. The `name` is the actual name of the project itself (more on that in a moment). The `default` entry is which task within this script is the default. Yup, it's that obvious. The next set of entries deal with setting various property tokens with values either from Flash Builder itself or from your operating system.

```
<property name="ProjectName" value="${ant.project.name}" />
<property name="TemplatesPath"
value="${user.home}/Development/Resources/Flex/Templates"/>
<property name="ExamplesPath" value="${basedir}/../examples"/>
<property name="ASDocs.dir" location="/Applications/Adobe Flash Builder 4/
sdks/4.0.0/bin/asdoc"/>
<property name="AppClasses.dir" location="${basedir}/../src"/>
<property name="Output.dir" location="${basedir}/../docs"/>
```

Again, the `name` value is the name of the property and the `value` or `location` entry refers to the value it represents. When resolving locations within the file system, you usually use `location`, and for just setting a property's value, you use the `value` attribute.

As you can see, four properties exist. The first takes its value from the actual project name; the second is the template files that ASDoc uses to generate the HTML and CSS. If you want to customize the HTML output ASDoc creates, you can copy the Templates folder from within the Flash Builder folder and reference it, like I am, from a different location. After the `templates` property, you have the property `ExamplesPath`. This is an advanced feature (and undocumented, so it may stop working in future versions of the Flex SDK) that I explain in the next section. First let's finish looking at the remaining properties. Next is the location of ASDoc on my machine. Obviously, if a newer version of the SDK is released, you need to update the location value to reflect this.

The next entry deals with the location of your actual classes and takes its path information based on the location of the actual build script. The last entry is the location where ASDoc is going to write the documentation to. In this case, it is in the root of the Flex project in a folder called `docs`. Don't worry about creating this folder. Ant generates it automatically when it is run.

```
<target name="Document Export [Full]" depends="Document Directory Rebuild,
 Document Only Export" description="Full document export including directory
 re-creation"/>

<target name="Document Directory Rebuild">
  <delete dir="${Output.dir}" failOnError="false" includeEmptyDirs="true"/>
  <mkdir dir="${Output.dir}"/>
</target>

<target name="Document Only Export">
  <exec executable="${ASDocs.dir}" failOnError="true">
    <arg line="-doc-sources '${AppClasses.dir}'"/>
    <arg line="-window-title '${ProjectName}'"/>
    <arg line="-output '${Output.dir}'"/>
    <arg line="-templates-path '${TemplatesPath}'"/>
    <arg line="-examples-path '${ExamplesPath}'"/>
  </exec>
</target>
```

The bottom of the script contains the actual tasks. These are represented by target tags, which encapsulate various attributes and parameters. Like all the other tags you've seen, the `name` attribute is the actual reference used to run the task. Notice that the top task has an additional attribute called `depends`. This basically enables you to run other tasks as part of this tasks process. Therefore, both of the other tasks must run and exit successfully as part of this task. It, in itself, doesn't perform any additional processing.

This logically brings us to the last two tasks. The first of these just deletes the folder, as defined by the `Output.dir` property and re-creates it prior to the last task running. This is a simple and quick way to make sure that no old files hang around when you build your documentation. Be *very* careful not to confuse `AppClasses.dir` and `Output.dir`; otherwise, you could accidentally delete all your classes by mistake. If the folder deletion fails, this particular task will not report an error - `failOnError=false`. However, the last of these tasks will, and with good reason. This task actually creates the documentation. It actually executes the ASDoc binary and passes it a set of parameters to use as part of the document-creation process. If this fails, it lets you know so that you can see what the issue is and rectify it. As you can see, this is where all the properties that were defined at the top of the script are used: providing values for the actual class directory, the output folder, custom templates, and even enabling you to set the title of the documents.

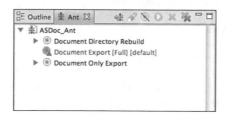

Figure 14.8   Ant panel showing your
Ant script open

Before you move on, let's talk about that advanced feature mentioned earlier. Notice that the last argument is passed to ASDoc by the task. That argument is -examples-path. As briefly mentioned, this is technically an undocumented feature, but it is useful; it enables you to supply an MXML file that provides an example block of code to illustrate the class you are documenting through the inclusion of an @includeExample tag. This differs from the @example tag because you have to include the code inline with @example.

Code included via the @includeExample requires that you place the sample file within a folder structure that reflects the same structure as the class itself. Therefore, if your component were in the package com.developingcomponents.components, you need to replicate that in a separate location and provide the path to the compiler; hence, the use of -example-path as a parameter of ASDoc. I tend to create a folder in the root of the project and call it examples, and if you review the properties of the Ant script, you'll see that is where I am pointing to in this script.

Now that you have seen the script, it's time to actually run it. To do this, drag the Ant script from the build folder, and drop it in to the Ant panel that you added earlier. As soon as you drop it, you should see something similar to Figure 14.7.

If you double-click Document Export [Full], after a few seconds, the Ant script runs. As soon as it finishes, two things happen: First, a folder called docs is created in the root of your project; second, a panel called Console opens and displays the output of the Ant script, which should end with a BUILD SUCCESSFUL message and the time it took to complete the task. If you get any errors, go back and check that all the property settings point to the correct locations on your machine.

If you expand the docs folder, right-click index.html, and choose Web Browser from the Open With entry on the menu. You can review the documentation generated from within Flash Builder. Notice that there is only one entry called ASDoc_Ant in the left panel and, if you click it to view the contents of that entry, nothing is in it beyond the package path, the class name, and inheritance path. To generate any code, you need to add some comments. Fortunately, I already knocked a few together in simple ActionScript class, which is shown here. Although it doesn't demonstrate all the tags that you can use with ASDoc, it gives you a bunch of them:

```
package com.developingcomponents.components
{
  import mx.core.UIComponent;

  [DefaultProperty("MyDefaultProperty")]
  /**
   * This is the class description. Use this to give an overview
   * of your class and provide any example code if need be.
   *
   * <p>If you want to apply formatting you can do that via <strong>HTML
   * tags</strong></p>
   *
   * @author FlashGen
   *
   * @mxml
   *   <pre>
   *   &lt;fgc:ASDocExample
   *     id="someValue"
   *     source="someOtherValue"
   *   /&gt;
   *   </pre>
   *
   * @see com.developingcomponents.components.ASDocSupportClass
   * @see http://developer.flashgen.com
   *
   * @includeExample ExampleOfASDocExample.mxml
   */
  public class ASDocExample extends UIComponent
  {
    /**
     * Event though I have comments for this variable, it won't
     * be exported the variable itself is private.
     */
    private var _myPrivateVar    :String;

    public var addedByASDoc      :Boolean;

    /**
     * This entry is added as it is not private or marked
     * &#64;private or uses the [Exclude] metadata tag.
     */
```

```
protected var myProtectedVar     :String = "myProtectedVar";


/**
 * @private
 * This entry is excluded as it is marked private.
 */
protected var myHiddenProtectedVar   :String = "myHiddenProtectedVar";



/**
 * This is the constructor, again you can add information
 * here about any parameters it may require and what they
 * are used for.
 */
public function ASDocExample()
{
  super();
}


/**
 * These are the only comments that are hand inserted. The
 * additional comments
 * about Binding are inserted because there is a [Bindable]
 * tag on this.
 *
 * <p>Below is an example of the &lt;Listing&gt; tag</p>
 *
 *
 * @example
 * <listing>
 *
 * public function get myValue():String
 * {
 *    _myPrivateVar;
 * }
 *
 * public function set myValue(val:String):void
 * {
 *    _myPrivateVar = val;
 * }
 * </listing>
 *
 */
[Bindable]
public function get myValue():String
{
```

```
    return _myPrivateVar;
  }

  public function set myValue(val:String):void
  {
    _myPrivateVar = val;
  }

  /**
   * This is an example method with a return type and
   * parameter.
   *
   * @param bool A Boolean value to be returned
   *
   * @return Returns a boolean value
   *
   *
   */
  public function MyMethod(bool:Boolean):Boolean
  {
    return true;
  }

  /**
   * @copy ASDocSupportClass#dummyMethod()
   *
   */
  public function myDummyMethod(someValue:String):Array
  {
    return new Array();
  }
 }
}
```

The one thing that I want to point out about this class example is that on its own it throws errors because it is missing the example MXML file and the other class that the @copy tag references. However, the full example is available for download, so just grab that—or just remove the @includeExample and @copy tags.

Summary

This chapter covered a lot of information about documentation and how to get ASDoc to do most—if not all—the work. You got a feel of how to use ASDoc and the tagging system that it uses, both on the command line and through the extension of Flash Builder, to allow access to Ant and hooking it into ASDoc directly.

You actually reached the end of this book. I hope you got as much out of it as I did writing it. All that is left to do is direct you to Appendix A, "Flex Resources," where you can find additional resources and links for further reading.

Thank you.

Flex Resources

This appendix provides helpful resources, including blogs, resource sites, frameworks, tools, and extensions.

Blogs

Here is a list of useful blogs that, although not all are component-specific, contains a wealth of information about the Flex framework. I broke it into sections: Adobe employee or team blogs and independent bloggers.

Adobe Blogs

The blogs listed here represent a slice of those that are available from the Adobe staff. I picked the ones that are Flex-focused and provide great content and insight. Obviously, I included myself and a few other evangelists, and those individuals who are directly involved in the development and release of Flash Builder and the Flex SDK.

Mike Jones (that's me)
Platform Evangelist
http://blog.flashgen.com

Mihai Corlan
Platform Evangelist
http://corlan.org

Christophe Coenraets
Enterprise Evangelist
http://coenraets.org/

Andrew Shorten
Product Manager for Flash Builder
http://andrewrshorten.wordpress.com/

Alex Harui
http://blogs.adobe.com/aharui/

Michael Chaize
Enterprise Evangelist
www.riagora.com

Piotr Walczyszyn
Platform Evangelist
www.riaspace.com/

James Ward
Enterprise Evangelist
www.jamesward.com/

Deepa Subramaniam
Product Manager for Flex SDK
http://iamdeepa.com/blog/

The Flex Team Blog
http://blogs.adobe.com/flex/

Independent Blogs

These are sites and blogs of people in the community who know their stuff when it comes to the Flash Platform. If they were not in your news feed already I'd add them as they provide great information.

Doug McCune
http://dougmccune.com/blog/

Neil Webb
www.nwebb.co.uk

Jeffrey Houser
www.jeffryhouser.com/

Richard Lord
www.richardlord.net/blog

Stefan Richter
www.flashcomguru.com/

Richard Leggett
http://richardleggett.co.uk/blog/

Grant Skinner
http://gskinner.com/blog/

Darron Schall
www.darronschall.com/weblog/

Ben Stucki
http://blog.benstucki.net/

Rich Tretola
http://blog.everythingflex.com/

Resource Sites

These sites provide information on various aspects of Flex development. Although there are many more, these provide a starting point.

InsideRIA
Covers a wealth of Rich Internet Application information
http://insideria.com/

ScaleNine
Great skinning & styling resource
www.scalenine.com/

Flex.org
Flex showcase site
http://flex.org/showcase

The Flex Show
Great podcast / blog
www.theflexshow.com/blog/

Flextras
Third-party Flex components
www.flextras.com/blog/

Flex Examples
All the examples you could ever need
http://blog.flexexamples.com/

Adobe Developer Connection
Flex Developer Center
www.adobe.com/devnet/flex.html

Flex Cookbook
Recipes for common problems
http://cookbooks.adobe.com/flex

Another URL worth adding to your RSS reader is the main Adobe XML News Aggregator (AXNA for short). This feeds on almost every Adobe technology and product, although the vast majority is Flash Platform–centric. The main page lists the entire feed, but you can select smart categories, products, or technologies from the side menus. You can even create your own feeds based on search criteria. Plus, if you want to have your blog aggregated by AXNA, you can submit it for approval from the menu entry in the top navigation.

You can access it by heading to http://feeds.adobe.com/.

Although not resource sites in the broad sense, these last two links provide information related to topics discussed in the book.

First there is the ActionScript 3.0 Coding Standards, which you can download from http://opensource.adobe.com/wiki/display/flexsdk/Coding+Conventions.

Finally, this link provides information regarding RSL optimization—something I mentioned in relation to SWC files. Although brief, it is worth knowing where to find it. I've converted it to a Bitly link because there were way too many alphanumeric characters for any one to type in: http://bit.ly/flex_optimize.

Frameworks

Although this book is about component development and, by it's very nature, not suited to the use of third-party frameworks, I did reference them in Chapter 9, "Manipulating Data." So, for those who want to know more about frameworks, here is a list of the current and most popular ones (in no particular order).

Cairngorm
http://sourceforge.net/adobe/cairngorm/home/

Swiz
http://swizframework.org/

Robotlegs
www.robotlegs.org/

Spring ActionScript
www.springactionscript.org/

PureMVC
www.puremvc.org

Mate
http://mate.asfusion.com/

Parsley
www.spicefactory.org/parsley/

Useful Tools and Extensions

Everyone has their own preferred working practices and, for software development, it's as much about the tools as it is the process.

Adobe Tools[1]

Although I assume that you have the applications used within this book, you might not. If that is the case, you can download the relevant tools from the following links:

- Flash Builder 4
  https://www.adobe.com/cfusion/tdrc/index.cfm?product=flash_builder
- Flash Professional CS5
  https://www.adobe.com/cfusion/tdrc/index.cfm?product=flash
- Flex Component Kit for Flash Professional★ (CS3/CS4)
  https://www.adobe.com/cfusion/entitlement/index.cfm?e=flex_skins

Third-Party Tools

Although the tools listed here don't necessarily relate to component development, they add features that enhance Flash Builder or are just useful tools to install.

Logwatcher

http://graysky.sourceforge.net/
   Logwatcher is a simple plug-in for Flash Builder that enables you to plumb into the Flash Player log. This is useful if you want to monitor trace statements without having to run your code in debug mode. Logwatcher is text-file agnostic, so you can easily get it to monitor alternative plain text files that aren't necessarily log files.

Regular Expression Tools

Having access to a good regular expressions tool can prove invaluable. Depending on how you like to work, you might opt for a plug-in for use directly in Flash Builder, like QuickREx, or a standalone tool, like RegExr. I use RegExr because it is specifically aimed at Flash Player's regular expression engine. It also provides the actual syntax needed to use within ActionScript, which is handy. RegExr is also available both as a desktop AIR application and as a web-based solution.

- QuickREx
  http://sourceforge.net/projects/quickrex/
- RegExr
  http://gskinner.com/RegExr/ (web version)
  www.gskinner.com/RegExr/desktop/ (desktop version)

---

[1] Be aware that you may need an Adobe ID to download software from Adobe.com.

Index

W-X-Y-Z

Mike Jones

Developing Flex 4 Components

Using ActionScript 3.0 and MXML to Extend Flex and AIR Applications

Developer's Library

FREE Online Edition

Your purchase of *Developing Flex 4 Components* includes access to a free online edition for 45 days through the Safari Books Online subscription service. Nearly every Addison-Wesley Professional book is available online through Safari Books Online, along with more than 5,000 other technical books and videos from publishers such as Cisco Press, Exam Cram, IBM Press, O'Reilly, Prentice Hall, Que, and Sams.

SAFARI BOOKS ONLINE allows you to search for a specific answer, cut and paste code, download chapters, and stay current with emerging technologies.

Activate your FREE Online Edition at
www.informit.com/safarifree

> **STEP 1:** Enter the coupon code: JLCNJFH.

> **STEP 2:** New Safari users, complete the brief registration form.
> Safari subscribers, just log in.

If you have difficulty registering on Safari or accessing the online edition,
please e-mail customer-service@safaribooksonline.com